Housing and Neighborhoods

Recent Titles in Contributions in Sociology
Series Editor: Don Martindale

Housing and Neighborhoods

THEORETICAL AND EMPIRICAL CONTRIBUTIONS

EDITED BY
Willem van Vliet—,
Harvey Choldin,
William Michelson,
and David Popenoe

Contributions in Sociology, Number 66

GREENWOOD PRESS
New York • Westport, Connecticut • London

Library of Congress Cataloging-in-Publication Data

Housing and neighborhoods.

(Contributions in sociology, ISSN 0084–9278 ; no. 66)
Bibliography: p.
Includes index.
1. Housing. 2. Neighborhood. I. Van Vliet, Willem.
II. Series.
HD7287.5.H47 1987   307.3′36   87–7527
ISBN 0–313–25459–1 (lib. bdg. : alk. paper)

British Library Cataloguing in Publication Data is available.

Library of Congress Catalog Card Number: 87–7527
ISBN: 0–313–25459–1
ISSN: 0084–9278

First published in 1987

Greenwood Press, Inc.
88 Post Road West, Westport, Connecticut 06881

Printed in the United States of America

The paper used in this book complies with the
Permanent Paper Standard issued by the National
Information Standards Organization (Z39.48-1984).

10 9 8 7 6 5 4 3 2 1

Contents

Tables and Figures

TABLES

FIGURES

Foreword

Housing, along with food, is a basic necessity for all people. Not only does it provide protection from the elements but it has psychological and social significance as well. It is a basis of personal identity, a source of status and pride, a spatial locale in which a variety of functions are carried on, and a major financial asset. Yet housing research has not been widely supported, especially that originating in the social sciences. What research has been done often is not utilized in government policy-making circles, a good example being the finding that high-rise housing is in many ways disadvantageous for most families. In disregard of this finding, governments around the world made costly policy miscalculations in the 1960s and 1970s when they heavily subsidized the construction of high-rise buildings. Housing researchers have often felt isolated from others in their disciplines, without a network of scholars to which they could turn.

The International Ad Hoc Committee on Housing and the Built Environment, the sponsor of the 1985 housing conference in Amsterdam where most of the chapters in this volume were originally presented, was founded to bring housing researchers together for an exchange of ideas and to increase the support for, and utilization of, housing research. Begun as a group of Americans meeting at the annual conferences of the American Sociological Association from the early 1970s onward, it became an international body in 1978 when it organized a number of sessions on housing research at the World Congress of Sociology in Uppsala, Sweden. A selection of papers from that congress was published in 1980 under the title *The Consumer Experience in Housing: Cross-National Perspectives* (edited by Clare Ungerson and Valerie Karn. Brookfield, VT: Gower Publishing Co.). The committee again organized sessions on housing research at the 1982 World Congress of the International Sociological Association, held in Mexico City. Drawing upon the papers given at that meeting another book was published: *Housing Needs and Policy Approaches: Trends in Thirteen Countries* (edited by Willem van Vliet—, Elizabeth Huttman, and Sylvia F. Fava. Durham, NC: Duke University Press, 1985). The next international meeting of the committee was held in 1985 in Amsterdam, as noted above, this time sponsored by the Netherlands Institute of Housing and the Built Environment. Over 140 housing researchers participated over a five-day period, representing more than 20 countries.

Recently made an official unit of the International Sociological Association, the Ad Hoc Committee on Housing and the Built Environment met again at the International Research Conference on Housing Policy organized by the National Swedish Institute for Building Research in Gävle, Sweden, in June 1986. Then in New Delhi, India, in August 1986, the committee again organized housing research sessions as part of the XIth World Congress of Sociology. There were eight housing research sessions under the committee's sponsorship in New Delhi, including two on Third World housing, plus a well-attended business meeting. The next major international meeting of the committee is scheduled for 1988 in the Netherlands.

The committee has provided housing researchers a lively network for intellectual exchange, with many members cooperating on projects and playing host to colleagues on international tours. An active advisory board includes a number of leading housing researchers from Europe and the Third World, as well as an American core. The committee's semiannual newsletter is now reproduced by members in a number of countries and sent to housing researchers across the world.

This book provides a sample of the excellent research that has been done by members of this committee and their colleagues. The chapters give an indication of how similar housing and built environment problems can be in different countries, and at the same time they show the wide diversity that housing programs and housing policies often take.

Elizabeth Huttman
Organizer and Founding Chairperson
International Ad Hoc Committee on Housing
and the Built Environment

Acknowledgments

A collection of edited papers such as this one is always the product of many people with direct or indirect contributions. Among these people is first of all Elizabeth Huttman, founding chairperson of the Ad Hoc Committee on Housing and the Built Environment, whose untiring efforts laid the basis that made possible the organization of the conference from which the chapters in this book emanate. Other long-standing members whose activities have helped to sustain this group and give it recognition include Harvey Choldin, Sylvia F. Fava, Herbert Gans, Suzanne Keller, William Michelson, and David Popenoe. Frans Grunfeld, professor emeritus of Tilburg University, the Netherlands, made the initial contact with the Gestructureerde Samenwerking Foundation (G. S.), which cosponsored the conference. Leon Deben and Dick van der Vaart, both of G. S., took responsibility for the Dutch role in organizing the conference, which was held in facilities made available by the Sociological Institute at the University of Amsterdam. Raymond Studer, current dean of the College of Environmental Design at the University of Colorado, Boulder, generously made available resources for preparatory work for the conference and to conduct the subsequent editorial work. John Crank tracked down missing bibliographic details of publications that more often than not had (dis)appeared halfway across the world. Monica Allebach and Lorraine Self provided superb clerical assistance. Finally, this book would not have come about if it were not for the support of Mary Sive, editor for the social and behavioral sciences at Greenwood Press, who extended our initial deadline for the manuscript with gracious understanding and who provided expert editorial guidance.

Willem van Vliet—

Housing and
Neighborhoods

Introduction: Some Comments on Recent and Current Research

WILLEM VAN VLIET—

The comments that follow are not intended as a complete review of all the literature on and developments in recent and current research on housing and neighborhoods.[1] The purpose here is not to provide such comprehensive coverage, but to sample, more or less representatively, from what appears relevant in order to help focus attention on the nature of housing and urban research at present and to give a sense of the directions in which the general field is evolving. As there is no space here to elaborate the issues and afford them the detailed attention that is warranted, even the reflections on these developments cannot be but very brief and partial, serving as a background for the chapters in this book.

The following discussion traces major developments in the field in North America and Western Europe during the last two decades to suggest that research on housing and urban issues is "alive and kicking." During this period, traditional urban research has regained popularity thanks to sustained empirical work and methodological and theoretical advances, and the field has been expanded and enriched by new approaches and by environment-behavior studies.

A BIRD'S-EYE VIEW OF RECENT DEVELOPMENTS

The United States

In the late 1960s, the field of urban studies and housing, ostensibly dormant for some time, was jolted by a number of societal and academic developments. Many European countries saw student protest erupting in the streets where the cause of academic reform often got linked up with urban renewal, industrial democracy, and other concerns of diverse urban groups. In the United States, student protest was more contained on campuses and more centered around the Vietnam War, but the black slums of large cities experienced riots and civil unrest. Friedland (1982), in a comprehensive analysis, found that the severity of the black urban riots during the 1960s was positively correlated to the amount of urban renewal and lack of low-rent housing. While these urban racial problems must be seen in the broad national context of structural inequalities and racism in the United States, neighborhood conditions and housing factors (quality, price, location) certainly played a role in the events that unfolded (National Advisory Commission on Civil Disorders 1968).

Against this background, Banfield, a political scientist disappointed by the failures of urban renewal and public housing in the United States and disenchanted with comprehensive planning more generally, published *The Unheavenly City* (1968) in which he diagnosed the ills of urban America. He prescribed a policy of "benign neglect" toward those "lower-class" population groups who had previously been the recipients of "generous" benefits under programs that failed to achieve their objectives. The book's thesis regarding a "culture of poverty," and its implications, proved highly controversial. Publishing a revised edition in 1974, Banfield responded to charges of racial prejudice and discrimination that followed the initial publication. *The Unheavenly City*, and the controversy it inspired, reinforced a heightened awareness of urban problems and questions of housing among policy makers in the United States and reflected increased interest in these issues among researchers. These concerns expressed themselves in, for example, the establishment in 1965 of the *Urban Affairs Quarterly* journal and the passing of the Housing and Urban Development Act of 1968.

At the same time, the concentration of the poor in discrete neighborhoods with physical boundaries (like major roads, railways, and industrial or commercial areas), identified with a particular racial or ethnic group or life-style, reinforced the need for decentralized services. These and other factors contributed to a view of neighborhoods as political entities (Rohe and Gates 1985). The idea of neighborhood-based local government reemerged as a hallmark of a nationwide movement beginning in the 1960s (Silver 1985).

Great Britain

While much of the research on housing and communities conducted in the United States during the late 1960s could be traced back to the Chicago School tradition, in Europe very different voices made themselves heard, likewise serving to bring urban issues and housing to the fore. In Britain, Rex and Moore published, in 1967, *Race, Community and Conflict*, a book that generated a great deal of discussion and was significant in two ways. First, it was highly critical of housing allocation policies in the city of Birmingham, exposing them as being racially discriminatory. More important, however, was the way in which their examination of the specifics of the local situation illustrated possibilities for advancing theoretical and empirical work on housing and urban issues. Rex and Moore introduced the concept of "housing classes," providing the impetus for a series of, not universally supportive, inquiries (for example, Couper and Brindley 1975). Their statement that "There is a class struggle over the use of houses and that this class struggle is the central process in the city as a social unit" oriented urban sociology to the study of urban communities as arenas defined by conflict between differentially empowered interests competing for limited resources. Thus, Rex and Moore directed attention to the control of access to scarce urban resources as a relevant and legitimate focus for urban research. In this context, Pahl (1969) initially identified "urban gatekeepers" as a valuable angle from which to study the management of resource allocation mechanisms, summing up the main propositions of his argument as follows:

(a) There are fundamental *spatial* constraints on access to scarce urban resources and facilities. Such constraints are generally expressed in time/cost distance.

(b) There are fundamental *social* constraints on access to scarce urban facilities. These reflect the distribution of power in society and are illustrated by:

—bureaucratic rules and procedures; and

—social gatekeepers who help to distribute and control urban resources.

(c) Populations in different localities differ in their access and opportunities to gain the scarce resources and facilities, holding their economic position on their position in the occupational structure constant. The situation that is structured out of (a) and (b) may be called a sociospatial or socioecological system. Populations limited in this access to scarce urban resources and facilities are the *dependent* variable; those controlling access, the *managers* of the system, would be the independent variable.

(d) Conflict in the urban system is inevitable. The more the resource or facility is valued by the *total* population in a given locality, or the higher the value and the scarcer the supply in relation to demand, the greater the conflict (Pahl 1969, 146–47).

Later on, Pahl himself, as well as others (for example, Mellor 1977), called into question the central role of such gatekeepers whose functioning came to be seen more realistically as taking place within constraints imposed by the broader political and economic frameworks in which they were situated.

West Germany

In West Germany, urban research during the 1960s was typically patterned according to canons of sound empirical research outlined by König (1962). There were also some new theoretical developments. Bahrdt (1969), for example, conceptualized urban communities in terms of the polarity and reciprocity of their public and private spheres, and Schmidt-Relenberg (1968) elaborated a systems model of housing and city planning drawing on Parsons's formulations. However, this work did not evolve into significant challenges on the agenda of the urban research community. The tradition of human ecological studies still remains a strong one, as represented in the work of, for example, Friedrichs (1977, 1982) and Hamm (1982). Recently, more policy-oriented analyses have gained in prominence, particularly with respect to housing (for example, Wollmann 1984). However, earlier contributions to the sociology of the built environment from Mitscherlich (1966), Berndt (1968), Berndt, Lorenzer, and Horn

(1968), and Bahrdt (1968) have gone largely unnoticed beyond the confines of West Germany and have had no impact to speak of in the international development of the field of environment-behavior studies. The same can be said of similar work done in the Netherlands and Sweden during that period.

French Contributions

Developments in France after 1968 proved to be more influential. Rapid urbanization, large-scale housing developments, and urban renewal programs, along with industrial unrest and urban disturbances, prompted authorities to channel considerable funds into urban social research. Resultant studies centered not on the city as a whole but on the mechanisms of urban development, with an emphasis on the part played by the state in a restructuring of the capitalist system (Kaufmann and Laigneau 1984). The theoretical anchorage of this work was delimited, for the most part, by Marxist perspectives. This point of view inspired an often-quoted article by Castells (1968) in which he challenged the legitimacy of the very subject matter with which urban sociologists had traditionally concerned themselves. Other French urban researchers, espousing variants of an essentially economistic framework, included Lojkine, Lefebre, Pinçon, Topalov, and Preteceille. Internationally, Marxist approaches to urban issues became very much *en vogue* as translations of this French work started appearing and were being added to in English (for example, Pickvance 1974; Harvey 1973). Although the neo-Marxist approaches (alias "new urban sociology" or "critical urban sociology") were ignored in some reviews of the field (for example, O'Brien and Roach 1984; Frisbie 1980), they seemed to become a dominant outlook for research, especially in Europe. It was felt by some critics that traditional urban sociology had failed to respond or remained impervious to lessons contained in developments and events during the 1960s. The challenges that the new urban sociologists posed met with few explicit responses (for example, Fischer 1978) and these never evolved into effective dialogue.

More recently, work along the lines of these new approaches has been hampered by a lack of progress and has become less prominent (see, for example, Harloe and Lebas 1981; Lebas 1982; Walton 1981). This stagnation led Szelenyi (1986) to entitle a critique of Harvey's recent work: "The Last of the Marxist Urban Sociologists?" and several attempts at reformulation of existing paradigms have appeared (Saunders 1981; Kemeny 1982; Gans 1984; Rose 1984). After Castells rescinded many of his earlier positions and others began disengaging themselves from rigid Marxist doctrines, traditional urban research returned to the limelight. The quality of people's daily lives in their neighborhood and community context, for example, not a salient concern in macrolevel Marxist analyses, has begun to receive renewed attention (for example, Ahlbrandt 1984; Banerjee and Baer 1984; Michelson 1985).

Environment-Behavior Studies

At about the same time that Castells (1968) and others began questioning the legitimacy of traditional urban sociology, other set out to explore, on quite different grounds, "what human ecology had left behind in the dust" (Michelson 1976). Work in this vein considered the ways and extent that the urban environment was congruent with people's needs. Various theoretical models were developed, as appropriate to the particular level of analysis and the questions at hand. Empirical research documented the implications of extant incongruities and probed the processes and structures underlying such incongruities. The institutionalization of environment-behavior studies, as this new field came to be called, was signaled by the regular organization of conferences, the founding of professional associations and new interdisciplinary academic programs, the endurance of funded research programs, and the establishment of a number of journals that became routine outlets for publication of the results of the studies being done. In the United States, environmental sociology and environmental psychology developed quickly into recognized subfields represented by sections in their respective national associations.

Research conducted under this broad banner was obviously diverse, exploring a variety of issues. Part of it dealt, for example, with the natural environment and is not immediately pertinent here, except perhaps on a theoretical level. However, as discussed later, another part blended with and supplemented traditional urban research.

SELECTED CHARACTERISTICS OF CURRENT RESEARCH

The New Urban Sociology

Against the background of the developments sketched above, what are some of the features characterizing urban studies and housing research over roughly the last decade? A significant contribution of the new urban sociology would appear to be its concern with macrolevel processes and structures that previously had received scant attention but that are nevertheless important factors molding the more immediate contexts and events studied by conventional urban sociology. (The Marxian concern with economic aspects represents a distinct political stance vis-à-vis a focus that is otherwise shared by many ecologists; compare Gans 1984.) The view on the role of the state in the process of private and corporate capital accumulation and the interpretation of urban conflict in terms of socioeconomic class take on various competing forms within the neo-Marxist tradition, none of which is necessarily shared by other schools of thinking (Krasner 1978). Nevertheless, it is important to recognize the new urban sociology for its insistence on studying these and other important urban phenomena that had received relatively less attention in previous urban research (for reviews, see Zukin 1980; Jaret 1983).

It is hard, for example, to conceive of an analysis of national housing systems that leaves out the role of the state.[2] There are, however, divergent theoretical perspectives on the role of the state (see, for example, Krasner 1978; Saunders 1979; Marcuse 1978). In addition, it is unclear whether observations regarding the role of the state in one sector, say, international trade, can be generalized to other sectors such as housing or urban development. There is also the question of whether notions about state intervention developed in Europe, where strong central government has a long and broadly legitimate tradition, can be transferred to much more decentralized free market economies such as found in North America and Australia (compare Gans 1984; Mullins 1983). Furthermore, there is nothing like a commonly accepted definition of what constitutes "the state." Definitions run the whole gamut from "president plus secretary of state," to "the political parties in control," to more "enduring structures of government organization," to none at all. The point is clear: The role of the state is variously important, as implicated by the question at hand, and the new urban sociology has helped direct attention to this role, but its theoretical interpretation of this role is one of several that are potentially valuable.

Observations such as those made above regarding the neo-Marxist emphasis on the state's role are, on a generic level, also applicable to other foci of housing and urban research. For instance, conflict has long been studied; however, it has generally been seen to arise from discrimination, racism, poor administrative or political organization, cultural differences, and competition for scarce resources, rather than economically determined class interests (Jaret 1983).

While acknowledging the contributions of the new urban sociology, it is equally important to recognize that it does not hold the exclusive rights to studies of, say, the state. For example, the reorientation of the state and its role in the privatization of British housing (Forrest and Murie 1987) are in plain view for anyone to see, and a critical analysis of what is going on is not necessarily predicated or contingent on a conceptual or methodological apparatus provided solely by neo-Marxist approaches. Nor do these approaches cover all of the relevant domains of inquiry. A study of a nation's high-rise construction program necessarily involves consideration of the central government's role, whether it be from a neo-Marxist or some other perspective. However, it seems odd to invoke theories of the state for studying the effects of high-rise living on family relations.

Traditional Urban Sociology

The nature of the various neo-Marxist approaches developed so far is such that, irrespective of their other variable characteristics, they selectively emphasize the economic dimensions of the subject matter in analyses that tend to be oriented to more macrolevel aspects. These angles are obviously important, but they are not all-inclusive. There exist many policy issues and theoretical questions with different parameters that are also important and that drive a plethora of housing and urban research programs.

Traditional concerns of urban sociology have by no means faded away. Domains of inquiry that were prominent in early urban studies have been advanced by sustained empirical research and informed by new theoretical analyses. For example, a concern with effects of housing and neighborhood conditions on physical and mental health was central in a number of early urban studies at the University of Chicago. While the conceptualization of the implied relationships has changed and, along with it, the methodological approaches as well, the same general concern underlies many studies conducted during the last 10 to 15 years (for example, Kasl, White, Will, and Marcuse 1982; Booth and Edwards 1976; Baldassare 1979; Gove, Hughes, and Galle 1979).

Similarly, early writings from the Chicago School (for example, Wirth 1938) dealt with social relations and community attachment—notably as these were affected by processes of urbanization, industrialization, and bureaucratization— building on a line of thinking developed by Simmel (1903) and Tönnies (1887). This focus is still very much in evidence in contemporary research. The "community question" continues to be a subject of research (Hunter 1975; Wellman and Leighton 1979; Christenson 1984; Lee, Oropesa, Metch, and Guest 1984; Tsai and Sigelman 1982), and also sense of, preference for, attachment to, and satisfaction with community are all actively studied (McMillan and Chavis 1986; *Population and Environment* 1984; Taylor, Gottfredson, and Brower 1985; Riger and Lavrakas 1981; Tremblay, Dillman, and Van Liere 1980; Goudy 1982). There has been extensive research on kinship (Stack 1974), neighboring (Unger and Wandersman 1985), and urban friendships (Fischer 1982), and the study of social networks more generally has been boosted by new developments in data analytic techniques. Social area analysis (Shevky and Bell 1955) has evolved into factorial ecology as computer-aided analyses permitted researchers to develop more sophisticated approaches taking in a larger range of variables (for example, Berry and Kasarda 1977).

The list could be expanded further. There are identifiable literatures with ongoing research on topics ranging from microlevel ethnographic studies of behavior settings as published in *Urban Life* (Wiseman 1979; Kenen 1982), to macrolevel urban policy analyses (Batty 1984; Clark 1985), including well-established research domains such as neighborhood safety (Loo 1986; Lavrakas 1982), suburbanization (Stahura 1986; Logan and Golden 1986), residential segregation (Peach, Robinson, and Smith 1982; Arnell-Gustafsson 1982; Taylor 1981), urban politics (Fasenfest 1986; Steinberger 1984), and urban revitalization (Gale 1984; Palen and London 1984).

Environment-Behavior Studies

In addition to studies such as those referred to above, research has broadened as social scientists' greater cognizance of the role of the built environment in social affairs converged with a growing realization among planners and design professionals that the production of the built environment was inextricably bound up with behavioral, cultural, political, and economic aspects on which the latter could claim little expertise. The studies that ensued, often inter- or at least multidisciplinary in nature, have been reviewed in several places (see, for example, Choldin 1978; Baldassare 1978; Dunlap and Catton 1979; Foley 1980; Stokols and Altman, in press; Moore, Tuttle, and Howell 1985; Huttman and Van Vliet— 1987). One possible classification of this work divides up the literature into six rubrics.

First, a large portion of the literature deals with the housing and neighborhood requirements of specific population groups. Examples are studies on the elderly, women, children, and the handicapped. There now exist very extensive international literatures, including also at least one journal devoted exclusively to each of these groups. A second body of literature can be characterized by its preoccupation with a specific behavior as it is affected by a range of factors derived from housing and neighborhood conditions. Examples include crime, social interaction, play, and health. A third strand in the literature examines a broader array of behaviors, but does so from a more restricted set of environmental conditions like, for example, land use patterns, population densities, street patterns, housing types, and so on. Fourth, and rather less developed, is theoretical work on the built environment. Much of this work appears to deal rather narrowly with design per se, rather than its relation to people and their broader context (see, for example, Dickens 1980). Fifth, there is a limited literature that covers methodological aspects of social scientific research of the built environment cum annexis (Michelson 1975; Zeisel 1980; Bechtel, Marans, and Michelson 1987). Finally, there is a category of studies focusing on a miscellany of "contextual" factors relating to the built environment. Topics grouped under this heading include ideologies and values of planners and architects (Howe and Kaufman 1981), the political economy of building form (King 1984), cross-national comparisons of urban form (Popenoe 1985), and a variety of other aspects of the processes through which the built environment is produced (Riemer 1976; Howell 1977; Blau 1976; Kantrowitz 1985; Zube 1982).

This Book

The papers presented at the international housing conference from which this book emanated (see Foreword) reflect the multifaceted nature of the field of which the preceding discussion has presented a brief sketch. There were, for example, presentations on studies of housing at a national level, often from a political-economic standpoint with special reference to the role of central government (a selection of these papers appears elsewhere; Van Vliet— 1987). But there were also many studies in the vein of traditional urban research and on the relations between the environment and human behavior. These last two domains provided the organizing focus for this volume. Thus there is a section with several theoretically and conceptually oriented studies that help to synthesize the, by and large, noncumulative outcomes of a host of empirical studies of the built environment. Subsequent chapters, structured around specific themes, often amplify these points, as they tie in with and attest to vibrant research programs in a field that has anything but ceased to exist.

NOTES

1. I am grateful to Harvey Choldin, William Michelson, and David Popenoe for their comments on an earlier draft of this introduction.

2. A concern with the state is particularly evident among political scientists who in the United States chose it as the theme for their national association's annual convention in 1981. Also the *International Political Science Review* (1986) just published a special issue on "the state and the public sphere." The title of a recent book on the topic, *Bringing the State Back In* (Evans, Rueschemeyer, and Skocpol 1985) aptly captures this new orientation.

REFERENCES

Ahlbrandt, R. S., Jr.
1984   *Neighborhoods, People and Community*. New York: Plenum Press.
Arnell-Gustafsson, U.
1982   "On Strategies Against Socio-economic Residential Segregation." *Acta Sociologica* 25: 33–40.
Bahrdt, Hans Paul
1968   *Humaner Städtebau*. Hamburg: Christian Wegner Verlag.
1969   *Die Moderne Grossstadt* (2nd ed.). Reinbek: Christian Wegner Verlag.
Baldassare, M.
1978   "Human Spatial Behavior." *Annual Review of Sociology* 4: 29–56.
1979   *Residential Crowding in Urban America*. Berkeley: University of California Press.
Banerjee, T., and Baer, W. C.
1984   *Beyond the Neighborhood Unit: Residential Environments and Public Policy*. New York: Plenum Press.
Banfield, E. C.
1974   *The Unheavenly City Revisited*. Boston: Little, Brown.
Batty, Michael
1984   "Urban Policies in the 1980s." *Town Planning Review* 55, no. 4, 489–98.
Bechtel, R., R. Marans, and W. Michelson (eds.)
1987   *Research Methods for the Built Environment*. New York: Van Nostrand Reinhart.
Berndt, Heide
1968   *Das Gesellschaftsbild bei Stadtplanern*. Stuttgart: Kramer.
Berndt, Heide, Alfred Lorenzer, and Klaus Horn
1968   *Architektur als Ideologie*. Frankfurt.
Berry, B. J. L., and J. D. Kasarda
1977   *Contemporary Urban Ecology*. New York: Macmillan.

Blau, Judith R.
1976   "Beautiful Buildings and Breaching the Laws: A Study of Architectural Firms."
        Revue Internationale de Sociologie 12, no. 1–2, 110–128.
Booth, A., and J. N. Edwards
1976   "Crowding and Family Relations." *American Sociological Review* 41, no. 2,
        308–21.
Castells, M.
1968   "Y a-t-il une sociologie urbaine?" *Sociologie du Travail* 3, 72–90.
Choldin, Harvey M.
1978   "Social Life and the Physical Environment." In *Handbook of Contemporary
        Urban Life*, edited by D. Street et al., 352–84. San Francisco: Jossey-Bass.
1985   *Cities and Suburbs: An Introduction to Urban Sociology*. New York: McGraw-
        Hill.
Christenson, James A.
1984   "Gemeinschaft and Gesellschaft: Testing the Spatial and Communal Hypotheses."
        Social Forces 63, no. 1, 160–68.
Clark, T.
1985   "Urban Policy Analysis." *Annual Review of Sociology* 11, 437–55.
Couper, M., and T. Brindley
1975   "Housing Classes and Housing Values." *Sociological Review* 29: 563–76.
Dickens, P. G.
1980   "Social Science and Design Theory." *Environment and Planning B* 7: 353–
        60.
Dunlap, R. E., and W. R. Catton, Jr.
1979   "Environmental Sociology." *Annual Review of Sociology* 5, 243–73.
Evans, Peter, Dietrich Rueschemeyer, and Thea Skocpol (eds.)
1985   *Bringing the State Back In*. New York: Cambridge University Press.
Fasenfest, D.
1986   "Community Politics and Urban Redevelopment." *Urban Affairs Quarterly* 22,
        no. 1, 101–23.
Fischer, C. S.
1978   "On the Marxian Challenge to Urban Sociology." *Comparative Urban Research*
        6, no. 2/3, 10–19.
1982   *To Dwell Among Friends: Personal Networks in Town and City*. Chicago: Uni-
        versity of Chicago Press.
Foley, Donald L.
1980   "The Sociology of Housing." *Annual Review of Sociology* 6, 457–78.
Forrest, R., and A. Murie
1987   "Fiscal Reorientation, Centralization, and the Privatization of Council Housing."
        In *Housing Markets and Policies under Fiscal Austerity*, edited by W. van Vliet—.
        Westport, CT: Greenwood Press.
Friedland, R.
1982   *Power and Crisis in the City*. London: Macmillan Press.
Friedrichs, Jürgen
1977   *Stadtanalyse: Soziale und Raumliche Organisation der Gesellschaft*. Reinbek:
        Rowohlt.
1982   *Spatial Disparities and Social Behavior*. Hamburg: Christians Verlag.

Frisbie, W. Parker
1980   "Urban Sociology in the United States." *American Behavioral Scientist* 24, no.
        2, 177–214.

Gale, D. F.
1984   *Neighborhood Revitalization and the Postindustrial City*. Lexington, MA: D. C.
        Heath.

Gans, Herbert J.
1984   "American Urban Theories and Urban Areas: Some Observations on Contem-
        porary Ecological and Marxist Paradigms." In *Cities in Recession: Critical Re-
        sponses to the Urban Policies of the New Right*, edited by I. Szeleny: 279–308.
        Beverly Hills, CA: Sage.

Goudy, Willis J.
1982   "Further Consideration of Indicators of Community Attachment." *Social Indi-
        cators Research* 11, 181–92.

Gove, W. R., M. Hughes, and O. R. Galle
1979   "Overcrowding in the Home: An Empirical Investigation of Its Possible Patho-
        logical Consequences." *American Sociological Review* 44, 59–80.

Hamm, B.
1982   *Einführung in die Siedlingssoziologie*. Munich: Beck.

Harloe, A., and E. Lebas (eds.)
1981   *City Class and Capital: New Developments in the Political Economy of Cities
        and Regions*. London: Edward Arnold.

Harvey, D.
1973   *Social Justice and the City*. London: Edward Arnold.

Howe, Elizabeth, and Jerome Kaufman
1981   "The Values on Contemporary American Planners." *Journal of the American
        Planning Association*, July, 266–78.

Howell, Sandra C.
1977   "Post Occupancy Evaluation Transfer Strategy." *Industrialization Forum* 8, no.
        1, 29–35.

Hunter, A.
1975   "The Loss of Community." *American Sociological Review* 40, 537–52.

Huttman, E., and W. van Vliet— (eds.)
1987   *Handbook of Housing and the Built Environment in the U.S.* Westport, CT:
        Greenwood Press.

Jaret, Charles
1983   "Recent Neo-Marxist Urban Analysis." *Annual Review of Sociology* 9, 499–525.

Kantrowitz, M.
1985   "Has Environment and Behavior Research 'Made a Difference'?" *Environment
        and Behavior* 17, no. 1, 25–46.

Kasl, Stanislav, Marni White, Julie Will, and Peter Marcuse
1982   "Quality of the Residential Environment and Mental Health." In *Advances in
        Environmental Psychology*, edited by A. S. Baum and J. Singer. Hillsdale, N. J.:
        Erlbaum.

Kaufmann, Jean-Claude, and Monique Laigneau
1984   "French Urban Sociology: Problems and Prospects." *Urban Affairs Quarterly*
        19, no. 3, 287–302.

Kemeny, Jim
1982 "A Critique and Reformulation of the New Urban Sociology." *Acta Sociologica* 25, no. 4: 419–30.
Kenen, R.
1982 "Soapsuds, Space and Sociability: A Participant Observation of the Laundromat." *Urban Life* 11, no. 2, 163–83.
King, A. D.
1984 "The Social Production of Building Form: Theory and Research." *Environment and Planning D: Society and Space* 2, 429–46.
König, R. (ed.)
1962 *Handbuch der empirischen Sozialforschung*. Stuttgart.
Krasner, S.
1978 *Defending the National Interest: Raw Materials, Investments and U.S. Foreign Policy*. Princeton, NJ: Princeton University Press.
Lavrakas, Paul J.
1982 "Fear of Crime and Behavioral Restrictions in Urban and Suburban Neighborhoods." *Population and Environment* 5, 242–64.
Lebas, E.
1982 "Urban and Regional Sociology in Advanced Industrial Societies: A Decade of Marxist and Critical Perspectives." *Current Sociology* 30 (Spring).
Lee, Barrett A., R. S. Oropesa, Barbara J. Metch, and Avery M. Guest
1984 "Testing the Decline-of-Community Thesis: Neighborhood Organizations in Seattle, 1929 and 1979." *American Journal of Sociology* 89, no. 5, 1161–88.
Logan, R. John, and Reid M. Golden
1986 "Change in Suburbs and Satellites." *American Sociological Review* 51, no. 3, 430–37.
Loo, Chalsa
1986 "Neighborhood Satisfaction and Safety: A Study of a Low-Income Ethnic Area." *Environment and Behavior* 18, no. 1, 109–31.
Marcuse, P.
1978 "Housing Policy and the Myth of the Benevolent State." *Social Policy* January/February, 21–26.
McMillan, David W., and David M. Chavis
1986 "Sense of Community: A Definition and Theory." *Journal of Community Psychology* 14, 6–23.
Mellor, J. R.
1977 *Urban Sociology in an Urbanized Society*. London: Routledge & Kegan Paul.
Michelson, W.
1975 *Behavioral Research Methods in Environmental Design*. Stroudsburg, PA: Dowden, Hutchinson and Ross.
1976 *Man and His Urban Environment* (rev. 1970 ed.). Reading, MA: Addison-Wesley.
1985 *From Sun to Sun: Daily Obligations and Community Structure in the Lives of Employed Women and Their Families*. Totowa, NJ: Rowman & Allanheld.
Mitscherlich, A.
1966 *Die Unwirtlichkeit unserer Städte*. Frankfurt.
Moore, G. T., D. P. Tuttle, and S. C. Howell
1985 *Environmental Design Research Directions; Process and Prospects*. New York: Praeger.

Mullins, Patrick
1983   "Theory and Australian Urbanisation: A Comment on Kemeny's Remarks." *Australian and New Zealand Journal of Sociology* 19, 3.
National Advisory Commission on Civil Disorders
1968   *Report of the Commission*. New York: Bantam Books
O'Brien, David J., and Mary Joan Roach
1984   "Recent Developments in Urban Sociology." *Journal of Urban History* 10, no. 2, 145–70.
Pahl, R. E.
1969   "Urban Social Theory and Research." *Environment and Planning*, 143–53.
Palen, J. and B. London
1984   *Gentrification, Displacement and Neighborhood Revitalization*. Albany: State University of New York Press.
Peach, C., V. Robinson, and S. Smith
1982   *Ethnic Segregation in Cities*. Athens: The University of Georgia Press
Pickvance, C. G.
1974   "On a Materialist Critique of Urban Sociology." *Sociological Review* 22, 203–20.
Popenoe, D.
1977   *The Suburban Environment*. Chicago: University of Chicago Press.
1985   *Private Pleasure, Public Plight: American Metropolitan Community Life in Comparative Perspective*. New Brunswick, NJ: Transaction.
Population and Environment
1984   Special issue on "Attachment to Place." Vol. 7, no. 2 (Summer).
Rex, J. and R. Moore
1967   *Race, Community and Conflict*. Oxford: Oxford University Press.
Riemer, Jeffrey W.
1976   "Mistakes at Work: The Social Organization of Error in Building Construction Work." *Social Problems* 23, 255–67.
Riger, Stephanie, and Paul J. Lavrakas
1981   "Community Ties: Patterns of Attachment and Social Interaction in Urban Neighborhoods." *American Journal of Community Psychology* 9, no. 1, 55–66.
Rohe, W. M., and L. B. Gates
1985   *Planning with Neighborhoods*. Chapel Hill: University of North Carolina Press.
Rose, D.
1984   "Rethinking Gentrification: Beyond the Uneven Development of Marxist Urban Theory." *Environment and Planning D: Society and Space* 1, 47–74.
Saunders, P.
1979   *Urban Politics*. London: Hutchinson.
1981   *Social Theory and the Urban Question*. New York: Holmes and Meier.
Schmidt-Relenberg, N.
1968   *Soziologie und Städtebau*. Stuttgart, West Germany: Kramer Verlag.
Shevky, E., and W. Bell
1955   *Social Area Analysis*. Stanford, CA: Stanford University Press.
Silver, C.
1985   "Neighborhood Planning in Historical Perspective." *Journal of the American Planning Association*, Spring, 161–74.
Simmel, G.
1903   *Die Grossstädte und das Geistesleben*. Dresden

Stack, C.
1974   *All Our Kin: Strategies for Survival in a Black Community*. New York: Harper and Row.

Stahura, John M.
1986   "Black Suburbanization." *American Sociological Review* 51, no. 1, 131–44.

Steinberger, Peter J.
1984   "Urban Politics and Communality." *Urban Affairs Quarterly* 20, no. 1, 4–21.

Stokols, D., and I. Altman (eds.)
n.d.   *Handbook of Environmental Psychology*. New York: John Wiley (forthcoming).

Szelenyi, Ivan
1986   "The Last of the Marxist Urban Sociologists?" *Contemporary Sociology* 15, 707–10.

Taylor, D. G.
1981   "Housing Choice. Residential Segregation." *Review of Public Data Use* 9, no. 4, 267–82.

Taylor, Ralph B., Stephen D. Gottfredson, and Sidney Brower
1985   "Attachment to Place: Discriminant Validity, and Impacts of Disorder and Diversity." *American Journal of Community Psychology* 13, no. 5, 521–38.

Tönnies, F.
1887   *Gemeinschaft and Gesellschaft* (Community and Society). Translated and edited by C. P. Loomis, 1957. New York: Harper Torch.

Tremblay, Kenneth R. Jr., Don A. Dillman, and Kent D. Van Liere
1980   "An Examination of the Relationship between Housing Preferences and Community-size Preferences." *Rural Sociology* 45, no. 3, 509–19.

Tsai, Yung-mei, and Lee Sigelman
1982   "The Community Question: A Perspective from National Survey Data—The Case of the USA." *The British Journal of Sociology* 33, no. 4, 579–88.

Unger, Donald G., and Abraham Wandersman
1985   "The Importance of Neighbors: The Social, Cognitive, and Affective Components of Neighboring." *American Journal of Community Psychology* 13, no. 2, 139–69.

Van Vliet—, W. (ed.)
1987   *Housing Markets and Policies Under Fiscal Austerity*. Westport, CT: Greenwood Press.

Walton, J.
1981   "The New Urban Sociology." *International Social Science Journal* 33, 374–90.

Wellman, B., and B. Leighton
1979   "Networks, Neighborhoods, and Communities: Approaches to the Study of the Community Question." *Urban Affairs Quarterly* 14, no. 3, 363–90.

Wirth, L.
1938   "Urbanism as a Way of Life." *American Journal of Sociology* 44, no. 1, 1–24.

Wiseman, J.
1979   "Close Encounters of the Quasi-Primary Kind: Sociability in Urban Second-Hand Clothing Stores." *Urban Life* 8, 23–51.

Wollmann, Hellmut
1984   "Housing Policy Between State Intervention and Market Forces." In *Policy-*

Making in the Federal Republic of Germany edited by K. von Beyme and M. Schmidt, 132–55. Beverly Hills, CA: Sage.

Zeisel, J.
1980   *Inquiry by Design: Tools for Environment-Behavior Research.* Monterey, CA: Brooks/Cole.

Zube, Ervin H.
1982   "Increasing the Effective Participation of Social Scientists in Environmental Research and Planning." *International Social Science Journal* 34, no. 3, 481–94.

Zukin, S.
1980   "A Decade of the New Urban Sociology." *Theory and Society* 9 (July), 575–601.

THEORETICAL AND CONCEPTUAL PERSPECTIVES

An old saw among sociologists is that there is nothing so practical as good theory. Unless the mind is organized to make sense of what it experiences, little sense emerges. One of the challenges to social scientists in putting their wits and tools to work in a field like housing, where others have long been placing their designs, is the need for insights that cut to the heart of the unknowns and dilemmas, leading to more fruitful responses, rather than simply more information and noise.

The three chapters in Part I all deal with conceptual strategies intended to generate critical information for housing betterment. They are all geared toward amelioration, but not with a fixed plan for all, or a political or economic ideology. They identify aspects of housing basic to the production of better conditions. Moreover, their emphases dovetail neatly.

Chapter 1 by Michelson, on congruence, traces the need for and emergence of a concept that puts into relief exactly which aspects of environmental context interact with people's lives and in what ways. The goodness or badness of plans, designs, and buildings do not occur in the abstract but rather in specific ways, as facilitating or constraining specific forms of behavior. Nonetheless, the presence of congruence or incongruence in a given setting has itself to be put into a larger context. The chapter therefore traces the evolution of this concept in view of subsequent research conducted by one of its early proponents.

In Chapter 2 Studer tackles the practical implications involved in assuring that congruent environments are constructed. He notes that while knowledge of behavioral congruence is essential, it is incomplete without an understanding of those structural conditions that spell the difference between the realization and nonrealization of optimal plans, designs, and buildings.

Chapter 3 turns in the direction of what environmental settings mean to those who use them. Francescato, Weidemann, and Anderson look specifically at satisfaction, a major construct that ostensibly reflects congruence or its absence. They show how diverse uses have cast doubt on the validity and utility of such a construct. However, instead of discarding satisfaction research approaches, they urge the same kind of specificity in dealing with objective measures of the physical environment, characteristics of the population, and behavior inherent in the conceptualization of the previous two chapters. Only in this way will the meaning of those aspects of environment that can be created and manipulated become explicit.

Thus all three chapters urge not simply more research but more strategic, conceptually relevant research toward the common objective to improve human environments.

1

Congruence: The Evolution of a Contextual Concept

WILLIAM MICHELSON

Abstract. The concept of congruence is examined in terms of its original purpose, uses and misuses, and evolution in the face of operational needs and subsequent findings. Behavior is now seen to be at the heart of the environmental contexts to which congruence pertains. Furthermore, the static condition of congruence must increasingly be understood within the larger perspectives of programmed change within the lives of individuals and families and of often unexpected change in societal structure. A family, for example, may alter its demands on its home as it proceeds through its life course and as society alters patterns of where and with whom people spend time.

INTRODUCTION

This chapter is about a concept called congruence, used in environmental research to refer to how well a given context accommodates the needs of a given person or group. Congruence was originally put forward to provide conceptual guidance to those seeking ways of understanding social implications of what architects and planners design, arrange, and build—at a time when there was uncertainty as to what these implications were, if any at all. Now that we have reached a point where there is much more experience in this interdisciplinary concern, not to speak of more knowledge of the substance involved, it might be useful to observe how, as an early proponent of this concept, I have found my own perspectives on it to evolve.

Therefore, I shall address five questions about congruence: (1) What was (is) the need for a concept like congruence? (2) What is it? What are its uses and misuses? (3) How did its original formulation become modified for operational use with respect to a concrete research application—a study of behavior in high-rise apartments? (4) What additional perspectives were shown necessary by this study? (5) How has the pool of relevant considerations expanded further as the result of a more recent study dealing with urban infrastructure more broadly?

WHY CONGRUENCE?

My concern with the need for a concept like congruence goes back to the mid–1960s. Housing has, of course, always been built, with or without this concept; and housing researchers suffered no lack of activity, having a variety of other foci and interests. Sociologists, for example, analyzed housing in such terms as its basic adequacy for human welfare, its status components, and life cycle stage (Beyer 1965; Rossi 1955). Geographers first concentrated on the locational attributes of housing and then turned to the more affective issues of stress and strain in conjunction with mobility (compare Goldstein and Mayer 1964; Simmons 1968; Clark and Cadwallader 1973; Wolpert 1966; Brown and Moore 1970). Other kinds of specialists were forced to be concerned with such aspects of housing as its investment qualities, design, labor and materials, and relationship to the more general economy.

What was largely missing was the conceptualization of housing in terms pertinent to the various behaviors intended or actually taking place there and the implementation of a systematic research and development cycle optimizing the behavioral outcomes of residential settings.

Research in the social sciences had similarly advanced and developed over many years, dealing with countless phenomena from the macrostructural considerations of nations, cultures, and the international order to the micro insights on individual perception and dyadic relationships. Surprisingly little emphasis, however, had been placed on the nature and patterns of ordinary, repetitive, everyday behavior, compared to more glamorous topics like class conflict, crime, and personality. Therefore, if what I wanted to know pertained to the relationship of housing environments and the kinds of behaviors recurring in them, there was relatively little conceptual or operational support emerging from the social sciences about either the behavioral content or linkages between environment and behavior.

Furthermore, the accumulated experience of persons explicitly and empirically dealing with the interface of housing environments and behavior was (to me) surprisingly meager. As one who had optimistic faith in rational science and planning (and hence of my teachers and forerunners), it came as a shock that a relationship so central to everyday life and human welfare had not received systematic attention. A prerequisite to this had to be a perspective that clarified the interaction of built environments and human behavior.

WHAT IS CONGRUENCE? WHAT ISN'T IT?

The word ''congruence'' was borrowed for use in a perspective centering on the assessment of whether phenomena in two systems (environmental and one of the so-called action systems) were mutually supportive (that is, symbiotic in ecological terms). For example, does housing provide sufficient spatial opportunity for behaviors that are desired by builders and/or users? If so, the match between the pertinent components of environment and behavior is said to be congruent. If not, the match is incongruent. Given the ingenuity and adaptability of human beings, incongruence is an extreme, limiting situation, perhaps rare but nonetheless crucial to avoid.

Congruence is not a deterministic formulation. While incongruent relationships may frustrate desired situations or outcomes, there is no regular expectation that the design of environment can force a given behavioral outcome. Many aspects of a context may be *necessary* for an activity to take place, but few if any are *sufficient* to determine that one will definitely occur. Human motivation and diversity preclude such determination, even if desired by certain actors. Thus, the congruence perspective is oriented to an increase in human freedoms and options (that is, making *possible* a greater range of the desirable), rather than to social engineering in any determinative sense.

Congruence was conceptualized as both experiential and mental. The former involves such congruence as is actually encountered, while the latter focuses on what people think are the fruitful forms of environment for themselves and/or others (hence, vital in making decisions about options).

My attention to congruence was crystallized in a book published in 1970 (and expanded in 1976) with the (blatantly sexist) title of *Man and His Urban Environment: A Sociological Approach*. My objectives were twofold.

First, I attempted to conceptualize built space so that it could be assessed in relation to human considerations. Built environment was observed by what I called an ego-centered view—its implications for the individual user. Space was assessed in terms of its implications for the relationship of people to other people physically, sensorily, and symbolically. It was similarly observed regarding people's access to and separation from specific land uses and activities.

From the ego-centered view, environments are considered as nesting sets, starting from the most micro and individual and extending outward to include and support more complex uses and larger numbers of persons. The point, however, is that the macro sets do not function any more satisfactorily than the micro unless the fulfillment of needs by the individuals at the specific settings encountered is assured by congruence. There are obviously different considerations as scale increases, from ergonomics to timetabling, but the considerations involved are connected, not discrete, ultimately depending on how they provide what the individual seeks and expects.

Second, the book aimed to document from a dispersed, existing literature evidence of congruence between specific dimensions of environment and of behavior. The central sections of the book were organized according to the latter consideration, and these were expressed in terms of some of the main structural bases for behavior: social class, life cycle stage, life-style, value orientations, and more. The aim in this case was to document relationships found to be congruent or incongruent, so as to provide evidence and precedent for future planning and design activities. It was hoped that this would in turn result in the creation of future environments that would be optimally congruent with desired outcomes.

All in all, congruence was put forward as a probabilistic perspective concerning particular outcomes, dependent on the environment and its capacity to facilitate human objectives. I further took as an article of faith (in part derived from existing studies) that congruence would be accompanied by satisfaction and well-being, while incongruence would foster the opposite. The actual process of determining the extent of congruence or incongruence in concrete situations, however, could not be formulated into theories insofar as settings and their users vary in so many ways, while determinative causation was thought even further from the mark. Improvement could be made by minimizing frustrating situations rather than by the creation of "perfect" environments that could determine "correct" behavior.

MODIFICATION OF CONGRUENCE FOR OPERATIONAL USE

I was anxious to utilize the congruence perspective to assess the situation of families with children living in high-rise apartments, in comparison to those living in the more customary (within the North American perspective) low-rise and detached housing. Did, for example, families in high-rise apartments have different objectives for their daily life than families in single-family homes, or were their objectives the same but with an incongruent interface with the different form of residential environment? A study design involved the comparison of matched family cohorts in single-family homes and high-rise apartments, each divided into central-city and suburban locations.

Operationalizing this research required an evolution in my previous treatment of congruence. The point was obvious once faced directly: *What happens in environments is behavior itself, not its typical structural causes.* Therefore, if we were to study what is facilitated or frustrated by residential environments, we had to gather behavioral data. The way I had formulated it in the book obscured the fact that it was the emergence or suppression of desired and/or characteristic behaviors that would indicate congruence or incongruence with the physical contexts involved. The partly causal factors like class, ethnicity, and the like I had outlined, which usually act in unpredictable combinations to produce behavior, are actually nominal categories, at least one step removed from behavior and at least two steps from the environment. In other words, class is not behavior; class is a structural predisposition that may cause certain kinds of behavior, alone or in combination with other structural factors. Thus it does not in and of itself interact with environmental design; such potential interaction would occur only through any behavior found to result from class.

Therefore, it became desirable to utilize a data-gathering technique that would address everyday behavior in necessary variety and detail, yet connect it to the settings in which it occurred. The time budget fulfilled this objective. Consisting of a chronological listing of activities a person undertakes during an actual period of time (for example, yesterday), including beginning and ending times for the respective episodes, who else was involved, where it took place, concurrent activities, and, ideally, some subjective assessment of the episode, this provides a quantitative picture of daily activity, with both interpersonal and contextual dimensions, and sometimes a qualitative dimension as well. Some of these data can be gathered by observation in very circumscribed settings, but more typical translocational behavior requires a more synoptic method like the time budget.

There is still room and interest to address the questions about which nominal characteristics of people are involved in the behaviors that enter environmental contexts. Relatively simple, traditional questioning elicits such material. But it was essential to recognize that if we wished to understand environment-behavior congruence, then we had to utilize a technique focusing directly on the dynamics of the context under examination. This is what the time-budget approach provided.

ADDITIONAL PERSPECTIVE(S) SHOWN NECESSARY

Our study, which utilized a longitudinal dimension to go with the comparison of residential environments, proved supportive of the concept of congruence (Michelson 1977). It showed congruence reflecting both self-selection to housing and location (Bell 1968) and the limitations and opportunities of specific settings. For example, families moving to their own houses reported more time spent entertaining, housekeeping, and making repairs, while those moving to apartments were more passive within them but spent more time elsewhere, including the health facilities so often included in North American high-rise complexes. Many of these behavioral differences were anticipated by movers to the environments in question, while other differences simply emerged as the path of least resistance.

However, when I wanted to ask about the human outcome of this kind of intersystem congruence (that is, what difference does it make for satisfaction?), I discovered that this could not be understood without including an interactive effect with still another consideration: people's aspirations.

In the case in point, most families moving to apartments wanted eventually to be home owners. Within the physical parameters of the apartment building, they would act in ways congruent with their existing setting; yet they would carry with them expectations of changed life-styles under future residential situations. If they expected to fulfill their residential aspirations, they would be satisfied with performing the behaviors congruent with their current residences. On the other hand, if they maintained the cultural aspiration of a single-family house but felt that they could not achieve it (that is, blocked aspirations), then they were dissatisfied with their apartments. In other words, the same behaviors in the same places had positive or negative outcomes depending on whether aspirations appeared fulfillable or blocked (compare Michelson 1980).

This additional perspective turned our attention beyond appropriate housing type and design to the consideration of what it is about the functioning of the housing market that makes families conclude that their future mobility is blocked. Although a focus on how poverty and handicap are treated in a market economy is useful for many cases, it was also important in our geographic area to note factors in the escalating costs of housing in general and single-family housing in particular. This included speculation in land by professionals and use of housing as an instrument of old-age security by ordinary citizens.

Thus, one of the implications of our study was that a direct way to increase satisfaction among residents of high-rise apartments was to increase the supply of low-cost houses!

All in all, our study of congruence in this high-rise versus low-rise comparison indicated that while such a concept had utility in understanding situation-specific behavior and its physical parameters, the interpretation of congruence required the additional perspective of how it fit into people's trajectory-of-life plans. Congruence is not a finite, closed phenomenon, in which people think only of the housing they now occupy. This makes congruence no less real, but its affective dimensions and hence implications are subject to intervening factors and considerations. Chapter 3 by Francescato, Weidemann, and Anderson deepens the context through which one might understand residential satisfaction.

EXPANDING THE POOL OF RELEVANT CONSIDERATIONS

The perspective in which congruence is found widened for me even more as a consequence of a recent project on the implications for women and their families of maternal employment, in view of various extrafamilial, community contexts and of intrafamilial division of labor (Michelson 1985). The time budget was used once more, as were a number of more subjective techniques, in this study of 538 representative families in Metropolitan Toronto, Canada.

Some previously unreported data are in my opinion extremely pertinent to the future direction of housing and the fulfillment of criteria for congruence. We could construct from the time budgets where and with whom our sample of married women with children up to 14 years of age spent their weekday time, broken down by whether they had full-time, part-time, or no employment.

Table 1.1 shows variations in the places where these women and their husbands spend their day, by the wife's employment status. The women show marked differences. Those with full-time jobs are at home one-third less time than those with no outside employment. They spend only about one-third the daily time in space immediately outside their home, such as a garden. In turn, the former spend correspondingly more time at a work site and traveling.

The centrality of home in people's lives is not thereby changed, but it is diminished. Furthermore, it is not buttressed by compensating time at home by the husbands. Men vary little according to the employment status of their wives in where they spend their days.

Table 1.1
Mean Minutes Spent on a Weekday by Husbands and Wives in Specific Places, by Employment Status of Wife

Places	Wives Employment Status of Wife Full-time Employment	Part-time Employment	No Employment
At home	839	1070	1206
Outside home	8	20	25
In neighborhood	4	2	7
Home of another	15	17	28
Public place outside neighborhood	74	99	85
Workplace	376	107	10
Transit	86	71	44
n =	(160)	(86)	(188)
Husbands			
At home	728	719	747
Outside home	25	27	27
In neighborhood	3	3	3
Home of another	12	9	11
Public place outside neighborhood	79	69	72
Workplace	423	462	456
In transit	107	80	84
n =	(141)	(80)	(173)

Table 1.2
Mean Minutes Spent on a Weekday by Husbands and Wives with Specific Persons, by Employment Status of Wife (includes combinations, hence not additive)

	Wives		
	Employment Status of Wife		
Places	Full-time Employment	Part-time Employment	No Employment
Immediate family	633	798	873
Other kin	22	51	48
Neighbors	0.4	2	17
Other friends	37	39	60
Workmates	340	102	8
Alone	206	299	303
n =	(160)	(86)	(188)
	Husbands		
Immediate family	533	583	583
Other kin	15	13	14
Neighbors	5	2	10
Other friends	26	20	30
Workmates	402	418	413
Alone	278	220	237
n =	(141)	(80)	(173)

Data in Table 1.2, showing with whom people spend time, complements those on place, in that traditional contacts frequently met at home are diminished in the lives of employed women. It must be noted that while employed women have far from eliminated everyday meetings with kin and friends, workmates have nonetheless assumed obviously greater proportions in their lives. Contact with neighbors was not a major form of contact even for housewives, but it declines almost to the point of extinction among employed others. Once again, the husbands show only minor variations in their patterns as defined by their wives' employment.

These data on where and with whom people spend time according to maternal employment status suggest that, with increasing maternal employment, the household may be losing its role as a critical locus of everyday activity and interaction.

More generally, what these data and the accompanying hypothesis point to is the need to place housing not only within the trajectory of change in the lifetime of a family but also in view of changing societal structures as well. For example, changing roles of women and conceptions of the family may well be altering traditional demands on what the "family home" should be and where it should be located for many in the population. A significant proportion of new population cohorts may envisage a new lifetime trajectory of change, as a consequence of evolving roles and structures. But we cannot take this for granted. Aspirations and trajectories, like congruence itself, are empirical matters, documented by research.

CONCLUDING REMARKS

Within the limited content of some subjects covered in my own research, an approach and accompanying subject matter that I once felt required legitimation and documentation may have become legitimate but must now, in my opinion, be placed rather modestly within a much larger perspective. The considerations mentioned here are but bare illustrations of the variety and complexity of factors impinging on the human value of housing. Even behavior, at the heart of environment-behavior congruence, is itself caused by many other factors in the real world beyond those pertinent to the context under study. Similarly, as Studer points out in Chapter 2, the environment is put into place (or not) for reasons well beyond human functioning.

Nonetheless, when we plan, design, and build, we contribute to people's lives by commission and by omission. The extent to which the behaviors that flow from particular junctures in a lifetime and in the evolution of a society can be realized is a sign of the degree of *support* offered by housing and urban environments. The biological sciences focus on life supports. Environmental planning is a step beyond. It has the potential to put in place support systems not only for life but for *living*.

If we as researchers and planners derive part of our living from the substance of our work, should we not do our utmost for the support of living among our fellow human beings? In this, an immediate first step is in the care and thought we give to our paradigms. In an age of fiscal austerity, when everything is no longer acknowledged possible, creativity in thinking must be turned to the basic purposes of environmental formation. This would be of benefit long past the end of austerity.

REFERENCES

Bell, Wendell
1968   "The City, the Suburb, and a Theory of Social Choice." In *The New Urbanization*, edited by Scott Greer, Dennis McElrath, David Minar, and Peter Orleans, 132–68. New York: St. Martin's Press.
Beyer, Glenn
1965   *Housing and Society*. New York: Macmillan.
Brown, L. A., and Eric Moore
1970   "The Intra-urban Migration Process: A Perspective." *General Systems* 15, 109–22.
Clark, William, and M. Cadwallader
1973   "Locational Stress and Residential Mobility." *Environment and Behavior* 5, 29–41.
Goldstein, S., and K. Mayer
1964   "Migration and the Journey to Work." *Social Forces* 42, 472–81.
Michelson, William
1970   *Man and His Urban Environment: A Sociological Approach*. Reading, Mass.: Addison-Wesley.
1977   *Environmental Choice, Human Behavior, and Residential Satisfaction*. New York: Oxford.
1980   "Long and Short Range Criteria for Housing Choice and Environmental Behavior." *Journal of Social Issues* 36, no. 3, 135–49.
1985   *From Sun to Sun: Daily Obligations and Community Structure in the Lives of Employed Women and their Families*. Totowa, NJ: Rowman and Allanheld.
Rossi, Peter
1955   *Why Families Move*. New York: The Free Press.
Simmons, J. W.
1968   "Changing Residence in the City, a Review of Intra-Urban Mobility." *The Geographical Review* 58, 622–51.
Wolpert, J.
1966   "Migration as an Adjustment to Environmental Stress." *Journal of Social Issues* 22, no. 4, 92–102.

2

Prospects for Realizing Congruent Housing Environments

RAYMOND G. STUDER

Abstract. Physical planning, design, production, and management are processes aimed at realizing congruence in sociophysical systems. Incongruences are seen to result from problems inherent in contemporary processes of environmental supply and demand; four such problems are identified. Arguments are developed for a generative decision-making model with particular emphasis on dialectical procedures, as holding potential for ameliorating problems intrinsic to environmental supply and demand processes.

INTRODUCTION

The processes of environmental organization have as their underlying purpose the realization and maintenance of a state of congruence between individual and collective behavioral goals and properties of the physical environment (Michelson 1977; Van Vliet— and Burgers 1986)—essentially a problem of (environmental) supply and (social) demand. Supply and demand relative to the built environment has been a major focus of urban economic analysis (for example, Alonso 1965); while this level of analysis certainly captures the *aggregate* reality of the problem, it provides only a limited understanding of its etiology and dynamics. The aim of this chapter is to identify several relevant issues and outline some directions for further research required to address them.

Committed as they are to systematic documentation of the social consequences of spatial organization, emerging programs of sociophysical research (see, for example, Dunlap and Catton 1979; Foley 1980) provide a deeper understanding of individual and collective sociophysical requirements, that is, the demand characteristics of the built environment. However, availability of this new knowledge does not automatically lead to sociophysical improvements. Also required are effective environmental supply processes—that is, instrumental and organizational means of realizing and maintaining physical systems and settings congruent with people's goals.

Figure 2.1
Unself-Conscious Decision Processes

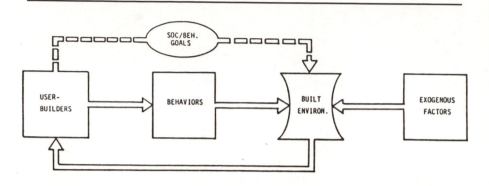

The processes that effect environmental supply include those of planning, design, production, and management of environmental systems and settings. These processes, driven by a complex array of actors, purposes, organizations, and institutions, operate in one form or another in all political economies. Regardless of their political economic context, all contemporary environmental supply systems embody certain common problems; none is fully effective in maintaining congruence between people's goals and the supporting built environment. To better understand the nature of environmental supply and social demand processes, let us briefly review major evolutionary developments in these processes.

THE EVOLUTION OF ENVIRONMENTAL SUPPLY PROCESSES

In his attempt to redress contemporary problems in physical design in the early 1960s, Christopher Alexander (1964) identified two fundamentally different evolutionary forms of physical decision making: *unself-conscious* and *self-conscious*. The direct, unself-conscious form-making process of indigenous cultures is guided by certain fairly complex and rigidly maintained "unspoken rules." Those covert "rules" produced physical settings integrally linked to explicit sociocultural conditions (and attendant behavioral requirements) on the one hand, and physical and technological constraints on the other. The resultant spatial arrangements and physical structures exhibited little variation and both the building norms and their products evolved over an extended time frame. The builders were close to their materials and techniques of construction, usually inhabited the shelters they produced, and subsequently altered them as required by unanticipated events and emerging dysfunctions. In short, the unself-conscious form-making process was one of direct, iterative responses to slowly evolving sociophysical requirements. Figure 2.1 depicts this process wherein user-builders respond to, produce, and alter physical settings predicated on their social, psychological, and physiological requirements.

A fundamentally different situation emerges when cultures experience a transformation from unself-conscious to self-conscious form-making processes. In the latter, the functions of inhabitant-builders are assumed by specialists, that is, master crafts people, responsible for the organization and construction of physical settings. The process of incremental, element-by-element, component-by-component, adaptive change—the continuous process of construction-testing-alteration—is replaced by one in which all elements of the system are in flux and require simultaneous comprehension and conceptual organization. Sociophysical accommodation was no longer slow, incremental, and adaptive, but rapid, synoptic, and willful. Moreover, new technologies vastly relaxed the physical constraints, thus elaborating and complicating the range of possible solutions. One of the characteristic norms of self-conscious processes (see below) is that physical structures became less alterable, thus dampening incremental adjustments to emerging sociophysical incongruities.

Faced with a far more complex organizational task, responsible specialists eventually got around to the search for principles, normative theories, and the like to provide guidance and render their problems tractable. Such prescriptions inevitably exhibit a certain arbitrariness, so serious debate and criticism ensued. Emergence of form-making specialists also led to the establishment of guilds, special educational requirements, and other institutionalized arrangements. The need to attain status within the guild produced a striving for identity and competition among prescriptive theories regarding how best to proceed and suceed. The success of the unself-conscious form-makers depended on their integral role in the sociocultural context. In contrast, the success of the self-conscious designers depends on the viability of the prescriptions guiding their efforts in the context of the norms of their guild.

The scientific and technological revolution produced vast changes in social organization. The greater differentiation and division of labor became manifest in new land use patterns, characterized by greater specialization and segregation. This trend was further reinforced by architect-planners like Le Corbusier who espoused the ideological principles embodied by the 1933 Athens Charter of the Congrès International d'Architects Modernes (CIAM). The increasingly complex functions of conceptualizing, organizing, and producing built environments also led to more specialized professionals, technicians, entrepreneurs, organizations, and processes. Figure 2.2 depicts self-conscious processes as they have evolved. In general, decision makers of various sorts interpret the requirements of user-stakeholders in organizing and producing built environments.

As positivist precepts came to dominate human affairs, decision-making processes became even more ''self-conscious'' (that is, scientific), and so-called rational approaches have been increasingly brought to bear on problems of supply and demand relative to the built environment (Faludi 1983). However, significant improvements in sociophysical congruence have not been realized. We will next

Figure 2.2
Contemporary Self-Conscious Decision Processes

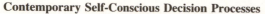

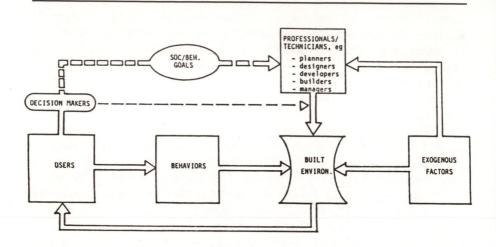

sketch out some of the possible reasons for this, then consider some emerging developments.

IMPEDIMENTS TO EFFECTIVE ENVIRONMENTAL SUPPLY PROCESSES

All contemporary environmental supply systems, *regardless* of political economic context, share certain intrinsic problems. They all: (1) are predicated on limited knowledge of sociophysical relations and processes; (2) embrace physical technologies dissynchronous with social demand dynamics; (3) operate in complex decision-making environments with conflicting goals and perspectives; and, (4) embody inappropriate decision-making instrumentalities.

Basic and applied knowledge of sociophysical systems is a necessary, if not sufficient, condition for addressing the environmental supply and demand problem. Nothing approaching nomological knowledge of the relevant relationships is available for application to real-world settings. Planning, design, and management of sociophysical systems involves certain kinds of predictions regarding the ensemble's performance prior to implementation. Such predictions require a *functional* understanding of sociophysical relationships and processes. What we generally have is a piecemeal *descriptive* account of these. Given our present knowledge base, the ability to model and predict sociophysical performance becomes even more problematic when dealing with larger aggregates. Social research programs focusing on environmental variables are committed to the generation of important new knowledge—a functional understanding—of environment-person-behavior relations at both disaggregate and aggregate levels.

The systematic linking of these research programs to instrumental decision making—the realization of a technology of environmental-behavioral programming and design—has yet to be fully consummated.

Dissynchronous social and physical system dynamics stem from the basic fact that the needs and goals of contemporary populations, both individually and collectively, are subject to considerable change, while physical environments, in contrast, are essentially static. The problem of environmental supply is thus made especially difficult by present physical technologies. To maintain congruence *over time*, and increase the probability of matching people to appropriately supportive environments, the obvious need is for physical systems capable of extensive adaptation along several continua; that is, spatial environments that can be readily and inexpensively reorganized or replaced in response to changing human goals and external conditions.[1] There is little doubt that appropriate, cost-effective, mass-produced physical technologies more responsive to the dynamics of demand could be developed.[2] However, their implementation is inhibited by a complex set of factors.

Attached to the built environment is a great deal of symbolism—certain aesthetic and sociocultural values. While user requirements related to such values are quite real, some of them appear to exacerbate environmental supply and demand problems. Consider, for example, permanence in the built environment. Architects are generally trained, rewarded, and even immortalized for creating sturdy, long-lasting structures, not for providing environments responsive to the dynamics of users' sociobehavioral goals. Paradoxically, users are also enamored with permanence and symbols thereof in their built environments. Through developers the marketplace responds accordingly. Building codes and other regulations, construction norms, financial institutions, and craft guilds all reinforce the same pattern. The result is a relatively permanent, expensive built environment, constructed with relatively unsophisticated building technologies on valuable land, which is responsive to some but certainly not all dimensions of human need.

If this analysis is accurate, we have a very basic and difficult problem: tenaciously held symbolic, aesthetic values on the part of certain stakeholders lead them to embrace goals in direct conflict with implementation of physical technologies responsive to other, seemingly more fundamental, goals. This is a classic ill-structured problem, one quite resilient to conventional, positivist decision-making procedures, and one that is not likely to be solved via free market mechanisms.

Decision-making environments within which physical planning, design, production, and management decision makers must operate are highly complex, with various decision centers and actors operating at cross purposes. In capitalist, private-sector contexts environmental supply and demand interact via market mechanisms involving entrepreneurs (for example, developers, building contractors, suppliers, investors) pursuing various goals that may or may not be congruent with those of users. Analogous to market forces in dominant capitalist economies are complex bureaucracies in socialist nations. Neither capitalist market mechanisms (Gans 1959) nor socialist allocation mechanisms (Szelenyi 1983) appear to provide an adequate response to people's sociophysical needs. The matter is made more complicated by the massive array of constraining building codes, policies, rules, and regulations, all developed in the public interest perhaps, but many tied to obsolete issues, practices, procedures, and various special interests (for example, labor union and entrepreneurial protectionism). These factors, together with the discontinuities across various decision centers, exacerbate supply and demand disparities and technological lag and complicate decision making generally.

Instrumental and normative decision-making processes as now effected present formidable difficulties in realizing and maintaining sociophysical congruence. It is through the processes of planning, design, and management that human knowledge (for example, experiential, practical, scientific) is brought to bear on human problems. Our ability to reduce disparities in environmental supply and demand systems is thus heavily dependent on the efficacy of these processes. Decision making necessarily involves both instrumental and normative dimensions, that is, the selection of instrumental means and the identification of normative ends.

A formidable instrumental difficulty grows out of the pervasive tendency of physical planners, designers, and managers to define their problem domains, and to evaluate their solutions, in terms of physical rather than sociobehavioral variables. This issue has been discussed in considerable detail elsewhere (see Studer 1970, 1971). The point is that this manner of defining sociophysical problems begs the very question a viable decision-making process is intended to answer; that is to say, effective instrumental decision making requires that physical problems be formulated, and solutions validated, in terms of sociobehavioral variables.

If we had nomological knowledge of environment-behavior systems, and could make precise if-then statements regarding the sociobehavioral consequences of particular spatial configurations, the problem of maintaining congruence would become more tractable, but it would not be solved. That is, the normative issue would not have been addressed. The normative issue in physical decision making comes down to the assessment of stakeholder perceptions of what ought to be done. Stakeholders are ''all parties who will be affected by or who affect an important decision'' (Mitroff and Emshoff 1979). Stakeholders in environmental supply and demand problems include: (1) users, (2) nonuser decision makers, and (3) professionals, technicians, and relevant social scientists. Considerable conflict can emerge within *and* among each of these classes of actors regarding both ends and means. Practical solutions to collective environmental supply problems require resolution of conflicts among these various stakeholders (recognizing that power is not equally distributed among them). Simon (1973) and Mason and Mitroff (1981) have classified such problems as *ill-structured*. They are characterized by one or more conditions: there are many decision makers whose identity and/or perspectives of a problem cannot be specified; multiple conflicting objectives; interdependent, uncertain, or unknown outcomes; and/or incalculable probabilities of achieving specified objectives (W. N. Dunn 1981). We are only beginning to fully comprehend the nature of such problem domains and the general charactersitics of decision-making instrumentalities required for dealing with them. What we do know is that conventional decision theoretic and policy analytic methods developed for well-structured problems are inadequate, if not irrelevant, to current problems of environmental supply and demand.

These multiple problem areas—impediments to effective environmental supply processes—together with more basic problems of distributive justice that challenge all contemporary political economies, present a picture of seeming intractability. Fortunately, emerging developments bearing on each of the above areas offer some encouragement. None is more pressing and fundamental, however, than the decision-making arrangements and processes involved. Let us now review recent developments bearing on these.

TOWARD GENERATIVE DECISION MAKING

As noted earlier, disparities in social demand and environmental supply systems are an important societal problem in *all* political economies. Blatant incongruences have been documented in countries with dominant capitalist economies (Gans 1959; Yancey 1971), in collectivist economies (Hegedus and Tosics 1983; Szelenyi 1983), as well as in less-developed nations (Brolin 1972; Grenell 1972). As has been argued, problems of supply and demand relative to the built environment cannot be fully understood and dealt with via an economic analysis of free market and other resource allocative mechanisms alone. It is also necessary to address the underlying organizational and procedural dimensions of environmental supply and demand systems.

The unself-conscious processes of indigenous cultures come to mind as an interesting (meta)model for approaching the problem. Are there principles and processes embodied therein that might be extrapolated to exponentially more complex postindustrial contexts? The issue of unself-conscious versus self-conscious form-making comes down to assessing the viability of *imposed* versus *generative* solutions to human environmental problems.

Imposed solutions characteristically emphasize empirical and instrumental dimensions and are developed by technicians external to the sociophysical problem and remote psychologically if not physically to those most directly impacted (Wengert 1976). Generative solutions, by contrast, characteristically emphasize the norms and values of all stakeholders and are developed via some form of direct participation in decision-making processes. The issues have sharpened in recent years as the forces of "scientification" and "pluralization" have come into direct confrontation. The limitations of instrumental rationalism have been illuminated (Leiss 1975; W. N. Dunn 1982) and the effectiveness of conventional "scientific" decision-making methods in dealing with ill-structured spatial problems has been seriously challenged (E. R. Alexander 1984; Hall 1983). Demands of alienated stakeholders for direct participation at various levels of decision making have, since the mid–1960s, became more extensive and intensive (Fagence 1977; Cantanese 1984). These demands for increased stakeholder participation appear to be transforming conventional problem-solving paradigms. The distinctive characteristic of one such paradigm, an evolutionary perspective developed by E. S. Dunn (1971), is that the direction of change is generated from *within* the human system, thus exhibiting self-organizing, self-regulating properties not characteristic of "deterministic social engineering" (that is, imposed processes). Depiction of sociophysical planning, design, and management as processes of social experimentation and learning places the organization of physical support systems in a social evolutionary context, one not unlike that of unself-conscious processes found in indigenous cultures. This is not so surprising; we are, after all, beginning to question the social achievements of "modernity" (McCarthy 1984). Whether our concern is the complex problem of sociophysical congruence via environmental supply and demand processes, or any number of other equally challenging societal problems, our task, it seems, is to realize planning, design, and management processes that support both the emancipatory *and* the technical interests of stakeholders.

The purpose of either generative or imposed modes of planning, design, and management decision making is the same: to move a system or setting from where it *is* to where it *should be*. Imposed processes, predicated on a posture of instrumental rationalism, bracket normative and instrumental aspects of decision processes, and they generally assume the latter as given. However, the so-called fact-value debate has firmly established that factual and valuative issues and claims are intertwined, indeed amalgamated, in all aspects and phases of decision making (Michalos 1981). Generative processes are required that address normative and instrumental dimensions of decision making with equal emphasis and methodological rigor. Such processes appear highly appropriate to address the ill-structured nature of sociospatial supply and demand problems.

METHODOLOGICAL AND ORGANIZATIONAL REQUIREMENTS

Ill-structured problems clearly require new methodologies that differ fundamentally from conventional ones. The nature of ill-structured problems requires not so much a theory of policy decision as a theory of policy search, that is, procedures that enable us to *structure* problems in the course of *solving* them. Proponents of *dialectical* methodologies (for example, Mason and Mitroff 1981; Rein and White 1977), a particular form of generative decision making, claim that such procedures are uniquely appropriate for addressing ill-structured problems. A dialectical methodology, in contrast to other modes of problem structuring, "is capable of producing a synthesis, *if* one is possible, which is based on full recognition and appreciation of conflicts, not by ignoring or trivializing them" (Mason and Mitroff 1981). Dialectically based methodologies, that is, those that facilitate reflective, intersubjective discourse and argument among

Figure 2.3
Generative Sociophysical Decision Processes

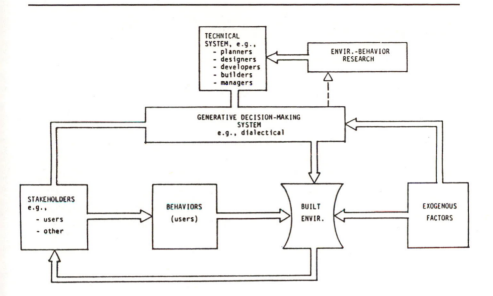

stakeholders with conflicting goals and objectives, hold great potential for supporting generative forms of sociophysical decision making (Goldstein 1984).[3] Figure 2.3 depicts generative processes in which users and other stakeholders in the environmental supply enterprise are linked into a decision-making process in which conflicting perspectives, objectives, and claims regarding ends and means are explicitly and systematically addressed.

Implementation of generative decision processes involving multiple stakeholder groups and directly linked to sociophysical knowledge generation functions (Studer, forthcoming) requires not only new conceptualizations of environmental supply processes, but new organizational arrangements as well. While it is not yet clear what particular organizational forms are required, it is clear that present hierarchically structured, compartmentalized, and discontinuous environmental supply functions have proven ineffective.

Thus, demands for participation and new power arrangements are complemented by a convergent interest in developing new decision-making instrumentalities more integrally linked to social evolutionary processes (for example, Dunn 1971; Campbell 1974; Habermas 1978; W. N. Dunn 1982). Critical theory, its refinements (Habermas 1984), and interpretation in the context of policy analysis, planning, and management decision making (for example, Mason and Mitroff 1981; Studer 1982) are producing a fundamental impact in areas highly relevant to the environmental supply and demand problem. These developments have produced a Zeitgeist of sorts that will most certainly transform decision-making styles and processes.

CONCLUSIONS

We are accumulating considerable evidence that pervasive incongruencies exist and persist between people's individual and collective goals and the built environment. The complex problems of environmental supply and demand have been quite resilient to reform in the past, and a society's investment in accommodating people's environmental needs must always be weighed against other, competing societal needs. These competing needs must, however, be weighed in light of an extensive, growing body of research findings indicating that sustained sociophysical incongruencies may carry significant economic, social, psychological, and physiological costs. In this chapter, it has been argued, these incongruencies and their implications stem, in part, from problems intrinsic to contemporary processes of environmental supply and demand operating in all political economies. Four such problems areas were identified, and the argument has been made that their solution via extent decision-making and resource distribution mechanisms is highly unlikely.

Examination of environmental supply and demand issues thus leads us to the core of contemporary societal tensions. These tensions are fostered in great part by the excesses of instrumental rationalism and all that is implied by this phenomenon, including its unresponsiveness to both the technical and emancipatory interests of stakeholders. The purpose of these comments has not been to provide a detailed explication of the instrumentation required to effect an alternative approach. The purpose was rather to identify issues requiring attention in future investigations of sociophysical congruence, and to argue for generative modes of decision making analogous to those found in indigenous cultures as holding great potential for ameliorating extant supply and demand incongruities.

NOTES

A different and longer version of this chapter, co-authored with Willem van Vliet—, appears in the journal *Architecture and Behavior/Architecture et Comportement* 3, no. 2, 1987.

1. Whatever constitutes an "appropriately supportive" environment, its requirements will most certainly change over time. Two conflicting arguments have been made for accommodating the dynamics of sociophysical systems. The first assumes the static nature of physical settings, and asserts that uncertainty regarding future sociospatial requirements can best be accommodated via highly *generalized* configurations permitting a wide range of behaviors. The counterargument is that such generalized configurations disregard the potential influence of physical variables in human affairs on the one hand, and introduce random (possibly counterproductive) influences on the other. According to this counterargument, what is needed are configurations explicitly supportive of goal-related behav-

iors, but capable of changing state when goals and/or other relevant conditions are altered (see Studer 1970).

2. Relevant in this context is Habraken's so-called supports principle. Its original explication appeared in Dutch in 1961 and was translated into English in 1972 under the title *Supports: An Alternative to Mass Housing* (New York: Praeger). See also Habraken et al. (1976). The extension of this principle to the neighborhood level has as yet not been discussed in English publications. However, information on this approach may be obtained by writing to Stichting Architecten Research, Postbus 429, 5600 AK, Eindhoven, The Netherlands.

3. For example, dialectical procedures would seem highly appropriate to address the earlier noted conflict between stakeholders' values and needs regarding, respectively, permanence and responsiveness of the environment.

REFERENCES

Alexander, C.
1964 *Notes of the Synthesis of Form.* Cambridge, MA: Harvard University Press.
Alexander, E. R.
1984 "After Rationality, What? A Review of Responses to Paradigm Breakdown." *Journal of the American Planning Association* 50, no. 1, 62–69.
Alonso, A.
1965 *Location and Land Use.* Cambridge, MA: Harvard University Press.
Brolin, B. C.
1972 "Chandigarh was Planned by Experts but Something Has Gone Wrong," *Smithsonian* 3, no. 3, 56–63.
Campbell, D. T.
1974 "Evolutionary Epistemology." In *The Philosophy of Karl Popper*, edited by P. Schilpps, 413–630. La Salle: Open Court Publishing Company.
Cantanese, A. J.
1984 *The Politics of Planning and Development.* Beverly Hills, CA: Sage.
Dunlap, R. E., and W. R. Catton, Jr.
1979 "Environmental Sociology." *Annual Review of Sociology* 5, 243–73.
Dunn, E. S.
1971 *Economic and Social Development.* Baltimore: Johns Hopkins University Press.
Dunn, W. N.
1981 *Public Policy Analysis: An Introduction.* Englewood Cliffs, NJ: Prentice Hall.
1982 "Reforms as Arguments." In *Evaluation Studies Review Annual*, Vol. 7, edited by E. R. House, S. Mathison, J. A. Pearsol, and H. Proskill, 117–28. Beverly Hills, CA: Sage Publications.
Fagence, M.
1977 *Citizen Participation in Planning.* New York: Pergamon.
Faludi, A.
1983 "Critical Rationalism and Planning Methodology." *Urban Studies* 20, 265–78.
Foley, D. L.
1980 "The Sociology of Housing." *Annual Review of Sociology* 6, 457–78.
Gans, H.
1959 "The Human Implications of Current Redevelopment and Relocation Planning." *Journal of American Institute of Planners* 25, 15–25.

Goldstein, H. A.
1984   "Planning as Argumentation." *Environment and Planning* 11, 297–312.
Grenell, P.
1972   "Planning for Invisible People: Some Consequences of Bureaucratic Values and Practices. In *Freedom to Build*, edited by J. Turner et al., 95–121. New York: Macmillan.
Habermas, J.
1978   "Toward a Reconstruction of Historical Materialism." In *From Contract to Community*, edited by F. Dallayr. New York: Dekker.
1984   *The Theory of Communicative Action*. Boston: Beacon.
Habraken, N. J., J. T. Boekholt, A. P. Thyssen, and P. J. Dinjens
1976   *Variations: The Systematic Design of Supports*. Cambridge, MA: Laboratory of Architecture and Planning, MIT.
Hall, P.
1983   "The Anglo-American Connection: Rival Rationalities in Planning Theory and Practice, 1955–1980," *Environment and Planning B* 10, 41–46.
Hegedus, J., and I. Tosics
1983   "Housing Classes and Housing Policy: Some Change in the Budapest Housing Market." *International Journal of Urban and Regional Research* 7, no. 4, 467–94.
Leiss, W.
1975   "The Problem of Man and Nature in the Work of the Frankfurt School." *Philosophy of Social Science* 5, 163–72.
Mason, Richard O., and Ian I. Mitroff
1981   *Challenging Strategic Planning: Concepts, Methods and Techniques*. New York: John Wiley.
McCarthy, T.
1984   "Translator's Introduction." In J. Habermas, *The Theory of Communicative Action*. Boston: Beacon.
Michalos, Alex C.
1981   "Facts, Values and Rational Decision Making." *Policy Studies* 9, no. 8, 544–51.
Michelson, W.
1977   "From Congruence to Antecedent Conditions: A Search for the Basis of Environmental Improvement." In *Perspectives on Environment and Behavior*, edited by D. Stokols, 205–19. New York: Plenum Press.
Mitroff, I., and J. Emshoff
1979   "On Strategic Assumption Making: A Dialectical Approach to Policy and Planning." *Academy of Management Review* 4, no. 1, 1–12.
Rein, M., and S. H. White
1977   "Policy Research: Belief and Doubt." *Policy Analysis* 3, no. 2, 239–72.
Simon, H.
1973   "The Structure of Ill-Structured Problems." *Artificial Intelligence* 4, 181–201.
Studer, R. G.
1970   "The Dynamics of Behavior-Contingent Physical Systems." In *Environmental Psychology: Man and His Physical Setting*, edited by H. Proshanksy, W. Ittelson, and L. Rivlin, 56–76. New York: Holt, Rinehart and Winston.

1971   "Human Systems Design and the Management of Change." *General Systems* 16, 131–43.
1982   "Normative Guidance for the Planning, Design and Management of Environment-Behavior Systems." Unpublished Ph.D. Dissertation, University of Pittsburgh.
n.d.   "Design of the Built Environment: The Search for Useable Knowledge." In *Handbook of Housing and the Built Environment*, edited by E. Huttman and W. van Vliet—. Westport, CT: Greenwood Press (forthcoming).
Szelenyi, I.
1983   *Urban Social Inequality Under Static Socialism.* New York: Oxford University Press.
Van Vliet—, W., and J. Burgers
1986   "Communities in Transition." In *Neighborhood and Community Environments*, edited by I. Altman and A. Wandersman. New York: Plenum Press.
Wengert, H.
1976   "Citizen Participation: Practice in Search of a Theory." *Natural Resources Fund* 16, 23–40.
Yancey, W. L.
1971   "Architecture, Interaction and Social Control." *Environment and Behavior* 3, no. 1, 3–21.

3

Residential Satisfaction: Its Uses and Limitations in Housing Research

GUIDO FRANCESCATO, SUE WEIDEMANN,
AND JAMES R. ANDERSON

Abstract. In periods of fiscal austerity, prudent management of scarce resources demands that policies and interventions maximize the benefits that
are to accrue to the targeted populations. Residential satisfaction measures
can provide useful guidelines for this purpose. The limitations of residents'
satisfaction research, as well as its appropriate utilization, are examined
within an overall view of housing as a complex system. In addition, suggestions are made for the refinement of conceptual models of residential
satisfaction and for the need to measure more comprehensive sets of variables
in future studies.

INTRODUCTION

An important aim of environment/behavior research is to contribute information
that can be applied to ameliorate and solve social problems. If policy can be
defined as "guides to action, rules of choice that apply priorities to specific
decisions" (Meehan 1979, 4), then it is appropriate that research focus on the
need to inform policy decisions. This focus is appropriate at all times, but it
becomes paramount when circumstances require that fiscal austerity policies be
followed. As resources become more and more limited, prudent fiscal management demands that available funds be directed toward interventions that are
likely to maximize the positive effects of policies and other actions.

Although policy is influenced by political ideologies, moral and aesthetic
values, economic constraints, and considerations of practical feasibility, research
findings can provide an empirical basis for decision making. Yet there has been
widespread concern that environment/behavior research has had little influence
on policy and practice.

One explanation offered for this state of affairs is that a number of unresolved
methodological issues have affected the technical quality of the research. Hence,
the confidence that can be placed on the reliability and validity of research
findings has been limited. If this explanation is correct, it follows that greater

attention needs to be paid to approrpiate research designs, protocols of data collection, and data analyses.

In recent years, however, another concern has emerged that is perhaps even more important than methodological rigor in fostering more useful and applicable research. This concern focuses on theoretical orientations and on conceptual frameworks, and on the need for greater integration among the variety of often disparate paradigms and approaches that inform research studies. As Canter and Kenny (1982) note, insufficient attention to these issues has resulted in lack of cumulative research findings and rarity of utilization of empirically generated information. The purpose of this chapter is to contribute to a reflection on conceptual issues in the domain of housing research.

More specifically, the chapter will focus on the construct of *residential satisfaction*, a construct that has been used with increasing frequency in a variety of housing studies, but also one that has been the target of numerous objections. We will examine a number of these objections in an effort to understand the usefulness and limitations of the construct. A distinction will be made between the use of residential satisfaction as a measurement *per se* to ascertain levels of satisfaction, and as a criterion to investigate relationships among a variety of components of satisfaction. Finally, recent work in modeling residential satisfaction will be examined and suggestions will be made in regard to the potential for increasing the robustness and usefulness of the concept of residential satisfaction in future research.

CONCEPTS UNDERLYING RESIDENTIAL SATISFACTION

The choice of the residential satisfaction construct derives from a specific view of "housing" that needs to be stated in order to frame the questions with which this chapter is concerned.

Implicitly or explicitly, housing has been defined in widely different ways. Rapoport (1980) notes that housing has been approached as a product (or even as a commodity), as a process, as a place (including concepts related to expression of identity, self-worth, and status), a territory, a private domain, a "behavior setting," or in terms of functional requirements. He suggests that this lack of uniformity and precision in defining housing may occur "possibly because since we all live in dwellings, we feel that we know what dwellings are."

We propose that housing, regardless of the perspective from which it is viewed, can be usefully approached on the basis of the notion of *system* as articulated by Churchman (1968). He defines a system as "a set of parts coordinated to accomplish a set of goals" (p. 29). Thus, housing can be thought of as a set of components of various nature, such as physical structures and their environments; the residents, managers, planners, architects, developers, and other entrepreneurs; the social and political organizations; the cultural characteristics; and so on (Figure 3.1).

Figure 3.1
Components of Housing Systems

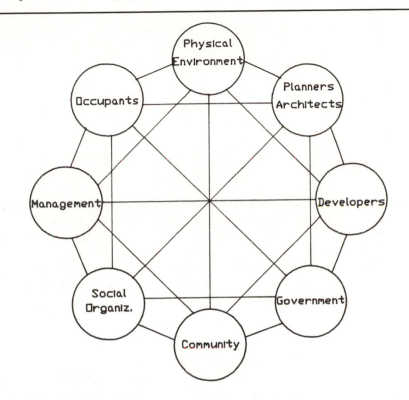

A systems approach introduces the need to think about "the total system objectives and, more specifically, the performance measures of the whole system" (Churchman 1968, p. 29). In turn, the determination of such objectives and performance measures is possible only if one can establish *whose* objectives are to be served, that is, who are the "customers" of the system.

Research that uses the construct of residential satisfaction is predicated on the notion that in a realm of such great personal and social significance as housing, the residents themselves are the main customers of the system. It follows that the residents' attitudes and behavior are important domains of study, which can be ignored only at substantial peril not only for the research community, but also—and more important—for the well-being of the social, political, and economic structures of a nation (Meehan 1979; Becker 1977; Michelson 1977; UN Economic Commission for Europe 1973; Sadacca and Isler 1972). This, in our view, constitutes the main justification for studying residents' satisfaction and represents the rationale for the use of this construct in an increasing number of recent studies.

NATURE AND MEANING OF SATISFACTION

Just as there are difficulties in defining housing, so there are disagreements about "satisfaction" itself. Disagreement about what satisfaction is and what it means is at the core of the definitional problem in satisfaction research. For instance, it has been observed that

as a term, consumers' satisfaction does have semantic and observational validity . . . however, as a concept, at the level of thought, the understanding of satisfaction becomes weaker. In a simple sense, it lacks substantive meaning—that immediate sense of being able to transfer to another exactly what it is that is known and experienced, why it is important, and how it is a thought worth sharing and doing something about (Czepiel and Rosenberg 1977, 93).

These concerns must be taken seriously, particularly when viewed against the hypothesis advanced by the same authors that measurement and modeling of satisfaction will produce findings that "tend to obtain in expensive and complicated ways the same answers provided by the market itself."

Earlier (Francescato 1981, 1982), we have suggested that a better understanding of the nature and meaning of residential satisfaction—and therefore of its potential usefulness—could be gained by focusing on its nature as an *attitudinal* indicator. Measures of attitudes have been studied by a number of psychologists, and there exists a large body of literature that could provide a framework for sharpening both operational definitions of the concept and interpretations of the meaning of its measurement.

The literature in social psychology recognizes three important facets, or dimensions, of attitudes: the affective, the cognitive, and the conative or behavioral intention (Rosenberg and Hovland 1960). With this framework in mind, it is possible to begin to attach concreteness and meaning to the term "satisfaction" and to examine the research based on the use of this construct. Indeed, even some studies that do not explicitly measure satisfaction may be shown to deal with aspects of these three facets. Thus they may contribute to shedding light on concepts and variables that, if measured in residential satisfaction studies, may result in more robust and comprehensive findings.

If one examines the housing research literature from the perspective of the measurement of attitudes, a taxonomy begins to emerge. For instance, some studies have focused on measuring cognitive aspects, or *perceptions and beliefs*. Among these, Gutek and Tyler (1979) dealt with the so-called internal referents, such as expectations, aspirations, and perceived control. Canter and Rees (1982) used facets analysis to investigate residents' perceptions. Ellis (1982) studied perceptions of outdoor spaces. Bernard and Gottesdiener (1982) investigated the aesthetic dimension in spontaneous evaluations of residential environments.

Affective measures, or *emotional* feelings about housing, have also been the object of study, though the actual measurement of affective variables in quantitative terms presents some unresolved difficulties. Among researchers who have dealt with affective variables, Cooper (1976) studied the house as symbol of the self, Becker (1977) investigated affective preferences for certain architectural and landscape features, Palmade (1979) focused on affective components of specific life-styles (*modes de vie*), and Korosec-Serfaty (1982) looked at emotions elicited by attics and cellars.

Among the studies that have measured conative variables, or *behavioral intentions*, most have concentrated on the intention to move and moving behavior (Rossi 1955; Wolpert 1966; Speare 1974; Michelson 1977; Newman and Duncan 1979). McDowell (1982) studied the intention to maintain and improve one's residence.

Some studies have used variables in a variety of domains. For example, our initial work (Francescato et al. 1974, 1979) investigated 37 publicly assisted, multifamily housing developments in the United States using an index of residents' satisfaction as a criterion variable. This study combined objective measures (such as age, sex, previous housing experience of the residents, and their psychological characteristics; size, height, density, and other physical characteristics of the developments; and management rules and practices), cognitive measures (such as perceptions or beliefs of residents and managers about the physical environment, the housing management, the respondents themselves, and other residents), and behavioral intention measures (such as desire for staying or moving, wish to live in a similar development if moving, and recommendations of the development to friends).

In addition to being useful as a classification scheme, viewing satisfaction as an attitude could assist in further exploring linkages between satisfaction and social behavior. Weidemann and Anderson (1985) suggest that recent work by Ajzen and Fishbein (1980) on their "theory of reasoned action" may be helpful in this regard. The theory of reasoned action requires that four sets of variables be measured if a full account of the relationships between attitudes and behavior is desired. Ajzen and Fishbein (1980, 97) list these as: (1) "behavioral and normative beliefs, outcome evaluations, and motivations to comply underlying the attitudinal and normative components; (2) the attitude toward the behavior and the subjective norm; (3) the intention to perform the behavior; and (4) the behavior itself." Perhaps the most important of their caveats is that only attitudes toward a specific behavior will have predictive power for that behavior. For instance, if, say, vandalism is the behavior one is interested in predicting, attitudes about vandalism—not attitudes about housing—will have to be measured.

These considerations point in the direction of theory building via the exploration of models of residential satisfaction that can be empirically tested, on the one hand, and that can be more easily interpreted—by reference to more general theories of attitudes and social behavior—on the other.

RESIDENTIAL SATISFACTION AS A MEASURE

Canter and Rees (1982, 185) suggest that housing satisfaction can be construed as "a reflection of the degree to which (the inhabitants) feel (their housing) is helping them to achieve their goals.'' This notion implies that measuring residential satisfaction is one way to assess the overall performance of the housing system. Indeed, one of the most common uses of satisfaction measures has been in assessing *levels* of satisfaction. High satisfaction levels have been considered as an indication of the success of specific policies, programs, or designs.

This use of the concept of satisfaction has been subjected to severe criticism, which is usually expressed in the following terms: (1) reported satisfaction tends to be uniformly high and therefore cannot be assumed to indicate the ''true'' state of affairs; (2) subjective measures of satisfaction do not correlate with objective measures of context and behavior, therefore they cannot be considered valid measures of the objective reality; (3) satisfaction with an object varies, for the same individual or social group, with time and with personal and social norms and expectations, thus it is too fickle an indicator on which to base action; (4) satisfaction tends to be higher the lower the respondent's awareness of ''better'' alternatives, thus it tends to reflect unenlightened assessments on which policy and decisions should not be based; and (5) focusing on satisfaction— rather than on attacking ''real'' problems—may result in suboptimal environments (for example, Galster 1984; Bernard and Gottesdiener 1982; Czepiel and Rosenberg 1977; Oländer 1976).

These objections frame some of the potential limitations of the construct. Therefore, it is appropriate to examine them in some detail. The first actually consists of two issues: the so-called Pollyanna effect, and the lack of variance in measured satisfaction.

The Pollyanna Effect Hypothesis, first advanced by Boucher and Osgood (1969), holds that most people are prone to using positive words in preference to negative ones whenever engaged in evaluation involving communication with others. Among those who have discussed this problem, Campbell et al. (1976) examined the issue at length and concluded that there is no evidence that high levels of satisfaction do not, in fact, accurately reflect the respondents' perceptions. Others, however, have taken a more cautious view. Bernard and Gottesdiener (1982), for example, report a predominance of positive aesthetic evaluations and note that the great majority of subjects tended to mask or deny any negative perceptions of the environment in order to reveal those that seemed to be more positive. It is, of course, possible that the Pollyanna effect may be more significant in the case of face-to-face interviews such as in the study by Bernard and Gottesdiener than in the instance of more interaction-neutral instruments (such as the anonymous questionnaires Campbell et al. used in their study).

Clearly, though, the issues raised by the Pollyanna Effect Hypothesis are more philosophical than empirical. Essentially, what is questioned is the validity of self-reports, that is, will people reveal their ''true'' perceptions when asked or will they, at least to some extent, lie. Since the referent of a perception is, by definition, not objectively measurable, it is unlikely that an empirical answer to this question will be forthcoming. This poses a limitation for which there seems to be no strictly verifiable solution.

The other facet of this objection is that satisfaction is uniformly high. However, this is not always the case. For instance, Francescato et al. (1979) found that levels of residential satisfaction in a sample of 1,907 residents of publicly assisted housing were relatively high (66 percent). But they were not as high as those reported by investigations of more "desirable" housing types such as Burby and Weiss' (1976) extensive study of new communities in which a higher proportion of respondents (65 to 75 percent) were satisfied with their rental housing. Campbell et al. (1976) reported that a still higher percentage (fully 76 percent) of respondents in a national (U.S.) sample representative of the entire population (both owners and renters) were satisfied with their housing. Even within a single study, sufficient variance in satisfaction has been found. When the 1,907 residents in the Francescato et al. (1979) study were disaggregated by sites and by assistance programs, levels of satisfaction *were not uniformly high*; mean scores of satisfaction varied from 2.7 to 4.4 on a five-point scale. Other subsequent studies have also found varying and not always high satisfaction levels (Anderson et al. 1983; Hourihan 1984). These examples show not only that sufficient variance exists for the purpose of statistical analysis, but also that the relative degree of satisfaction is a more useful indicator than the absolute satisfaction level for a given study.

The second objection to satisfaction measurements is that they exhibit very low levels of correlation with objective measures. Oländer (1976) cites Robinson's (1973–74) findings that about 90 percent of a U.S. national sample reported they were satisfied with their jobs, with their marriages, and with their dwellings. He compares these statistics with those of rising absenteeism, 33 percent divorce rate, and 20 percent yearly rate of moving among American households. At first glance, this comparison seems very compelling. However, if it is examined in light of the caveats mentioned earlier (Ajzen and Fishbein 1980) in regard to the lack of correlations between general measures of attitudes and specific behavior, it is clear that the low level of correlation between these measures of satisfaction and these specific behaviors *should be expected*. Indeed, this objection seems to point to the need for models capable of accounting for different levels of specificity. For example, it should be possible to discriminate between outcomes and behavior since in many instances actual behavior may be influenced by external conditions. Moving behavior is a case in point: Dissatisfaction with one's dwelling is not the only reason for the large percentage of household moves reported, since a number of moves may be related to changes in jobs, family composition, and life cycle.

Again, though, the criticism that subjective and objective measures do not often correlate has at its core a philosophical issue: What the "objective" variables actually measure is not necessarily empirical, but rather what has been assumed to reflect reality. For instance, objective measures of dwelling quality and conditions have been used for decades in the collection of census data in the United States and in a variety of European countries. The choice of these objectives measures was determined by "experts," and the measures themselves have been found wanting as to their validity and reliability (U.S. Bureau of the Census 1967; UN Economic Commission for Europe 1973). Thus, the notorious lack of correlation between these measures and reported satisfaction levels is not surprising and cannot be construed as a serious objection, unless one is willing to concede that the "experts know better."

The third criticism refers to the finding that levels of satisfaction with an object or service vary, for an individual or a social group, according to time and to personal and social norms and expectations. This objection seems to rest on a misunderstanding of the nature and purpose of evaluation research. The critics seem to be looking for a fixed *meter* with which to assess social structure and human behavior. For instance, Olander (1976, 415) laments: "There is seldom, or ever, a yardstick which is common to different groups or which stays put over time. Is it then possible for a policy-maker—or anybody else—to make much sense out of satisfaction ratings as measures of society's achievements?" Satisfaction measures can be used in evaluation only if one conceives society as a dynamic entity not only (diachronically) over time, but also (synchronically) across population groups. Personal and social norms are constantly changing. In this regard, the fact that satisfaction is influenced by all these factors should be seen as an advantage, since any measure that disregarded social and personal changes would be useless indeed as a criterion on which to base action. The proper mode for evaluation research is the *monitoring* of conditions. Hence a criterion that is sensitive to change is precisely what is wanted.

The fourth objection to measuring satisfaction is that the population does not, by-and-large, have a clear knowledge of the alternatives. Ignoring, or not having experienced, a "better" set of conditions, respondents tend to be more satisfied than if they had a clear view of situations that are "objectively" better. This, or course, is correct, and should be taken into account when interpreting the findings of satisfaction research. But it should also be remembered that measurements of satisfaction are specific to a certain sample and a certain time. It is certainly not intended that they provide anything other than the respondents' perceptions—conditioned as they may be not only by unawareness of alternative options, but also by other intervening constraints that may or may not exist were the circumstances to be different. Hence the desirability of integrating findings from satisfaction research with results of other modes of inquiry such as residents' participation, simulations, and so on.

Finally, the proposition that satisfaction is not desirable because the elimination of problems, rather than the elimination of dissatisfaction, is the target of the policy maker can be addressed by referring to the earlier discussion of a system's objectives. A problem does not exist until it is recognized as such by someone. In order to eliminate a problem one must first define what the problem is. The housing literature only too clearly shows that failures of policies and programs can often be traced to having misstated the problem to begin with. Measuring the perceptions of the residents should increase, rather than decrease, the likelihood that problems will be more accurately identified and that the policies, strategies and programs aimed at their elimination or amelioration will be successful.

Another facet of the objections to measures of residential satisfaction is that they represent an indirect approach to the problem of generating housing that is satisfying to the residents. Authors holding this view prefer to rely on direct residents' participation in the decision-making process leading to policy, planning, and design. There is no question that users' participation can be used successfully to direct decisions toward outcomes responsive to the users' values and interests. Unfortunately, residents' participation is a slow and cumbersome process, owing to a variety of practical constraints that have often been mentioned in the literature. In addition, it requires elaborate simulation and projection techniques for the prospective users to be able to visualize and assess the outcome of alternative proposals. Whenever possible, it would seem advisable to conduct both residents' participation and residents' satisfaction measurements. Indeed, reported satisfaction may be one technique to use in order to examine empirically the assumed success of a residents' participation effort.

In summary, while the objections discussed above do point to some limitations—which should be taken into account when interpreting the findings of satisfaction research—they do not seem to be serious enough to cause the construct of residential satisfaction to lose its usefulness as a measure of housing performance.

RESIDENTIAL SATISFACTION AS A CRITERION

Measuring levels of satisfaction—useful as this may be—is not, however, the most important utilization of the residential satisfaction construct. Determining which components of the housing system most strongly and consistently predict residents' satisfaction is perhaps more useful as a guide for action because it can be used to direct efforts in those directions and to those aspects in which an intervention is likely to yield the most beneficial effect.

Conceptually, it is important to know what elements and aspects of housing are meaningful to people. Understanding what the residents perceive as desirable and what they feel is linked to their attitudes about housing can provide a greater measure of human purpose to the knowledge base on which policy should be founded. Residential satisfaction models are a way to represent and investigate this understanding.

In their recent discussion of a number of models of residential satisfaction, Weidemann and Anderson (1985) point out that model building requires the use of appropriate data analysis techniques. They note that descriptive statistics, such as frequency distributions, percentages, measures of control tendencies, and such, cannot be relied upon to identify the relative importance of components of residential satisfaction. They caution that it is not necessarily appropriate to assume that factors found to be unsatisfactory are the ones that should receive remedial attention, since it is possible that unsatisfactory aspects are simply not important for, or related to, overall satisfaction.

Recent empirical work reinforces this concern. Galster (1984) studied 971 households in Wooster, Ohio, and measured their perception of four general dimensions of their residential environment and six specific features of their homes in terms of both satisfaction and ranking for improvement. He expected that what people were most dissatisfied with would be what needed improvement and attention. Contrary to this expectation, however, when he compared means of satisfaction and rank variables, he found that correlation between relative satisfaction and improvement priority was very weak. Galster concluded that "if efficacy of a limited amount of resources invested in a housing policy is to be maximized, we generally should not employ satisfaction as our primary guideline." This conclusion was reached because within the terms of this study "satisfaction" was simply a level measure of a number of items. There was no indication that these items *predicted* overall satisfaction.

Other researchers who were interested precisely in maximizing the potential benefits of limited resources did successfully use satisfaction measures. For instance, Weidemann et al. (1982) reported a case study in which such measures were used to guide the allocation of modernization funds in a public housing development in Lake County, Illinois. In this case, however, the information used in identifying areas in need of improvement were not the raw measures of satisfaction with specific items. Rather, principal component analysis and multiple regression were utilized to identify those aspects that most strongly contributed to overall satisfaction.

Thus, when appropriate multivariate techniques are used to analyze the data, it is possible to identify aspects that need improvement on the basis of their relationship to overall satisfaction. These aspects are not necessarily confined to physical improvements. They may—and usually do—involve variables related to organizational structures, such as management and tenant organizations; personal characteristics of the residents, such as demographic variables, employment, health, and socioeconomic conditions; community perceptions about the residents; and so on. Two aspects of the universe of variables considered by a study should be examined. The first aspect is the relative importance of predictor variables in accounting for the variation in overall satisfaction. The second is the degree (or percentage) to which the same predictor variables, taken together, explain the variation in overall satisfaction. In this sense, residential satisfaction becomes a *criterion variable*, and all components, aspects, factors, dimensions, or variables of a study are examined for their ability to predict variation in the criterion. Provided that a study's universe of variables is sufficiently comprehensive to yield a relatively high degree of overall prediction, those aspects that most strongly *predict* satisfaction are indeed the aspects most likely to maximize

Figure 3.2
Path Model of Residential Satisfaction

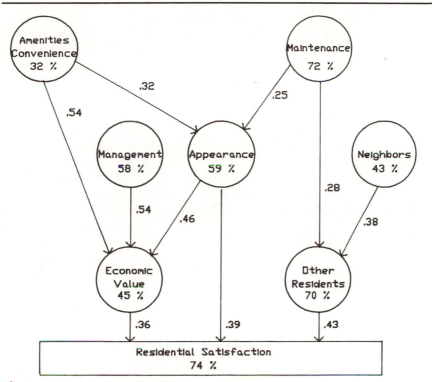

R² values shown in nodes; path coefficients at links.
Source: Francescato et al. 1979.

the benefit of interventions, regardless of the specific satisfaction levels found
with each specific aspect.

An important application of considering residential satisfaction as a criterion
variable is the ability to test theoretical models empirically and thus sharpen the
understanding of the interrelationships among various aspects of the total housing
system. Models can be used as reference frameworks when interpreting the results
of a study. They can also serve as an indication of areas in which future research
is needed to elucidate relationships among aspects (Figure 3.2).

To this end, greater integration of existing models and standardization of terms
used by different researchers would be extremely helpful. Weidemann and Anderson (1985) have initiated the task of synthesizing a number of models that,
implicitly or explicitly, have been used in recent studies. When comparisons are
made among the studies cited by these authors, it is interesting to note that there
are large differences in the amount of variance (R^2) in "overall satisfaction"

accounted for by the measured variables. R^2 values ranging from 13 percent to 74 percent have been reported. While it appears that those studies in which more comprehensive sets of variables were measured also exhibit higher R^2 values, it is apparent that there remains a proportion of variance that is not accounted for.

As empirical evidence becomes available about variables and components that do not strongly contribute to overall satisfaction, it becomes advisable to discard those variables and replace them in future studies with as yet unmeasured ones. Among these, Weidemann and Anderson (1985) suggest that greater attention should be paid to objective measures of the physical environment and the characteristics of the population. They also indicate that it would be useful to focus more strongly on behavioral intention variables. The domain of affective variables, while perhaps the most difficult to express in quantitative measures, should also receive greater attention. This domain is of particular importance in relation to the issue of clarifying the *meaning* that certain aspects of housing, both socially and in terms of physical design, may have for people.

In summary, if measures of residential satisfaction are used as criterion variables, it becomes possible to identify what aspects of the housing system are more important in the eyes of the inhabitants. The relative degree of importance attributed to these aspects can be ascertained. The overall strength of a number of aspects in predicting satisfaction with one's housing can be estimated. Thus policy and interventions can be directed to affect those aspects that are more likely to enhance overall satisfaction.

CONCLUSION

We suggested that viewing housing as a complex system composed of many interactive factors leads to question the purpose of housing systems. Research that uses the residential satisfaction construct assumes that such a purpose must, above all, include the satisfaction of the inhabitants' goals.

We addressed a number of objections that have been raised against using residential satisfaction as a measure of the degree to which the inhabitants' goals have been met. We concluded that these objections frame some limits that must be taken into account when interpreting and applying research results, but that they do not invalidate the usefulness of satisfaction measures.

We noted that these measures have a more important role than that of determining levels of overall satisfaction. When used as criterion variables in appropriate multivariate analyses, they can be a means to determine what aspects of housing systems are more important for the inhabitants and thus more likely— when addressed by policy and programs—to result in housing responsive to social purpose and to the public interest. We pointed out that the literature and ongoing work in the measurement of attitudes can shed light on the nature and meaning of satisfaction as well as on its relationship to social behavior.

Finally, we touched upon the need for greater attention to two endeavors within housing research: the integration and refinement of theoretical models and the search for more comprehensive and more sensitive universes of measured variables in future studies.

REFERENCES

Ajzen, I. A., and M. Fishbein
1980   *Understanding Attitudes and Predicting Social Behavior*. Englewood Cliffs, N.J.: Prentice Hall.
Anderson, J. R., S. Weidemann, and D. I. Butterfield
1983   "Using Residents' Satisfaction to Obtain Priorities for Housing Rehabilitation." In *Renewal, Rehabilitation and Maintenance*, Vol. 1, Gavle, Sweden: The National Swedish Institute for Building Research.
Becker, F. D.
1977   *Housing Messages*. Stroudsburg, PA: Dowden, Hutchins, & Ross.
Bernard, Y., and A. Gottesdiener
1982   "Rôle de la dimension esthetique dans l'evaluation spontanee d'un habitat." *International Review of Applied Psychology* 31, no. 2, 169–83.
Boucher, J., and C. E. Osgood
1969   "The Pollyanna Hypothesis." *Journal of Verbal Learning and Verbal Behavior*, no. 8, 1–8.
Burby, R. J., III, and S. F. Weiss
1976   *New Communities USA*. Lexington, MA: Lexington Books.
Campbell, A., P. E. Converse, and W. L. Rodgers
1976   *The Quality of American Life: Perceptions, Evaluations, and Satisfactions*. New York: Russell Sage.
Canter, D., and C. Kenny
1982   "Approaches to Environmental Evaluation: An Introduction." *International Review of Applied Psychology* 31, no. 2, 145–51.
Canter, D., and K. Rees
1982   "A Multivariate Model of Housing Satisfaction." *International Review of Applied Psychology* 31, no. 2, 185–207.
Churchman, C. W.
1968   *The Systems Approach*. New York: Dell.
Cooper, C.
1976   "The House as a Symbol of the Self." In *Environmental Psychology*, edited by H. Proshansky, W. H. Ittelson, and L. G. Rivlin. New York: Holt, Rinehart & Winston.
Czepiel, J. A., and L. J. Rosenberg
1977   "The Study of Consumer Satisfaction: Addressing the 'So What' Question." In *Conceptualization and Measurement of Consumer Satisfaction and Dissatisfaction*, edited by H. K. Hunt. Cambridge, MA: Marketing Science Institute.
Ellis, P.
1982   "Shared Outdoor Space and Shared Meaning." *International Review of Applied Psychology* 31, no. 2, 209–22.
Francescato, G.
1981   "Satisfaction Guaranteed or Your Money Back; Problems, Opportunities, and Usefulness in Measuring Residential Satisfaction." Paper presented at the 12th

Annual Conference of the Environmental Design Research Association. Ames, Iowa (Mimeo).

1982   "Residential Satisfaction as a Criterion of Quality." Paper presented at the Congress of the International Association of Applied Psychology. Edinburgh, U.K. (Mimeo).

Francescato, G., S. Weidemann, J. R. Anderson, and R. Chenoweth

1974   "Evaluating Residents' Satisfaction in Housing for Low and Moderate Income Families: A Multimethod Approach." In *Man-Environment Interactions: Evaluations and Applications*, Vol. 5 (Methods and Measures), general editor D. H. Carson, 285–96. Washington, DC: Environmental Design Research Association.

1979   *Residents' Satisfaction in HUD Assisted Housing: Design and Management Factors*. Washington, DC: U.S. Department of Housing and Urban Development.

Galster, G. C.

1984   "Housing Satisfaction, Improvement Priorities and Policy Formulation." Urban Studies Program, College of Wooster, Ohio (Mimeo).

Gutek, B., and T. R. Tyler

1979   *The Importance of Internal Referents as Determinants of Satisfaction*. Los Angeles: University of California, Los Angeles (Mimeo).

Hourihan, K.

1984   "Context-dependent Models of Residential Satisfaction." *Environment and Behavior*, 16, no. 3, 369–93.

Korosec-Serfaty, P.

1982   "The Home, from Attic to Cellar." Université Louis Pasteur, Strasbourg, France (Mimeo).

McDowell, K.

1982   "Perceived Satisfaction, Control, and Quality in the Home Environment." University of Saskatchewan, Canada (Mimeo).

Meehan, E. J.

1979   *The Quality of Federal Policymaking: Programmed Failure in Public Housing*. Columbia: The University of Missouri Press.

Michelson, W.

1977   *Environmental Choice, Human Behavior, and Residential Satisfaction*. New York: Oxford University Press.

Newman, S., and G. J. Duncan

1979   "Residential Problems, Dissatisfaction and Mobility." *Journal of the American Institute of Planners*, April, 154–66.

Oländer, F.

1976   "Consumer Satisfaction—A Skeptic's View." In *Conceptualization and Measurement of Consumer Satisfaction and Dissatisfaction*, edited by H. K. Hunt. Cambridge, MA: Marketing Science Institute.

Palmade, J.

1979   "Fonctionnalité et Symbolicité de l'Habitat." Paris: Centre Scientifique et Technique du Bâtiment (Mimeo).

Rapoport, A.

1980   "Towards a Cross-Culturally Valid Definition of Housing." *Proceedings of the 11th Environmental Design Research Association*. Washington, DC: EDRA Inc.

Robinson, J. P.
1973–74   "On the Correspondence Between Subjective and Objective Social Indicators." *Public Opinion Quarterly* 37, 451–54 (Abstract).

Rosenberg, M. J., and C. I. Hovland
1960   "Cognitive, Affective, and Behavioral Components of Attitudes." In *Attitude Organization and Change*, edited by C. I. Hovland and M. J. Rosenberg. New Haven, CT: Yale University Press.

Rossi, P. H.
1955   *Why Families Move*. Glencoe, IL: The Free Press.

Sadacca, R., and M. Isler
1972   *Management Performance in Multi-Family Housing Developments*. Working Paper No. 209–4. Washington, DC: The Urban Institute.

Speare, A., Jr.
1974   "Residential Satisfaction as an Intervening Variable in Residential Mobility." *Demographic* 11, 173–88.

UN Economic Commission for Europe.
1973   *Housing Requirements and Demand: Current Methods of Assessment and Problems of Estimation*. Geneva: United Nations.

U.S. Bureau of the Census.
1967   *Measuring the Quality of Housing, An Appraisal of Census Statistics and Method*. Washington, DC: U.S. Bureau of the Census, Work Paper No. 25.

Weidemann, S., and J. R. Anderson
1985   "A Conceptual Framework for Residential Satisfaction. "In *Home Environments*, edited by I. Altman and C. Werner. New York: Plenum Press.

Weidemann, S., J. R. Anderson, D. I. Butterfield, and P. O'Donnell
1982   "Residents' Perceptions of Satisfaction and Safety: A Basis for Change in Multifamily Housing." *Environment and Behavior* 14, no. 6, 695–724.

Wolpert, J.
1966   "Migration as an Adjustment to Environmental Stress." *Journal of Social Issues* 22, no. 4, 92–102.

PART II

REVITALIZATION IN THE INNER CITY

The four chapters in Part II all examine the same question: What happens to older neighborhoods in city centers? The authors, social scientists in the Netherlands, Great Britain, and Canada, refer to theories that assume that as a neighborhood ages, or, more specifically, as its housing stock ages, the entire situation tends to deteriorate, environmentally and socially. Nonetheless, the authors do not necessarily assume that aging represents an inexorable force. They assume that communities can act efficaciously to produce change in desired directions; but, at least in two of the chapters in this section, the authors show that they are often disappointed by the results of such action.

Three of the chapters present case studies of older neighborhoods. Their authors employ various kinds of social and environmental data, including census statistics, municipal plans and reports, surveys of residents, in-depth interviews with activists and officials, all focused upon particular older neighborhoods. From each case study, the reader gets a well-drawn portrait of one or more residential areas.

While these portraits depict neighborhood conditions, none of them is static. The studies emphasize processes of change. In each case, the neighborhood populations change through the aging of the old-timers and the introduction of newcomers. In some cases the newcomers are dark-skinned immigrants settling in formerly all-white areas. In others, the newcomers are of a higher social class than the old-timers. In one Canadian case, the newcomers are not very different from the residents, except for being somewhat younger and slightly wealthier.

Other conditions also change; the greater community may impact upon the neighborhood. Nearby districts, particularly downtowns, may change through investment or disinvestment. City plans and governmental policies may change. And "change agents," such as city planners, architects, social workers, and others may come to the neighborhoods, attempting to create changes.

Three chapters in Part II deal with governmental policies and practices affecting redevelopment of housing and neighborhoods. Machielse (Chapter 4) provides a dispassionately written overview of redevelopment trends affecting different social classes in various cities in the Netherlands. At least one author, Taner Oc (Chapter 6), is profoundly pessimistic, emphasizing British national policies and local practices that have failed to help those minority groups who have the worst housing. Likewise, Wuertz and Van der Pennen (Chapter 7) analyze the community-level planning model utilized in Dutch cities and show how and why it fails to form an effective line of communications between planners and immigrant residents.

Ironically, the one author writing optimistically, Bunting (Chapter 5), reports on neighborhoods where change is occurring in a positive direction, without conflict between old and new residents, and without the sponsorship of a specific governmental program.

4

The Multiformity of Neighborhood Revitalization in the Netherlands

E. C. M. MACHIELSE

Abstract. The study of neighborhood revitalization in the Netherlands is almost exclusively directed to Amsterdam, where conditions for gentrification are highly favorable. However, more Dutch cities are being confronted with an increasing demand from middle- and high-income households for housing accommodation in the center. As a result of different local conditions these cities are not able to house the newcomers in physically renovated buildings and therefore they assimilate this well-to-do population category in another way. This results in a multiformity of residential revitalization in the Netherlands that is manifest at both inter- and intracity levels.

INTRODUCTION

During the past 15 years neighborhood revitalization—brought about largely through the investment of private capital—has been a major subject of study. By the late 1970s, numerous cities and towns in the United States were showing signs of private revitalization activities and a huge number of American theoretical and empirical analyses have filled us in on various aspects of the process, such as characteristics of the parties involved, causes, consequences, federal and local policies, and so on.

One of the main forms of neighborhood revitalization is gentrification, a process involving the physical renovation of houses, many of which were previously in the privately rented sector, to meet the standards required by the new owner-occupying middle-class residents. Because the new inhabitants bring a distinctive life-style and set of tastes with them, gentrification in addition to being a physical and social process also affects the cultural life in revitalizing areas (Hamnett and Williams 1980, 471).

Because it contravenes both the traditional residential location theories and substantial years of experience with urban decline, gentrification has been very much in the public eye, more than one would expect on the grounds of the scale of the process. This excessive attention is at the expense of other forms of residential revitalization, like the construction of new high-quality housing, apartment conversion, loft conversion, and incumbent upgrading (with reinvestment coming from long-term residents instead of high-income newcomers). At the same time it means that, in studying residential revitalization, attention is chiefly paid to those cities where conditions for gentrification are highly favorable (that is, cities with a city center where many distinguished, historically valuable houses are available). However, more cities are being confronted with an increasing demand from middle- and high-income households for housing accommodation in the center. Since they are not able to house these newcomers in physically renovated buildings, it would be particularly interesting to see how their inner cities assimilate this well-to-do population category. Such a study would probably result in the discovery that residential revitalization is a process characterized by a multiformity of manifestations.

Hereafter I shall discuss residential revitalization in the Netherlands, emphasizing the influence of different local conditions on the form taken by the residential reinvestment activities. This discussion is preceded by a section on revitalization in Europe, to place the Dutch situation in a broader context.

REVITALIZATION IN EUROPE

In trying to make a comparative analysis of neighborhood revitalization in Western Europe, Gale (1984, 119) comes to the conclusion that, with the exception of England, empirical studies on revitalization are not available in other advanced industrial nations. Several years later there is hardly any change in the situation; the study of social change in London by Hamnett and Williams (1973, 1979, 1980) is still the main contribution to the European revitalization literature. Hamnett and Williams examined the scale and significance of gentrification in London and found that, besides real gentrification (colonization of working-class inner areas by the middle classes), intensification of existing high-status residential areas has been an important development. These areas already had a high initial percentage of managers and professionals and are therefore not considered to have experienced gentrification. The location of the really gentrified wards points both to the extension of existing high-status areas into adjacent working-class areas and to the upgrading of previously isolated working-class areas.

It appears that important governmental regulation in the private rental sector has not discouraged the London gentrification process. On the contrary, the decrease in the supply of privately rented property is partly the result of national and local policies. Rent regulations, for example, try to protect the tenant population by placing a ceiling on rental income. However, this has caused the market value of rented property to rise above the rent income value, giving the landlords a good reason for selling off their property to individual owner-occupiers. This development is further accentuated by the operation of improvement grants, one of the provisions of the 1969 Housing Act. Up to 1974, a complete lack of restrictions allowed owners to sell immediately after improvement without any obligation to pay back the grant. Developers and landlords were completely free to give notice to existing tenants and either to sell or rent at a much higher rate.

In this way, several policies aimed at protecting or improving the housing conditions of low-income residents actually result in their displacement. But even an intensification of state intervention (for example, by imposing restrictions on improvement grants) does not decrease the sale of improved or converted dwelling units to higher socioeconomic groups. The demand for property for renovation exceeds supply and the process itself is so powerful and lucrative that individual owners, landlords, and developers are not dependent on financial incentives to keep the process going.

The lack of empirical studies on neighborhood revitalization in other European countries does not mean that gentrification, apartment conversion, or any other form of revitalization is not in evidence in these nations. Paris, Bordeaux, Antwerp, Amsterdam, Munich, Stockholm, Copenhagen, and other cities are all known to have small though impressive revitalization areas, where improvement in the quality of the physical fabric and upward socioeconomic transition have coincided. However, official policies consider private residential investments, which do not benefit the original residents, undesirable. Revitalization must prevent the continued degradation of buildings and the associated social impoverishment, providing that the continued survival of the indigenous population can be assured. In this respect, private revitalization has not succeeded: Destroying the human aspects and failing to create a dignified living environment for everyone, it does not form part of the official, socially oriented housing and renewal policies. However, the government role is not all-embracing and the example of England clearly demonstrates that pursued policies may have unforseeable consequences. Therefore, neighborhood revitalization also occurs in West European cities, either on the edge of public urban renewal areas (for example, in Munich and Stockholm), brought about by large-scale urban development projects (Pompidou Center and Forum des Halles in Paris, or Barbican Center and Covent Garden in London) or stimulated by urban conservation policies (such as the designation of safeguarded sectors like The Marais in Paris). Sometimes commercial restoration is the only way to protect an area from total dilapidation because, in spite of money as incentive, local residents and owners are not interested in improving the quality of their property, not even to statutory norms of amenity. In such a case middle-class households and investment companies acquire the houses and rehabilitate them at their own expense and for their own use or for sale or rental purposes (Clout 1984, 89).

Given the relatively strong social component of the housing and renewal policies, revitalization activities in Europe certainly do have a moderate character when compared to the American situation. When social criteria become as important as those of architectural quality or historical interest, simpler rehabilitation schemes are obvious. They provide the only way to keep the houses within reach of the low- and moderate-income local households. The social-democratic political principles also affect European neighborhood revitalization in that they succeed in reducing the income range, especially in the Netherlands, Denmark, and Sweden. As a consequence, revitalization is less lavish both in exterior restoration and renovation and in the proliferation of luxury and specialty shops, restaurants, night clubs, cultural centers, and such. This is also partly because cities like Munich, Amsterdam, and especially Copenhagen and Stockholm, as opposed to Paris and London, are best characterized as national capitals and national centers of commerce, finance, and culture. Although they attract a lot of international tourism and business traffic, Paris and London are undisputedly the leading European centers attracting cosmopolitans with an international outlook. It seems only natural that white-collar households—of major importance for the revitalization process—have settled there in great numbers (Gale 1984, 140).

A final reason for the less rigorous character of European revitalization is one of a different kind; in most West European cities physical decay and social impoverishment never reached the level found in some North American inner cities. Given these relatively moderate prerevitalization conditions, the results produced by rehabilitation activities will also be less striking.

REVITALIZATION IN THE NETHERLANDS

Before going into the situation in Amsterdam and several other Dutch cities, I will briefly discuss three essential aspects of the course of neighborhood revitalization in the Netherlands. First of all it will be clear that Dutch cities play only a minor role in international business and tourism economies. Therefore, the stream of well-paid foreign employees—often a well-represented group in revitalizing areas—is limited and so is their role in the Dutch urban revitalization process. Internationally, the Netherlands is too small a country to share in the structural shifts in the international economy or to profit from them, via the revitalization of some of its cities (Cortie and Ostendorf 1986, 71).

Dutch urban revitalization is then for the greater part the result of internal developments. However, for a sound appreciation of this internally induced revitalization, one needs to be familiar with the specific urban structure of the Netherlands. Unlike London or Paris, where the traditional functions of a metropolis, such as government administration, industry, and services, are concentrated in a single center, in the Netherlands these functions are spread over several cities. Amsterdam is a city of commerce and a center of sociocultural facilities, The Hague is the center of government administration, and Rotterdam is a port and center of industrial activities. Therefore, the Netherlands has no primate city like most other European countries.

The deviating urban structure has influenced the Dutch revitalization process to a high degree. As a result of the allocation of tasks, each city has a different character and when these cities are confronted with a growing interest in the residential function of their inner city, this process manifests itself in different ways, owing to different local circumstances. Later on I shall discuss this multiformity of revitalization in the Netherlands more extensively.

The influence of national and local housing policies on the development of neighborhood revitalization is a third and final item getting some attention, before going on to a discussion of the Amsterdam situation. Despite active government participation and a considerable number of rules and regulations, the authorities do not seem to have a direct influence on private investment activities, either by stimulating or by acting as a brake. The general aim of housing policy is to provide housing, both in sufficient number and of adequate quality, for all sections of the population. In practice, all attention is directed to housing the low- and moderate-income households, because the authorities take the line that higher incomes are very well able to provide their own housing needs.

The housing policy of the larger municipalities reflects this conviction to a high degree. Both in the Amsterdam and Rotterdam city councils, the left wing has been in the majority for quite a while now, meaning that they have been able to give profile to the political ideology of their party. Housing the low-income households and public urban renewal have been central themes and, although this policy as such is a laudable effort, it is also one of the reasons for the higher income households leaving the central city. Because urban renewal is based on the policy of improving housing conditions for the benefit of the original population and the house-building programs almost completely consist of housing-act dwellings or premium-assisted housing, for which high-income households are not eligible, their housing opportunities within the city are minimal. They leave the central city stimulated by a national urbanization policy that gives priority to (clustered) decentralization via building in growth centers, where, in addition, politics are relatively well-disposed toward the higher incomes.

The spatial urbanization policy for the coming years has been laid down in the Structural Outline Sketch for Urban Areas, drawn up by Parliament in 1985 (Ministry of Housing, Physical Planning and Environment 1985). This document appears to ring in a new era, in which the deconcentration policy is exchanged for building in, and contiguous to, the urban areas, giving the central cities support. If the central cities want to benefit fully from this renewed attention, they must be prepared to create housing opportunities for a wide range of income categories, because that will be the only way to check the social one-sidedness, caused by many years of selective migration. Especially in Rotterdam, where the lack of high-quality housing cannot be compensated for by the expensive restoration of old architecturally distinctive properties, middle- and high-income households are completely dependent on local housing plans and programs. The municipalities seem to be waking up to this situation and gradually and very carefully (after all, this is a very sensitive issue politically) they adapt their housing policy accordingly. A general change of mentality, brought about by the problems and disadvantages of a socially one-sided population, helps them in doing so.

Amsterdam

Population and Employment Trends. It is probably due to the emphasis on gentrification in American literature that Dutch research concerning neighborhood revitalization is almost exclusively directed to Amsterdam, where conditions for gentrification are highly favorable. First, the inner city offers both a lot of distinguished, historically valuable houses and commercial properties, which can be converted into dwelling units. Second, a significant shift in the employment structure has turned Amsterdam into a service-oriented postindustrial city where white-collar service occupations supersede blue-collar manufacturing occupations to a high degree. Many of these services are public rather than private: education, public administration, medical services, and so forth.

The employees within these new branches of industry are highly educated, both men and women. Often they form part of dual-earner households and, given their relative lack of time, a central residential location offers them several benefits. They have a greater accessibility to their job location—saving them the commuting costs both in time and expense—and to shops, restaurants, laundries, and so on. This gives them the opportunity of contracting out part of their household chores. Besides, living in the inner city, they enjoy the proximity of cultural and recreational services, highly valued because of their emphasis on consumption and amenity.

A recent publication by Cortie et al. (1984) reveals that the inner city of Amsterdam is indeed being revitalized. Since the beginning of the 1970s there has been a tremendous increase in the level of education achieved by the inner-city working force. Furthermore, there is a great excess of scientific and other specialists. A significant proportion of these specialists consists of members of the creative professions (such as artists, authors, journalists). In all branches of industry, the managerial staff quite often live in the inner city; the indigenous unskilled laborers have almost all disappeared (see Table 4.1).

In addition, it is seen that immigrants from Surinam, The Antilles, and the Mediterranean countries no longer move into the inner city as they used to up to the 1970s. Since then, their numbers have even decreased, not only relatively but also absolutely. The inner city is becoming more and more a place for young singles (20–29) and childless couples, and there is also a slight concentration of somewhat older people (30–45), who are not part of a conventional nuclear family. These people form the dual-earner households mentioned earlier. Since both partners work and there are few if any children to support, these households have more time and money to devote to other interests, such as their careers, voluntary activities, traveling, entertainment, and improving their properties.

Housing Stock. Besides changing the household composition of the inner-city population, the increasing interest in the residential function of the inner city has also influenced the character of the housing stock. The preliminary results of my own investigation provide me with some information concerning the nature of these changes.

Table 4.1
Occupations of the Working Population of the Inner City and of Amsterdam as a Whole, 1981

Occupation	Inner City	Amsterdam
Authors, journalists, artists etc.	11.1	3.8
Teaching staff	9.9	6.1
Technicians, medicals and other professional specialists	10.7	8.9
Lawyers, accountants, economists	3.4	1.3
Scientific specialists	6.3	3.7
Executive staff	5.6	4.7
Clerical staff	16.1	22.9
Managers, (wholesale) tradesmen	5.1	3.0
Employees (wholesale) trade	4.9	6.8
Managers, employers hotel and catering industry	4.0	1.5
Other service occupations	9.5	13.4
Crafts, industrial and transportation occupations	13.4	23.9
Total	100.0	100.0

Source: Cortie et al. 1984, 24.

Given the fact that the local administration gives first priority to the housing of low-income households and given the limited spatial possibilities for newly built houses, those moving in depend almost entirely upon existing privately rented property. The increasing pressure on the extant housing stock is reflected in changes in property renovation, sales activities, and tenure conversions, but these activities do not create extra dwelling units for the rising number of households who wish to live in the inner city. Nevertheless, the figures demonstrate that extra dwelling units have indeed been created (see Tables 4.2, 4.3, and 4.4). During the 1970–82 period as many as 634 extra units were the result of rebuilding activities, and between 1970 and 1984 almost 1,000 units were created by projects, which we could refer to as loft conversion, although not all the converted buildings may have been former lofts; in all cases the converted buildings had no residential function before the conversion took place.

Both the rebuilding activities and the conversions were heavily concentrated in the historical inner city, although, during the last five years, the nineteenth-century neighborhoods to the west and south of the inner city of Amsterdam have shown an increase in the number of conversions. This might mean that the activities have extended into the more recent, and maybe less desirable (less central), areas of the city because of the overwhelming and continuous demand for these housing forms. That the extensions go in a westerly and southerly direction is probably caused by the fact that the revitalization activities of the last 15 years were concentrated in the western and southern part of the inner city. Historically these neighborhoods have been characterized by industrial activities and merchants' offices. However, the decline and exodus of these activities have led to a substantial number of empty stores and office buildings. With great pressure on the nearby housing stock, these buildings become very attractive for conversion purposes, especially since the deterioration resulted in lower prices. In other parts of the inner city (such as the ring of canals) where many banks and service industries (lawyers, estate agents, advertising agencies) are concentrated, such a decline has never taken place. These activities need the elegant office buildings that are available here in great numbers. Demand still exceeds supply, resulting in price increases, so there is not much chance of an increasing residential function within these neighborhoods (Eising and Hietbrink 1985).

Other Dutch Cities

It has often been assumed that, given the different character of the housing stock, the employment structure, or the cultural and educational facilities, chances for revitalization in other Dutch cities are limited. These arguments are probably valid as long as they concern gentrification, but residential revitalization is a process with many manifestations, gentrification being just one of them. The possibility that other Dutch cities may have potential for other forms of revitalization is one we should not overlook.

Rotterdam is a city with almost no historical center left, as a result of World War II. Opportunities for gentrification are therefore limited. At the same time, the spatial possibilities for the construction of new houses are almost unrestricted. Up to the 1980s these possibilities were hardly used, but, since then, an enormous increase in new construction activities can be observed: from 1981 to 1984 institutional and private investors have built as many as 2,565 middle- and high-

Table 4.2
Number of Dwelling Units Created in the Inner City and Adjacent Nineteenth-century Neighborhoods in Amsterdam

	1970–74	1975–78	1979–82	1970–1982
Newly-built houses*	374	619	539	1532
Dwelling units created by rebuilding or conversion activities**	391	307	715	1413
Total	765	926	1254	2945

Table 4.3
Number of Dwelling Units Created in the Inner City and Adjacent Nineteenth-century Neighborhoods in Rotterdam

	1973–76	1977–80	1981–84	1973–1984
Newly-built houses*	346	1034	2565	3945
Dwelling units created by dwelling or conversion activities**	47	125	140	312
Total	393	1159	2705	4257

Table 4.4
Number of Dwelling Units Created in the Inner City and Adjacent Nineteenth-century Neighborhoods in The Hague

	1970–74	1975–79	1980–84	1970–1984
Newly-built houses*	318	1352	624	2294
Dwelling units created by rebuilding or conversion activities**	46	108	338	492
Total	364	1460	962	2786

*Low-price rental properties are not included.
**It is impossible to distinguish between private and public initiatives.

priced dwelling units in the inner city and adjacent nineteenth-century neigh-borhoods (Table 4.3).

Without doubt, conditions in Rotterdam are rather unique and we should therefore not expect similar developments elsewhere in the Netherlands. Still, in The Hague, a city with far more limited new construction possibilities, the number of houses built for more affluent households also greatly exceeds the number of units created by rebuilding or conversion (Table 4.4). This is probably due to the presence of an older and more conventional population, which prefers new expensive apartments over converted warehouses or renovated historically valuable houses, so much beloved by the young, highly-educated, dual-earner households of Amsterdam. It is because The Hague, in contrast to Amsterdam and Rotterdam, has conducted a relatively conservative policy over the past years that these centrally located, expensive apartments have been built.

While several cities in the Netherlands are experiencing an increasing demand for housing in their inner cities among middle- and high-income households, as a result of different local conditions, this results in one place in gentrification and in another in the construction of new, high-quality housing or another form of residential revitalization. In Amsterdam young, highly educated, dual-earner households, employed in public services or in artistic or design professions, live in converted warehouses or renovated architecturally distinctive houses; middle-priced, modern, newly built houses find ready buyers in Rotterdam, and in The Hague older and more conventional couples (sometimes with grown-up children) are concentrated in expensive apartments.

Among the local circumstances that influence the manifestation of the process are housing stock characteristics, spatial possibilities for the construction of new housing, population or employment structure, local policies, and cultural and recreational facilities. They cause differences in residential revitalization when we compare the situation in several cities. However, it is also possible that, as a result of changing local circumstances, different revitalization forms are man-ifest within a city. In Amsterdam, for example, the construction of new housing or apartments for high-income households was until recently considered impos-sible. The city was completely built up, leaving only a few new construction possibilities in public urban renewal areas (meant for the existing population) or at the urban fringe. Nowadays, local authorities think otherwise. Stimulated by the concentration policy of the central government they have "discovered" several inner-city areas where new construction activities can be realized, one of the main examples being the eastern harbor area. In contrast to the local policy of the past 10 to 15 years, the redevelopment of this area will be realized via cooperation between the public and private sectors. Add to this the change of mentality and political climate that has now developed to such a degree that building for high-income groups is considered acceptable again, and it will be clear that, in the future, high-income households in Amsterdam will no longer be completely dependent on the extant convertible warehouses or renewable buildings.

The city of Rotterdam also shows a change of policy, which may influence the revitalization process. The recently published Housing Program Rotterdam 1986–1990 (1986) suggests that the city should build more high-quality owner-occupied housing to stop the selective migration of the past two decades. The housing department has reached the conclusion that many migrants were not leaving the city because of their need or wish to live away from the city but because of the lack of suitable dwellings in Rotterdam itself. Besides a continuing emphasis on housing the low- and moderate-income households, this diagnosis probably means a shift from middle- to high-priced dwelling units in the house-building program.

In The Hague, where the conservative city council just has been replaced by a council dominated by the liberals, the situation is almost the reverse.

CONCLUSION

Although this discussion on neighborhood revitalization has been limited, the Dutch situation clearly demonstrates the various nuances of this process. The cities, which are confronted with a growing interest in the residential function of their inner cities, may all react in a different way as a result of differing local circumstances. Conditions like population or employment structure, housing-stock characteristics, spatial possibilities for the construction of new houses, local policies, and cultural and recreational services give each city a different starting position from which it faces the increasing demand for middle- and high-priced, centrally located housing accommodation. The result is a multiformity in neighborhood revitalization, manifest at both inter- and intracity levels.

REFERENCES

City of Rotterdam
1986   *Huisvestingsplan Rotterdam 1986–1990. Naar een voorraadbeleid* (Housing Program Rotterdam). Rotterdam: Dienst Volkshuisvesting; Afdeling Onderzoek.
Clout, H.
1984   "Bordeaux: Urban Renovation, Conservation and Rehabilitation." *Planning Outlook* 27, 84–92.
Cortie, C., R. van Engelsdorp Gastelaars, P. Terhorst, and J. van de Ven
1984   *Nieuwe bewoners in de binnenstad van Amsterdam.* Amsterdam: Social Geography Institute, University of Amsterdam.
Cortie, C., and W. Ostendorf
1986   "Suburbanisatie en Gentrification: Sociaal-ruimtelijke Dynamiek in de Randstad na 1970." *K. N. A. G. Geografisch Tijdschrift* 20, 64–83
Eising, H., and S. Hietbrink
1985   "Funktieverandering in de Amsterdamse grachtengordel." *Rooilijn* 18, 7–13
Gale, D. E.
1984   *Neighborhood Revitalization and the Postindustrial City: A Multinational Perspective.* Lexington, MA: Lexington Books.

Hamnett, C.
1973   "Improvement Grants as an Indicator of Gentrification in Inner London." *Area* 5, 252–61.
Hamnett, C., and P. Williams
1979   *Gentrification in London 1961–1971, an Empirical and Theoretical Analysis of Social Change*. Research Memorandum 71, Centre for Urban and Regional Studies, University of Birmingham.
1980   "Social Change in London, A Study of Gentrification." *Urban Affairs Quarterly* 15, 469–87.
Ministry of Housing, Physical Planning and Environment
1985   *Structuurschets stedelijke gebieden 1983, deel d: regeringsbeslissing*. The Hague: Government Printing Office.

5

Changing Patterns in Inner-City Housing: A Canadian Example

TRUDI E. BUNTING

Abstract. An examination of changing household and housing characteristics in the inner residential zones of the City of Kitchener, Ontario, over the period 1971–81 produces evidence of revitalization as well as decline. A more detailed survey of the two innermost census tracts produces stronger evidence of modest, yet substantial, upgrading undertaken by newly resident home owners. This somewhat inconspicuous form of upgrading is put forward as an alternative type of inner-city change that is quite different from the well-recognized extremes of gentrification and deterioration. In the broader context, it is thought that this style of upgrading may be more typical of medium-, rather than large-sized, cities and may be more likely to be found in Canada, rather than the United States.

INTRODUCTION

This chapter is concerned with upgrading of inner-city housing that occurs in conjunction with modest investment in home renovation by households purchasing dwellings in central-city neighborhoods. Traditional theories of neighborhood evolution assume a negative correlation between age of the housing stock and residential investment activity, which ultimately ends in large-scale disinvestment in the inner city (Andrews 1971; Birch 1971; Hoover and Vernon 1959). The extent that these neighborhood stage models are believed to hold true is such that inner-city areas in North America are generally described in a state of decline that characterizes both the physical housing stock and the demographic composition of the population (Bourne 1982). The last 20 years have witnessed exceptions to this downward trend as evidenced in well-publicized cases of middle-class revitalization or gentrification of inner-city neighborhoods. Rates of reinvestment are substantial in such cases, but the process is circumscribed to larger cities with growing central business districts and to select neighborhoods within these cities. Even though the estimated extensiveness of gentrification is low, its presence is widely recognized in the research literature. Thus it comes about that the map of the inner city today is said to reflect "gentrification amid decline" (Lang 1982) rather than uniform downgrading. This chapter challenges both the uniqueness of gentrification as an upgrading process and the residual universality of inner-city decline.

RESEARCH ON INNER-CITY HOUSING

Current research on inner-city housing and neighborhoods raises many questions. First, from a categorical point of view, relatively little is known about inner-city housing in Canadian, as opposed to U.S., cities or in smaller (population 50,000–500,000), as opposed to larger, metropolitan areas across North America. Second are questions relating to the status of housing in "grey areas" of neither gentrified nor deteriorated neighborhoods extant throughout the inner city. The processes described in this chapter occur in a medium-sized Canadian city, Kitchener, Ontario. The central neighborhoods in this city have relatively little deteriorated housing and few visible signs of gentrification.

The North American housing literature suggests that urban housing problems are geographically concentrated in the inner city. Inner-city neighborhoods are most likely to contain substandard housing since dwelling units are old and more prone to obsolescence and disrepair. A significant proportion of this housing stock is usually found to be rented and its value decreasing relative to the metropolitan average. Slum landlords serve to accelerate this process. Inner-city neighborhoods generally show substantial loss in population, which has been further interpreted as a lack of demand for older types of housing. Neoclassical economic models of housing change and turnover (Andrews 1971; Birch 1971; Hoover and Vernon 1959; Lang 1982; Leven et al. 1976; Lowry 1960; Ratcliffe 1949; Solomon and Vandell 1982) postulate a "filtering-down" of housing quality and occupant households, which results in deterioration and disinvestment in inner-city neighborhoods (compare Chapter 12 by Van Kempen in this book). The scale of deterioration at the end of this cycle is such that massive amounts of public or private funds are required to redevelop or rehabilitate the housing stock. In instances where private redevelopment occurs, the replacement land use is usually either nonresidential or high-rise residential; either way, the original character of the neighborhood and its occupants is changed dramatically through redevelopment.

Despite the fact that the neoclassical models negate any reversal in the downward filtering process, "filtering up" has been observed with increasing frequency over the last two decades. The term "gentrification" or alternatives such as "whitepainting," "brownstoning," "revitalization," and the like are all used to describe the process whereby inner-city housing is upgraded for occupancy by residents of considerably higher socioeconomic status than the population being displaced. While academics tend to differ as to the precise definition of the term, all seem to agree that gentrification entails the process wherein lower income housing is rehabilitated by higher income homeowners, landlords, or professional developers (Clay 1979; Lang 1982; Smith 1982). Extensive and highly visible renovation, both interior and exterior, is a fundamental characteristic of the process. Expressions like whitepainting and brownstoning quite literally attest to the symbolic and visual impact of this renovation process.

Numerous studies carried out in Canada in the United States show that gentrifying households tend to be small (1–2 person), young (25–40 years), childless, and well-educated, with above-average incomes and high occupational status (Gale 1979, 1984; Holcomb and Beauregard 1981; Kennedy 1983; Ley 1986; Ornstein 1977; Palen and London 1984). Some studies have noted a temporal staging in the gentrification process that permits a distinction between relatively small-scale reinvestments undertaken by a minority of risk-taking households through to fully established upper-middle-income neighborhoods exhibiting housing quality comparable to that generally found only in newly developed communities (Gale 1979; Zeitz 1979).

In addition to the work on gentrification, there is a much smaller body of research that deals with a very different type of housing improvement, incumbent upgrading. As the term implies, incumbent upgrading refers to a process of housing rehabilitation undertaken by resident (low-income) homeowners. Incumbent upgrading has been associated with active local community groups who apply political pressures to release public monies for neighborhood and property improvement (Johnson 1983; Solomon and Vandell 1982). In Canada, federal programs like NIP (Neighborhood Improvement Program) and RRAP (Residential Rehabilitation Assistance Program) have similar aims, though the process is directed from the top-down rather than vice versa. The impact of such programs tends to be diffuse and is not always directly visible in the neighborhood (Mercer and Phillips 1981; McConney 1985; Phipps 1983).

Deterioration, gentrification, and incumbent upgrading are three distinct processes that are known to characterize inner-city housing and neighborhoods. All are easily identifiable—the first two in direct visual terms and the last through specific policy measures. Questions then arise as to the status of inner-city neighborhoods not visibly affected by any of these distinctive processes. In the Canadian context, a more comprehensive picture of inner-city housing was attained in a federal study of pre-World War II housing (McLemore et al. 1975). This yielded a fourfold classification of neighborhood types defined as: deteriorating, redeveloped, revitalizing (i.e. gentrifying), and stable. Current observation suggests that the former pair (those postulated in neoclassical economic theory) are perhaps not as evident as they were a decade ago, whereas the range of types between the latter pair of revitalizing and stable neighborhoods may need considerable expansion (Hung 1986; Ley 1986; Palen and London 1984; Rose 1984). Recent work in Australia suggests that inner-city neighborhoods can be arrayed along an extensive continuum ranging from stable to revitalized (Badcock and Cloher 1981; Kendig 1984). The current study presents a similar perspective on inner-city neighborhoods within a Canadian city.

EMPIRICAL METHODOLOGY

Existing studies of residential upgrading, mainly studies of gentrification, have tended to adopt one of two approaches to the topic. The first entails identification of upgrading via change in critical socioeconomic indicators. This type of research is usually carried out as comparative analysis at the census tract or some larger geographic scale (Badcock and Cloher 1981; Hung 1986; Ley 1986; Lipton 1977; McLemore et al. 1975). Indexes of on-going gentrification include: increased educational, occupational, and income status; decreased household size, age, and family status; and increased value and quality of the residential stock. The second approach, which can be termed sociopsychological, is more concerned with residential decision making or why gentrification occurs (Chevan 1982; MacLennan 1985; Mercer and Phillips 1981). This type of study identifies factors that range from (1) perceived savings in housing cost through (2) ease of access to work place to (3) possession of strong preferences for a distinctively older housing style and neighborhood design.

A further concern, not as yet widely dealt with in the literature, concerns the nature of upgrading. As upgrading takes place through households' investment of time and money in home improvement, surveys that deal directly with renovation activity are needed for this type of analysis (see also Chapter 6 in this book). Information about reinvestment in renovation becomes critically important when, as in the present case, interest is focused on a style of residential upgrading that is not as easily identifiable as the well-recognized gentrification.

In the findings presented here, large-scale, tract-level analysis is supplemented with a more detailed survey aimed at investigating the how and why of upgrading. Census data are examined over the period 1971–81 for the entire Census Metropolitan Area (CMA), the inner city, and the two tracts selected for further survey. The surveyed tracts are the oldest and innermost neighborhoods abutting the central business district. The survey portion of the study elicits information about households' renovation activities (type of activity, cost, paid and unpaid labor) as well as their sociodemographic characteristics and reasons for purchasing an inner-city home. Portions of the survey dealing with reinvestment rates have been modeled after Phipps (1983). Respondents to the survey are drawn from home-owning households who had purchased a home in central Kitchener in the last five years. This group was identified from City Directories for 1979 and 1983 and a 20 percent sample (N = 65) was randomly drawn. Each sampled tract had a 13 percent turnover in owner-occupied housing over the period of investigation.

STUDY AREA

By Canadian standards, the City of Kitchener is a medium-sized city comprising the core of a larger metropolitan area. In 1981 the respective populations were 139,734 for the city and 287,000 for the CMA. The city is located 100 kilometers west of Toronto and has its economic base firmly entrenched in manufacturing. It is notable that this city fails to conform to the profile said to characterize gentrifying cities—it is neither large nor white-collar and its labor force and employment centers are geographically dispersed.

Housing in inner-city areas of Canadian cities is mainly in the order of 50–100 years old. Change of one sort or another is imminent because of the relatively obsolescent nature of a housing stock developed to late Victorian or early twentieth-century standards and because of demographic turnover brought about by the demise of the first or second generation of original occupants. The housing stock in inner-city Kitchener fits this picture. The areas selected for detailed examination lie immediately to the east and west of downtown. Neither surveyed tract exhibits significant amounts of architecturally interesting housing or other local amenities that have been found to attract gentrifiers to inner-city neighborhoods (Palen and London 1984). Tract 16 has some originally exclusive housing and is homogeneously residential; Tract 11 has more working-class-style housing, mixed industrial land use, and a significant number of recent Portuguese immigrants. Both tracts have high proportions of elderly and low numbers of children.

It is important to consider briefly the context within which the surveyed housing stock has aged. Like most North American cities, the City of Kitchener experienced large-scale suburbanization of capital and households during the 1950s and 1960s. Since that time a series of changes has impacted more positively on the relative attractiveness of the central city (Bunting 1984). First, in conjunction with planning policy, new suburban housing densities have risen on average above those characterizing the original housing stock in the inner city. At the same time, the price of new homes has inflated faster than the Consumer Price Index. A second change has come about through a series of major redevelopment projects in the central business district, undertaken in 1970, 1978, and 1985. (Further plans are currently under way for another large infill project scheduled to be completed within the next five years.) A third factor is secondary-level planning in the core neighborhoods, which has resulted in widespread downzoning of residential properties. Finally, no inner-city school has been closed; in fact, the largest of the central elementary schools is being renovated under historic properties guidelines. Processes of change like these that might be said to enhance the inner city do not appear to be unique to the City of Kitchener. Similar redevelopment trends and policies have been observed in other Canadian cities (Goldberg and Mercer 1986; Hung 1986; Ley 1986; Phipps 1986).

THE INNER-CITY TRACTS

Census tract data (shown in Table 5.1) have been used to provide a broad perspective on housing and social change in the City of Kitchener over the decade 1971–81 and to characterize the status of inner-city tracts relative to the entire metropolitan average. In comparison to the entire CMA, Kitchener's inner-city neighborhoods exhibit several attributes of so-called deterioration and decline: population loss, above-average proportion of the population 65+ years, lower family incomes and levels of education, lower rates of owner-occupied housing, and smaller household size. On the whole, however, the differences between the metropolitan average and the inner city are not as large as the research literature might lead us to expect. In fact, inner-city tracts go against the citywide norm and show an increase in children under the age of 15. The percentage of adults in the 25–34 age range is well above the metropolitan average (23.8 percent contrasted with 17.8 percent). The inner city has the same proportion of females with high-status professional jobs as the rest of the metro areas and almost the same proportion of males in such occupations. Gentrification aside, one can only conclude that the inner city has not become entirely undesirable to young households and middle-income professionals. While this conclusion tends to contradict the mainstream interpretation of inner-city change, it accords with several more recent studies carried out in Canada, the United States, Britain, and Australia (Badcock and Cloher 1981; Hodge 1981; Goldberg and Mercer 1980; Palen and London 1984; Phipps 1983; Rose 1984; Solomon and Vandell 1982).

Inner-city tracts have lower than average rates of home ownership. This is not surprising given the relative predominance of rental, high-rise apartments. The two- and three-story style of single-family housing that characterizes Kitchener's inner-city neighborhoods is also quite adaptable to conversion to duplexed accommodation. Under conditions shown in Table 5.1 where 49 percent of the dwelling units are apartments, an owner occupancy rate of 46 percent seems quite high. Inflation rates on house prices, while not up to the CMA average of 163 percent over the decade 1971–81, show a dwelling unit value increase of 150 percent, suggesting that disinvestment is definitely not occurring on a large scale. It is also notable that the inner city shows a 60 percent rate of undoubling or decrease in the number of homes accommodating two or more households.

At a general level, change in the two innermost neighborhoods is manifest in the census tract data. While visual inspection of these neighborhoods does not reveal the intense style of renovation that characterizes housing in gentrified areas of larger and more cosmopolitan places, there is some suggestion of a middle class, professional resurgence in Tract 16. Table 5.1 shows little difference between median family incomes in this tract and the metropolitan area as a whole; dwelling unit values are somewhat lower but are inflating at a rate close to the metropolitan average. In contrast to the metropolitan average, this tract has more people with professional status jobs and university degrees. The percentage of the population in the age range 25–34 is the same as is found throughout the CMA, though households are smaller and there are fewer children. In contrast to Tract 16, Tract 11 manifests characteristics that might be thought indicative of inner-city decline. As Table 5.1 shows, the population in this neighborhood is older, poorer, and less well-educated with predominantly blue-collar occupations. Unlike the rest of the inner city, this tract shows no increase

Table 5.1
City of Kitchener, Inner-City Housing Characteristics, 1981

	Kitchener CMA	Total Kitchener Inner City *	Tract 011	Tract 016
Population	287,800	25,391	5,295	6,010
Population Change 1971-81	+26.8%	-20.3%	-16.9%	-17.3%
Population<15 yrs. 1971	28.9	21.4	22.5	21.3
Population<15 yrs. 1981	23.5	24.7	16.7	15.1
Population>65 yrs. 1971	7.4	12.7	10.5	15.1
Population>65 yrs. 1981	8.9	13.7	16.5	21.8
Population 25 - 34 yrs. 1971	14.7	12.8	14.5	12.5
Population 25 - 34 yrs. 1981	17.8	23.8	16.8	17.5
Median Family Income	$24,761	$20,823	$23,773	$23,660
Education:<Gr. 9	18.5%	27.7%	32.7%	23.1%
University Degree	8.5	7.5	4.5	10.8
Professional Occupations (Males)**	23.3	19.5	16.1	26.5
Professional Occupations (Females)	19.6	19.6	11.1	24.3
Housing Owner Occupied	60.8	46.2	50.7	40.1
Apartments ***	30.7	49.2	50.1	53.9

Table 5.1 cont'd.

Change Families Per Household 1971 - 81:				
0	+111	+38	+40	+51
1	+38	-16	-11	-14
2+	-19	-61	-50	-60
Value of Dwelling	$62,936	$51,910	$57,288	$56,478
Change Dwelling Value 1971-81	163%	150%	156%	159%
Dwellings Built Before 1946	21	53	49	54
Foreign Born	22	25	36	23

*An Inner City Tract is defined as having at least double the census metropolitan area for housing built prior to 1946 (McLemore et al. 1975).

**1981 Statistics Canada Occupations: Managements, Administrative and Related; Teaching and Related; Occupations in Health and Medicine; Technological, Social, Religious, Artistic, and Related.

***1981 Statistics Canada: Apartments >5 Stories, Apartments <5 Stories, and Duplexes.

Source: Statistics Canada (1981).

in occupationally high-status females but rather an increase (10 percent) in female blue-collar employment. However, owner-occupancy runs at 51 percent and median family incomes and housing values are well above the inner-city average.

In relative terms housing quality in both innermost tracts is good. In 1980 the City of Kitchener conducted a building survey of its inner-city neighborhoods. Housing quality was generally high: in Tract 16, 82 percent of all units were classified as good or fair (24 percent good, 58 percent fair); 83 percent were similarly classified in Tract 11 (39 percent good, 44 percent fair). However, the dwelling unit stock is aging—the majority of units are 60–90 years old. Most units require significant upgrading, at least above an annual maintenance level, to counter the evolutionary trend toward obsolescence and deterioration.

On the one hand, statistical enumeration of Kitchener's inner-city tracts suggests some demographic revitalization (children under age 15, adults aged 25–34, occupational status); on the other hand, the inner tracts evince many characteristics associated with ''decline'' such as population loss and reduced income. Some of these signs of decline—namely, population loss, nonfamily households, and reduced levels of income and education—can at least partially be attributed to the predominance of elderly households (14 percent 65 + years; 24 percent 55 + years). Issues then arise regarding housing and population turnover as these older households relocate or, quite literally, die off.

REINVESTMENT BY RECENT MOVERS

Dramatic changes in neighborhood quality, such as slum housing at one extreme or gentrification at the other, are easily recognized both visually in the streetscape and statistically through a census of housing. If less-extensive change is incurred such exercise may produce rather ambivalent conclusions. This is the case with the census data presented above. Where upgrading is concerned, households with limited financial resources generally begin the process of home improvement with interior renovation. Interior change is not directly observable to the untrained eye. Nor is there any readily available statistical index of home renovation activity. Building permits, though required by law in Canada, are notoriously unreliable as homeowners and contractors alike avoid the tax reassessment procedures that a building permit instigates. Accordingly, the household survey administered in this study has been designed to provide detailed information on homeowners' renovation activity.

Table 5.2 is a summary of findings compiled from the survey of home renovation practices. The data in this table represent conservative estimates of upgrading as only direct, out-of-pocket, financial outlays are tabulated. A majority of households engaging in home improvement report use of their own unpaid labor, even with more technical aspects of renovation involving such things as plumbing and heating. Moreover, although reinvestment has been tabulated over a five-year period, many households have been resident for con-

Table 5.2
Total Investments in Home Improvement

	Tract 11 (N = 37)	Tract 16 (N = 28)
Interior Change		
nil	19%	18%
$100 - $500	6	7
$501 - $1,000	8	11
$1,001 - $5,000	39	25
$5,001 - $10,000	11	25
$10,000+	9	14
Exterior Change		
nil	28	25
$100 - $500	14	7
$501 - $1,000	8	14
$1,001 - $5,000	44	36
$5,001 - $10,000	6	11
$10,000+	0	7
Combined Expenditure		
nil	14	18
$100 - $500	0	4
$501 - $1,000	8	0
$1,001 - $5,000	36	25
$5,001 - $10,000	19	25
$10,000+	22	29

Source: T. Bunting, *Residential Investment in Older Neighborhoods*. Ottawa: Canada Mortgage and Housing Corporation.

siderably less than five years, which further serves to reduce their overall financial outlay.

The fact that reinvestment activity has probably been underestimated in this study only underscores the significance of changing housing quality in inner-city tracts. As was expected, there is a marked emphasis on interior, rather than exterior, renovation. This helps to explain the "invisible" quality of the up-grading alluded to earlier. It is difficult to gauge the relative rates of reinvestment shown in Table 5.2 as little is known about household investment in maintenance and repair as opposed to outright purchase (Seek 1983). The Canadian building industry estimates that homeowners should spend approximately 1 percent of the dwelling unit value annually on maintenance and repair though, in reality, it is believed that these standards are seldom met. Morrison's (1978) work with a survey of homeowners spread geographically across metropolitan Toronto found that 55 percent of those surveyed spent no money on maintenance and repair in the previous year. Of those showing some expenditure, 56 percent claimed less than $500.

The average purchase price of homes surveyed in inner-city Kitchener is in the order of $60,000, implying an annual maintenance cost of $600 or something on the order of $1,000-$5,000 for the five-year period of accounting. Close to half of the surveyed households (46.9 percent) claim to have spent considerably more than this maximum $5,000. Because of shared empirical methodology these findings lend themselves to more direct comparison with recent work by Phipps (1983) in Saskatoon. With regard to interior renovation, Phipps classified 35 percent of households in his survey as "large-scale renovators" and 65 percent as "normal maintainers." Comparable analysis of reinvestment rates found in this study produces 66 percent large-scale renovators, 15 percent normal maintainers, and 19 percent nonmaintainers. Similar relationships exist between the findings of the two studies in regard to exterior renovation. While it is difficult at this stage to say why one finds both more upgrading and downgrading (non-maintenance) in inner-city Kitchener, it is clear that substantial renovation has taken place.

In Tract 16, where purchasing households tend to have higher incomes, 53.6 percent of the surveyed households have invested more than $5,000 on housing renovation (25 percent, $5,000–10,000; 28.6 percent, $10,000 +). In the more working-class Tract 11, though households are older and somewhat less affluent, 41.6 percent have invested more than $5,000 (19.4 percent, $5,000–$10,000; 22.2 percent, $10,000 +). There is a considerable amount of variation within the tracts as well. Not surprisingly, differential rates of reinvestment tend to be associated with household characteristics. Findings suggest a direct correlation with household income, age, and length of residence. These patterns accord with the findings of related studies (Mendelsohn 1977; Morrison 1978; Phipps 1983; Seek 1983).

Where sociodemographic characteristics are concerned, there is a lack of correspondence between the attributes of this sample and attributes of middle-class gentrifiers who are generally found to be childless, well-educated singles or couples with well-above-average incomes. Most surprising in this respect is the family status dimension. Households surveyed in Kitchener's innermost neighborhoods exhibit a degree of familism lifestyle that, in North America, is usually associated with a suburban place of residence and life-style. Some 66 percent of families have children under the age of 16; over 80 percent are married; a majority of households consist of three–four persons, and, among the younger and more affluent households in Tract 16, half of the female heads of household are traditional housewives. (In the entire metropolitan area, 65 percent of households have children under the age of 18; 41 percent of the female population is classified as not in the labor force.) As a group, these households are reasonably well-educated (15.6 percent have university degrees as contrasted with 8.5 percent throughout the CMA). Tract 16 households are predominantly white-collar (39.3 percent of males in professional occupations, some 15 percent higher than the metro average), whereas Tract 11 shows an equivalent blue-collar dominance (39 percent males and 31 percent females in manufacturing occupations) with a large foreign-born (Portuguese) contingent. Residents in both tracts have slightly above-average incomes—34.4 percent of families report more than $30,000 per annum. However, relative to the home-owning population across Kitchener, this affluence is not outstanding (for example, only 17 percent report family incomes greater than $40,000, with 6 percent over $50,000). By way of comparison, the income profile shown here is extremely modest in comparison to the degree of affluence characteristically associated with gentrification.

While the surveyed households do not resemble the picture so often painted in the literature of the gentrifying or back-to-the-city movement, neither do they resemble the incumbent population (as characterized in Table 5.1). Here the contrast is marked in three important ways: age, socioeconomic status, and, again, life cycle. The surveyed population comprises youthful, family-oriented households who possess a degree of affluence at least equivalent to the metropolitan average. The incumbent households are older and smaller with lower levels of education and income.

Debate wages in the literature over the long-term permanence of central-city revitalization (see, for example, Berry 1980; Smith 1982). As far as the surveyed households are concerned, their residential choice is relatively fixed. Although 30 percent remain uncertain about future mobility plans, only 25 percent plan to move within the next five years and another 16 percent in a subsequent five-year period. It is noteworthy that over half of the households planning a move intend to stay in the inner city. Moreover, it tends to be the blue-collar, foreign-born households who express an ultimate desire for a suburban neighborhood.

Reasons for moving to the inner city are many. For purposes of the present research, household respondents were asked open-ended questions about reasons for choosing their current home and neighborhood and, conversely, their reasons for not choosing a suburban location. Four reasons predominate among surveyed households: a preference for older housing and neighborhood types; access to downtown in both the symbolic and functional sense; a perceived savings in the cost and quality of housing; and access to place of work.

When asked about reasons for choosing their particular dwelling unit, close to one-third of the sample mention accessibility to work, services, and downtown. Next in order of importance is the attraction to the older, generally pre-World War I style of home and the relatively low price. Differences between the blue-collar Tract 11 and white-collar Tract 16 are marked on the housing preference dimension. About 33 percent of the white-collar respondents express an affinity for antiquarian housing; 25 percent mention accessibility, mostly in terms of access to a wide variety of services and to downtown; 14 percent mention perceived savings in purchase price. The responses are reversed for Tract 11. Approximately 33 percent mention accessibility, in this case mainly to work place, often the work place of the female head of the household; 25 percent cite a lower purchase price, while less than 10 percent mention the merit of older architectural styles. Both tracts view access as the outstanding feature of the neighborhood, though respondents in Tract 16 are not much concerned with access to work. Just as these Tract 16 households emphasize distinctive style in their housing choice, they cite an aversion to suburban landscape and life-styles when asked why they chose not to settle in suburbia. On this dimension their responses tend to reinforce Allen's (1980) arguments regarding an "ideology" of high-density living. Access and cost factors predominate among reasons given by Tract 11 residents for not buying in the suburbs.

Economic constraints, environmental preference, and spatial access are cited by residents as factors underlying their decisions to purchase property in the inner city. Even the better-off, white-collar households who say less about the premium on inner-city housing costs appear somewhat constrained in terms of their total family income; by today's standards, a surprising number of these households have only one, rather than two, wage earners. The fact that most renovation is carried out in the interior rather than the exterior would seem in itself a reflection of economic constraint.

CONCLUSIONS

The research presented here attests to a form of modest upgrading taking place in inner-city tracts in the city of Kitchener, Ontario. The immediate implication is that in other cities there too may be vast uncharted "grey" areas experiencing neither extreme of deterioration nor gentrification, but rather modest refurbishing of the original housing stock. It can be postulated that the processes described here are more typical of Canadian, as opposed to U.S., cities and of medium, rather than large-sized, cities. The various economic, demographic, racial, and other pressures exerted on inner-city neighborhoods in large cities, especially in the United States, need not be elaborated here. What this study further suggests is, first, that aging, both of housing and occupant households, is a natural phenomenon and that some developments commonly seen as "decline" are simply a function of this aging process. Second, this research illustrates that critical processes of change may be put in place by the replacement population whose presence may not be immediately visible, especially if the improvement they undertake is on a modest scale. Finally, there appears to be a diversity of household types—middle versus working class, child-rearing versus childless, immigrant versus native born, housewife versus working mothers, and so on— who have been motivated to seek housing in the inner city through different forces of preference and constraint.

From a policy perspective there are several implications. The processes of change described here appear to avoid both the problems of widespread deterioration that result from downgrading, and the displacement of vulnerable, incumbent households that accompanies gentrification. However, programs will be needed to provide services (day-care, recreation) for younger and more affluent households while at the same time continuing to provide for the less-well-off occupants of the neighborhoods. It may be, as Rose (1984) has pointed out, that the newcomers will act as agents for the incumbent population in agitating for neighborhood improvement. Or it may be that strong policy initiatives will be needed to maintain the delicate balance of new and old. Further concerns could be raised about the differential needs of a variety of inner-city neighborhood types, demarcated along the lines of the two identified here.

From both a policy and theoretical perspective, more recognition needs to be given to the diversity and the resilience of inner-city housing and neighborhoods and to the context in which change, be it upgrading, downgrading, or apparent stability, occurs. Current impressions of the inner city at best reflect a picture of gentrification amid decline. This needs to be revised to accommodate other types of more modest and less visible processes.

NOTE

This project was carried out with the assistance of a grant from Canada Mortgage and Housing Corporation under the terms of the External Research Program. The views expressed are those of the author and do not represent the official views of the Corporation. Research assistance was ably provided by Andrew Barker and Anne Craig.

REFERENCES

Allen, I.
1980 "The Ideology of Dense Neighborhood Redevelopment: Cultural Diversity and Transcendent Community Experience." *Urban Affairs Quarterly* 15, 409–28.
Andrews, R. B.
1971 *Urban Land Economics and Public Policy*. New York: The Free Press.
Badcock, B., and D. Cloher
1981 "Neighborhood Change in Inner Adelaide." *Urban Studies* 18, 41–55.

Berry, B.
1980   "Inner City Futures: An American Dilemma Revisited." *Transactions of the Institute of British Geographers* 5, 1–18.
Birch, D.
1971   "Toward a Stage Model of Urban Growth." *Journal, American Institute of Planners* 37, 78–87.
Bourne, L.
1982   "The Inner City." In *Modern Metropolitan Systems*, edited by C. Christian and R. Harper, 223–50. Columbus, Ohio: Charles Merrill.
Bunting, T.
1984   *Kitchener-Waterloo: A Geography of Mainstreet*. Waterloo: University of Waterloo, Department of Geography Occasional Paper No. 3.
Chevan, A.
1982   "Age, Housing Choice and Neighborhood Age Structure." *American Journal of Sociology* 87, 1133–49.
Clay, P.
1979   *Neighborhood Renewal: Middle Class Resettlement and Incumbent Upgrading in American Neighborhoods*. Lexington, MA: D. C. Heath.
Gale, D.
1979   "Middle Class Resettlement in Older Urban Neighborhoods." *Journal, American Institute of Planners* 45, 313–28.
1984   *Neighborhood Revitalization and the Post Industrial City*. Lexington, MA: D. C. Heath.
Goldberg, M., and J. Mercer
1980   "Canadian and U.S. Cities." *Papers and Proceedings, Regional Science Association* 45, 159–83.
1986   *The Myth of the North American City*. Vancouver: University of British Columbia Press.
Hodge, D.
1981   "Residential Revitalization and Displacement in a Growth Region." *Geographical Review* 71, 188–200.
Holcomb, H. B., and R. A. Beauregard
1981   *Revitalizing Cities*. Washington, DC: Association of American Geographers.
Hoover, E., and R. Vernon
1959   *Anatomy of a Metropolis*. New York: McGraw-Hill
Hung, K.
1986   "Toward a Stage Model of Residential Development—The Ottawa Experience." Unpublished Ph.D. thesis, Department of Geography, University of Waterloo.
Johnson, J. H.
1983   "The Role of Community Action in Neighborhood Revitalization." *Urban Geography* 4, 16–39.
Kendig, H.
1984   "Gentrification in Australia." In *Gentrification, Displacement and Neighborhood Revitalization*, edited by J. Palen and B. London, 235–54. Albany, N.Y.: SUNY Press.
Kennedy, L.
1983   *The Urban Kaleidoscope: Canadian Perspectives*. Toronto: McGraw-Hill.
Lang, M.
1982   *Gentrification Amid Urban Decline*. Cambridge, Mass.: Ballinger.

Leven, C., J. T. Little, H. O. Nourse, and R. B. Read
1967   *Neighborhood Change: Lessons in the Dynamics of Urban Decay.* New York: Praeger.

Ley, D.
1986   *Gentrification in Canadian Inner Cities.* Department of Geography, University of British Columbia.

Lipton, S.
1977   "Evidence of Central City Revival." *Journal, American Institute of Planners* 43, 136–47.

Lowry, I.
1960   "Filtering and Housing Costs: A Conceptual Analysis." *Land Economics* 36, 362–70.

MacLennan, D.
1985   "Urban Housing Rehabilitation: An Encouraging British Example." *Social Policy and Administration* 19, 413–29.

McConney, M.
1985   "An Empirical Look at Housing Rehabilitation as a Spatial Process." *Urban Studies* 22, 39–48.

McLemore, R. V., C. Aass, and P. Keilhofer
1975   *The Changing Canadian Inner City.* Ottawa: Ministry of State for Urban Affairs.

Mendelsohn R.
1977   "Empirical Evidence on Home Improvement." *Journal of Urban Economics* 4, 459–68.

Mercer, J., and D. Phillips
1981   "Attitudes of Homeowners and the Decision to Rehabilitate Property." *Urban Geography* 2, 216–36.

Morrison, P.
1978   *Expenditures on Housing Maintenance and Repairs: Some Recent Evidence. An Analysis of Expenditures Made by Home Owners in Toronto in 1973.* Toronto: University of Toronto, Centre for Urban and Community Studies.

Ornstein, M.
1977   *Entrance into the Labor Market.* New York: Academic Press.

Palen, J., and B. London (eds.)
1984   *Gentrification, Displacement and Neighborhood Revitalization.* Albany: State University of New York Press.

Phipps, A.
1983   "Housing Renovation by Recent Movers into the Core Neighborhoods of Saskatoon." *The Canadian Geographer* 27, 240–62.
1986   *Government Involvement in Residential Renovation.* Department of Geography, University of Saskatchewan.

Ratcliffe, R.
1949   *Urban Land Economics.* New York: McGraw-Hill.

Rose, D.
1984   "Rethinking Gentrification: Beyond the Uneven Development of Marxist Urban Theory." *Environment and Planning D* 2, 47–74.

Seek, N.
1983   "Adjusting Housing Consumption: Improve or Move." *Urban Studies* 20, 455–69.

Smith, N.
1983   "Gentrification and Uneven Development." *Economic Geography* 58, 139–55.
Solomon, A. and K. Vandell
1982   "Alternative Perspectives on Neighborhood Decline." *Journal, American Institute of Planners* 48, 81–98.
Zeitz, E.
1979   *Private Urban Renewal*. Lexington, MA: Lexington Books.

6

Ethnic Minorities, Scarce Housing Resources, and Urban Renewal in Britain

TANER OC

Abstract. This chapter examines the impact of housing improvement on the ethnic minorities in Britain who today constitute a large percentage of those living in the dilapidated inner-city areas and have very limited choice in the housing market. After a brief look at housing improvement policies and especially the Housing Action Areas, the chapter examines the experience in three cities: Leicester, Bristol, and London. Housing Action Areas in the predominantly black neighborhoods of these three cities fail to reach the black residents. Even with 90 percent grants, finding the balance to improve their housing conditions is not possible for a majority of black owner occupiers and resident landlords. The chapter concludes that current housing improvement policies in Britain should be amended to overcome the problems suffered by ethnic minorities.

INTRODUCTION

In Britain, the wholesale clearance and redevelopment approach to urban renewal that displaced large numbers of poor inner-city residents has been abandoned for over a decade. Today, even much-needed redevelopment is undertaken with great reluctance and very often it is strongly opposed. As Stoker and Brindley (1985) show, a proposal for limited clearance of structurally defective properties can be obstructed through skilled manipulation of the local political system by the residents, who in this case happened to be predominantly Asian. As a consequence, currently most local authorities are trying to improve their dilapidated housing stock and the run-down inner-city neighborhoods by using grants for area-based improvement schemes.

Compared to redevelopment, housing improvement (rehabilitation) is a much gentler approach, at least on the surface, and its social costs are less obvious to the outsiders. This chapter examines the impact of housing improvement on the ethnic minorities in Britain. Today, ethnic minorities constitute a large percentage of those living in the dilapidated inner-city areas and they also constitute the groups who have the least degree of choice in the housing market. We point out that the present approaches to housing improvement in Britain fail to improve their housing conditions.

ETHNIC MINORITIES IN THE INNER-CITY AREAS

Ethnic minorities in Britain tend to congregate in the large cities in the major industrial areas. Within these cities, the black population tends to be concentrated in certain parts of the inner city. This concentration of black homes has important consequences in terms of housing and other policies. Very often segregation of groups of people is a consequence of the sort of jobs they do. Because they tend to occupy the bottom end of the labor market, black immigrants can afford only the relatively inexpensive accommodation in the run-down inner-city neighborhoods (The Runnymede Trust 1980a). The different values and social habits of minority groups strengthen this concentration. As Department of the Environment's (DOE) White Paper "Race Relations and Housing" (1975) outlines, a continued influx of people into such areas coupled with the high birth rates to minority women residents has put severe strains on already scarce accommodation, accelerating deterioration.

Black people live in poorer housing with poorer amenities and at higher densities than the majority of whites in the inner city (Lornes 1975; Smith 1976; DOE 1979; DOE 1971). This poor quality of housing is not only related to their low socioeconomic grouping and financial circumstances, but also to direct and indirect social discrimination. Despite the 1968 and 1976 Race Relations Acts, only certain types of property are available to the ethnic minorities. As a result, they tend to concentrate in poor housing available in certain areas. This is clearly undesirable and often labels them as the cause rather than victims of inner-city decline.

To be able to understand the implications of housing improvement programs for ethnic minorities whose housing conditions are clearly below the acceptable level we must also note their tenure preferences. Great Britain is a country of owner occupiers—61 percent of the population either own or are in the process of buying their houses. Generally the higher the social class the more owner occupation and less council tenancy. With West Indians, we see that there is a similar council house tenancy between classes, and owner occupation replaces private renting the higher the social class. Among Asians we see that the lower the social class the higher is owner occupation, mostly of pre–1919 property (see Table 6.1).

Studies show that Asian owner occupiers live in older housing and with worse problems, lacking basic amenities compared not only to the white population but also to West Indian owner occupiers. However, housing occupied by both Asian and West Indian groups needs major structural repairs. Together with bad housing conditions we must note the particulars of housing finance for ethnic minorities. Building societies are reluctant to lend money to ethnic minorities because they are termed as high risk. Therefore, these people, especially Asians,

Table 6.1
Housing Conditions of All Households, West Indians, and Asians

Housing Conditions	All Households	West Indians	Asians
Sole use of all basic amenities	91%	87%	76%
Some basic amenities shared, none lacked	3%	9%	13%
Below bedroom standard	5%	18%	30%
Pre-1919 property	27%	47%	62%

Source: DOE (1979).

are forced to depend on expensive ''back-street finance'' to buy their dilapidated houses in the inner cities. They also rely on their own social networks (see also Chapter 7 in this book) and have to put together a number of small loans, often at exorbitant rates (Clark 1977). Repayments can be met only by subdividing houses into lodgings rented at high rents and ignoring their maintenance or improvement. Local authority mortgages try to redress the balance by lending to ethnic minorities and for older property but this has been a declining source of finance since 1979. There is also some indication that ethnic minorities pay about 5 percent in excess of the going purchase price for their property (Fenton 1977). On the whole, owner occupation does not increase choice for ethnic minorities, as some argue; their situation is ''involuntary owner occupation'' as the private rented sector declines and the public rented sector fails to satisfy their demands.

Many blacks have no prospect of ever obtaining a mortgage or a council house and, therefore, are dependent on the continued existence of privately rented accommodation. In the case of Asians, landlords may be related or friends. West Indians, on the other hand, are more likely to have been trapped in the private furnished sector for much longer periods than Asians since they are less likely to rent from friends or relatives or to obtain loans from friends/relatives to help buy a house. We must note that although owners of large inner-city houses who subdivide and rent may be regarded as slum landlords, they do offer the only source of accommodation for people excluded from every other type of housing.

The chapter then continues with a short review of housing improvement policies in Britain, before taking a close look at three Housing Action Areas (HAAs). These areas from three different cities (Leicester, Bristol, and London) are predominantly ethnic minority neighborhoods. Examining these areas in terms of rates of improvement and changing tenure patterns indicates a degree of failure to meet the needs of ethnic minorities. Several measures are recommended in the concluding section to redress this failure to deal with the housing problem of ethnic minorities in the inner cities.

HOUSING IMPROVEMENT POLICIES IN BRITAIN

Since the Housing of the Working Classes Act of 1890, local authorities have tried to find ways of providing satisfactory housing accommodation for those residents who are not able to satisfy their housing needs themselves. Currently there are two major avenues for local authorities of providing satisfactory accommodation to their less-well-off residents; first is providing them with council housing; second is helping them with housing improvement or rehabilitation. Here we will focus on the second approach and examine how ethnic minorities fare in terms of rehabilitation.

Housing improvement/rehabilitation is tackled by the local authorities through: (1) the improvement of individual, structurally "fit" but unsatisfactory houses; (2) the repair or demolition of individual "unfit" houses; and (3) clearance or rehabilitation of "slum" areas.

The individual house that is structurally sound but unsatisfactory owing to lack of one or more of the basic amenities (inside bathroom and toilet, sink, running hot and cold water) may be dealt with by means of a grant from the District Council. If a house is unfit as a result of structural defects and lack of facilities, the District Council may require the persons having control of the house to carry out necessary repairs to make it fit, provided this can be done at reasonable expense. If the house is beyond redemption, the District Council has a duty either to make a demolition order or a closing order. A closing order requires that the house may not be used for human habitation until it has been rendered fit. Local authorities use both avenues to effect rehabilitation.

The more common local authority intervention to rehabilitate urban housing is through area-based policies. An area may be defined a General Improvement Area (GIA), in which case the authority has the power to acquire land, encourage house improvement, provide necessary buildings, make traffic orders, improve the street furniture, and so on. If in an area the social conditions as well as the physical conditions of houses are required to be taken into account, as is the case in many ethnic minority concentration areas, the local authority may declare an HAA. In HAAs with grants up to 90 percent and with increased powers of intervention the local authority tries to rehabilitate the area in five years. Areas adjoining HAAs are Priority Neighborhoods where local authorities have similar powers without the same degree of urgency (Garner 1981).

Before we turn to several case studies of Housing Action Areas, it is important to point out that the accepted policy toward ethnic minorities is to include them in policies of general improvements (see Chapter 7). The argument is that to improve housing conditions generally will lead to improving the position of black people among others. This approach is not augmented with policies to improve the position of black people in the housing market by catering for their particular needs.

HOUSING ACTION AREAS AND ETHNIC MINORITIES: CASE STUDIES

Government and professionals are concerned that there is a great need to reach ethnic minority communities with housing improvement (rehabilitation) policies. Considering the state of ethnic minority housing conditions, it is no surprise that there is a certain effort to improve their houses. However, this effort as yet is not well coordinated and the results are varied, as will be shown in this chapter. We will examine three different HAAs where there are majorities of black residents.

These case studies are compiled from local authority reports. Before an area is designated as an HAA, local authorities undertake both social and house condition surveys. Based on these surveys, planning committees declare areas as HAAs and set up special teams. During the five-year period there are annual reports and before the area is designated a GIA, a final report is prepared to assess the progress. These reports cover the take up of grants, improvements, changes in tenure, changes in population, and, in some cases, changes in the social structure of the area. Improvements in each are examined over time and current conditions are compared with conditions that existed before the areas were designated as HAAs.

Down Street, Cossington Street, and Catherine Street HAAs, Leicester

The three areas in Leicester are situated in the Belgrave area and exhibit many of the characteristics described above. In total they amount to 1,529 properties. Of these, over 65 percent are in owner occupation and over 50 percent are inhabited by people whose ethnic origin is Asian. The highest Asian percentage is in Down Street at 66 percent. This HAA also has the highest proportion of owner occupancy at 73 percent.

The *Declaration Report* (Leicester City Council 1979) stated that

the high concentration of Asian households has changed the character of the area considerably as evidenced, for example, by the number of shops in the area and the other facilities expressly orientated to the Asian community. This provision of facilities reinforces the attractiveness of the area for Asians and . . . it is expected that the proportion of Asians will continue to grow over the next few years. . . .

A majority of the houses are flush-fronted two-story terraces. The general picture in many ways is much the same as other HAAs in other cities. There are, however, certain features peculiar to HAAs with predominantly Asian pop-

Table 6.2
Tenure Patterns, Down Street, Cossington Street, and Catherine Street HAAs

	Households			
	1979		1983	
	N	%	N	%
Owner-occupation	868	57	968	63
Privately rented dwellings and vacant dwellings	409	27	270	18
Housing Association dwellings	93	6	147	10
Council owned dwellings	162	10	144	9
TOTAL	1532		1529	

Source: Leicester City Council (1983).

ulations, such as the level of overcrowding, which stands at 8 percent (that is 1.5 or more persons per room) as compared to the city average of 2 percent. This can be explained, to some extent, by the tendency among Asian households for three generations of the family to live together.

Upon the *Declaration* the City Council held three public meetings that were attended by over 300 residents and schedules of desirable renovation work were sent to every owner occupier and landlord whose property had been surveyed. Previous to the *Declaration* a majority of households had been visited at least once during a house condition survey, and many were visited again during the course of a social survey. Three newly formed resident committees were contacted and made aware of the proposals to improve the area and of the role they could play. Surrounding the house improvement scheme there were a number of other independent schemes aimed at improving the overall quality of life using a combination of private and Inner Area Programme funding.

At the end of the fourth year a modest success can be claimed. If the number of houses not needing improvement is added to those that have been improved and those that are in process of being improved, the overall figure of improved houses comes to roughly 61 percent. In fact, this figure indicates a higher success rate when one takes into account the fact that 16 percent of the occupiers in the area do not want improvements. Unfortunately about 23 percent of households, despite the availability of the 90 percent hardship grant, are still either unable to finance the extra 10 percent or have not been able to find an appropriate loan.

Table 6.2 shows that the transfer of tenure has been mainly from the privately rented and vacant sectors to the owner-occupied and housing association sectors. This reflects the general trend found in a majority of HAAs nationwide, and the continuing downward proportion of houses that are rented privately.

Three main difficulties were identified by the renewal officers in relation to the Asian community and house improvement. First, there is a problem involved with the "participatory" element of the improvement scheme. As in other cities, the Asian community is extremely reluctant to get publicly involved and there is very poor attendance at public meetings and residents' committee meetings (see also Chapter 7). A second difficulty is the problems encountered by Asians in understanding the concept of a grant and what it will cover—indeed what an HAA is, what obligations an owner has, and what powers the local authority has. The greatest difficulty experienced by Asians, however, is that of funding their contribution to the renewal work, a problem they share with other low-income households. Those Asians who have a second mortgage or even a first mortgage from a high-interest loan source will already be spending a large proportion of their income on housing (Wolfe 1984).

St. Paul's HAA, Bristol

St. Paul's HAA is characterized by a large percentage of households renting their accommodation privately, much of which is multioccupied. A 1973 survey of 206 houses showed 105 of them to be in multiple occupation. Of these, 51 were owner-occupied, 52 privately rented, and 2 council rented; 380 households lived in these 105 houses. Consequently, there were large numbers of households sharing or lacking amenities (155 households shared or lacked cooking facilities, 323 households bath facilities, and 294 households toilet facilities). When one adds the figures for overcrowding, it becomes rapidly obvious that there were considerable social and housing problems (Bristol City Council 1976).

It is impossible to ascertain the precise ethnic dimension in these acute problems, but with the high concentration of West Indians and their offspring in the area, it should be expected that they will experience similar, if not greater, deprivation than the indigenous population. If one considers that minority groups can statistically be expected to figure more prominently in unemployment and bad housing conditions, then it should be expected that minorities (especially West Indian one-parent families) in the area will experience degrees of multiple deprivation and special problems above that of the general population (Ashcroft 1982).

By the end of the five-year period there was a marked change, both in the tenure pattern and the conditions of the housing stock. City council and various housing associations had acquired about 53 percent of the stock and improved over 90 percent of their properties, the rest being scheduled for improvement. The owner occupiers, encouraged by the efforts of the city council and the housing associations, improved 57 percent of the housing stock. Another 22 percent were being repaired.

The figures do not allow an analysis of improvements to the dwellings of the area's West Indians. Nevertheless, the very high improvement rate generally is a clear indication that various ethnic groups will have benefited along with the indigenous population. The long-term commitment of the city council to the regeneration of the HAA was highlighted by the area's declaration as a GIA in September 1981. This should allow a host of environmental improvements in this generally shabby area (Bristol City Council 1981).

Hubert Grove HAA, Lambeth (London)

Hubert Grove HAA was declared in March 1977. It was an area of 343 properties at the time of declaration, and the percentage of New Commonwealth origin population (1981 Census) was 56.7 percent, a majority of which was of West Indian origin. The Declaration Report (Lambeth Borough Council 1977) states the following:

The survey of household characteristics shows that there was a large privately rented sector in the area (41 percent) comprised mainly of small households (73 percent) and most of these were tenants of absentee landlords (65 percent). The area, therefore, serves an important function in providing privately rented accommodation for single people and childless couples. Physical housing conditions were, however, particularly bad amongst tenants of absentee landlords and many of these tenants shared amenities.

A predesignation survey carried out by Lambeth City Council of residents' attitudes to staying in the area showed that 38 percent wanted to leave the area, of whom 53 percent were council tenants. Within the private sector fewer owner occupiers (21 percent) or resident landlords (5 percent) wanted to leave as compared to private tenants (40 percent). So overall it was the tenants, both private and council, who were most dissatisfied and wanted to move. This suggests that many residents viewed their housing conditions very much as a stop-gap solution until they were able to find something better or until they could find council housing elsewhere.

Table 6.3 shows which properties had been improved after five years and the respective improvement rates of each type of property. The overall success of improvement is 47 percent if we allow for those properties that are not in need of improvement. There is an even split among owner occupiers and privately rented households: Just under 40 percent of both sectors are still in need of improvement. This figure is all the more interesting when one considers Table 6.4, which shows changes in tenure over the five-year HAA duration. Owner occupation has jumped from 21 percent of the total households in 1977 to 36 percent of the total in 1982 (Wolfe 1984). The increase in the owner-occupant sector virtually matches the decline in the privately rented sector.

This change in tenure is explained in the extension report as being due to a process of gentrification. The report also states that ''experience shows in other

Table 6.3
Summary of House Improvement Progress, Hubert Grove HAA

	Local authority		Housing association		Owner-occupied		Privately rented		TOTAL	
	N	%	N	%	N	%	N	%	N	%
Improved	43	32	3	15	68	58	34	58.5	148	45
Not improved	89	66	17	85	46	39	22	38	174	53
Not needing improvement	3	2			3	3	2	3.5	8	2
TOTAL	135	100	20	100	117	100	58	100	330	100

Source: Lambeth Borough Council (1982).

Table 6.4
Changes in Tenure Patterns, Hubert Grove HAA: 1977–81

	Local authority		Housing association		Owner-occupied		Privately rented		TOTAL	
	N	%	N	%	N	%	N	%	N	%
March '77	132	39	0	0	72	21	139	40	343	100
Sept '81	135	41	20	6	117	36	58	17	330	100

Source: Lambeth Borough Council (1982).

HAAs that these 'new' owner-occupiers are the more likely to take up house renovation grants'' (Lambeth Borough Council 1982). The report shows that those owner occupiers who have been in the area for a long while are those who are reluctant to, or do not have the means to, improve their property even with the grant assistance.

The report argues that continuing and increasing unemployment of the ethnic minorities, their distrust of local authorities, their inability to use the loan systems adequately, and the local authority's benign failure to communicate with them— all contribute to the lack of success in the current housing improvement efforts in this area where ethnic minorities constitute large numbers (Lambeth Borough Council 1982).

FAILURE TO MEET THE NEEDS OF ETHNIC MINORITIES

Despite substantial investments in council housing and some effort for reha-bilitation, a majority of the British cities are failing to provide adequate housing for the ethnic minorities, particularly the black population. Lord Scarman pointed out this failure as a factor contributing to the current racial tension (The Scarman Report 1982). Research concurs that "the housing situation is plainly one of the root causes of the social tensions and individual problems" in the ethnic minority neighborhoods (John 1973).

The economic position in which black people are placed in British society is the cause of their low standards of housing. In other words, as Rex and others argue, blacks in Britain constitute a distinct housing class whose access to housing is restricted as a result of competition with other classes in the city (Deakin and Ungerson 1973). They fare badly in access to local authority housing. Those housed by the local authorities usually get housing in various degrees of disrepair, either ripe for demolition or programmed for rehabilitation (The Runnymede Trust 1980b). On the other hand, a majority of them do worse than the bad local authority housing; they end up either as involuntary owners of, or tenants in, unfit housing. The owners who can ill afford these dilapidated houses usually try to meet their costs by renting (Lambert, Paris, and Blackaby 1978). Con-sequently, large numbers of ethnic minority involuntary owner occupiers are forced by circumstances to multioccupation. At the bottom of the heap we have black people who rent from the slum landlords, some of the landlords being the involuntary owners of the dilapidated houses.

Multioccupied houses in ethnic minority concentration areas

give rise to the greatest concern. Occupiers complain of exploitation by landlords, of lack of adequate space and facilities, of too many people sharing basic amenities. When these properties are purchased they are already in need of extensive repair and, in many cases, renovation. It is therefore all the more difficult for people with few resources to rehabilitate such properties (John 1973).

Even in HAAs very often the owners find it beyond their means to carry out the necessary repairs in spite of grants covering 90 percent of the cost.

Ethnic minority tenants in single-family rented property usually suffer because the landlords in many cases fail to provide adequate basic amenities. As a result of rent control and security of tenure, investment in such property does not yield any returns even for minimal investment in rehabilitation. In many areas, especially in HAAs, local authorities end up by using their powers to acquire these properties. However, this is a lengthy process. After such property comes into council ownership the residents have to wait for a council rehabilitation program to reach them. In most cases, this wait is long and frustrating.

The subgroup of ethnic minority population in single-family owner-occupied housing in inner-city areas is potentially in a better position. Owners with regular incomes make use of grants and rehabilitate their housing. Very often such residents are very active in local associations and try to have their areas declared HAAs so that they can get maximum grants. In some cases, black owner occupiers who would like rehabilitation grants come into direct conflict with black residents who rent, because this latter group prefers their houses to be condemned for demolition so that the council would have to rehouse them, one hopes in better accommodation. These black tenants also come into direct conflict with their black landlords. Although black landlords cannot afford to rehabilitate their houses, they object to being rehoused in council property, with better amenities, because such a move would increase their housing expenditure.

Improvement grants and area-based policies, which fail to bring about rehabilitation of ethnic minority housing, are more successfully used by middle and lower-middle income groups. This was the case in Hubert Grove, where a degree of gentrification was under way. However, in Britain, gentrification does not lead to the direct and devastating displacement we see in other countries. Tenants are protected by rent control and security of tenure.

Ethnic minorities in Britain are not served adequately by the present policies. As Barr (1978) argues,

racial negativism among white residents inhibits rehabilitation of the neighborhood by its effect on mobility patterns and attitudes towards the area. In turn these affect the propensity of residents to invest in improvement. Failure to invest reinforces the process of physical decline which in turn increases inter-ethnic tensions and bitterness. Unable to buy out of the area, poorest (usually older) residents become "trapped." Due to the disparity in attitudes between white and Asian communities a free market process of race housing segregation is occurring.

The only way out seems to be more interventionist policies aimed at housing improvement/rehabilitation.

As was the case in St. Paul's, housing associations play a positive role in the rehabilitation of the inner-city housing stock. These charitable, nonprofit organizations use council grants and programs to bring into use and to improve the housing stock, which individuals cannot afford and which councils are too slow and unwilling to undertake. Once they rehabilitate such properties, they rent them to individuals and families with special needs. Ethnic minorities, single-parent families, and the elderly are very often beneficiaries of the housing association rehabilitation schemes.

CONCLUSIONS

In Britain, a majority of black people are condemned to dilapidated housing in the inner cities. Rent control and security of tenants protect the poor from the evils of private market rehabilitation and displacement. However, present policies fail to bring about large-scale rehabilitation of the dilapidated inner-city housing stock. Therefore, ethnic minorities continue to experience some of the worst housing in Britain.

The experience indicates that government must design policies that enable the poor and the ethnic minorities to rehabilitate their housing. Government must ensure that the present commitment to rehabilitation continues and that a more concerted effort is made. It would be advisable to take a fresh look at rehabilitation and give more money to local authorities for housing improvements. Present policy should be amended to give the local authorities powers for making 100 percent grants as well as a combination of loans and grants in case of hardships so that the number of improved houses can be increased and the process can be accelerated. Local authorities may experiment with co-ownership policies. They may fund improvements in certain cases in return for a stake in the property. Although some ethnic minority residents would be reluctant to share their ownership, if adequately explained some people may see the benefits and opt for it. These measures would solve some of the problems faced by owner occupiers and resident landlords.

Government must also provide special funds to the housing associations working in ethnic minority neighborhoods, because housing associations can cater to special needs in these areas. Last, there must be a reassessment of the policy of not having special programs for ethnic minorities. The case studies, especially Hubert Grove, illustrate that the current HAA approach is less successful in reaching ethnic minorities than it is in reaching the white population. As was noted in the case of the Belgrave area, local authorities are doing their best to reach the ethnic minorities through publicity and encouragement, but in the end their efforts are frustrated by the ethnic minority residents' inability to find even the 10 percent of the cost of improvements. Urgent attention is required to rehabilitate the housing stock and neighborhoods before they deteriorate any further and the ethnic minorities trapped in poverty of the inner cities suffer any more.

REFERENCES

Ashcroft, Andrew P.
1982   "Ethnic Minorities, Public Participation and Local Planning." Dissertation, University of Nottingham.

Barr, Anthony
1978   *Housing Improvement and Multi-Racial Community*. Oldham: Community Development Project.

Bristol City Council
1976   *HAA No 2, Declaration Report*. Bristol: City Council.
1981   *St. Paul's Draft District Plan: Preferred Strategy*. Bristol: City Council.

Clark, David
1977   "Immigrant Responses to the British Housing Market." *SSRC Reports*. Bristol: University of Bristol, pp. 1–5.

Deakin, Nicholas, and Clare Ungerson
1973   "Beyond the Ghetto: Illusion of Choice." In *London Urban Patterns, Problems and Policies*, edited by D. Donnison and D. Eversley, 215–47. London: Heinemann Press.

Department of the Environment (DOE)
1971   *Census Indicators of Urban Deprivation*. London: HMSO
1975   *Race Relations and Housing*. London: HMSO
1979   *National Dwelling and Housing Survey*. London: HMSO

Fenton, M.
1977   "Asian Household in Owner-occupation: A Study of the Patterns, Costs and Experiences of Households in Greater Manchester." *SSRC Reports*. Bristol: University of Bristol, pp. 1–12.

Garner, J. F.
1981   *Practical Planning Law*. London: Croom Helm.

John, Augustine
1973   *Race in the Inner City*. London: The Runnymede Trust.

Lambert, John, Chris Paris, and Bob Blackaby
1978   *Housing Policy and the State*, 121–39. London: Macmillan.

Lambeth Borough Council
1977   *Hubert Grove HAA Action Programme*. Lambeth, London: Borough Council.
1982   *Hubert Grove HAA Progress Report*. Lambeth, London: Borough Council.

Leicester City Council
1979   *Down Street HAA, Tudor Road and Ross Walk HAA Declaration Report*. Leicester: City Council.
1983   *Housing Department Renewal Strategy Team Seventh Annual Report*. Leicester: City Council.

Lornes, B. B. G.
1975   *Housing Action Areas*. London: Commission for Racial Equality.

The Runnymede Trust
1980a   *Britain's Black Population*. London: Heinemann Educational Books.
1980b   *Inner Cities and Black Minorities Workshop*. London: The Runnymede Trust.

The Scarman Report
1982   "The Brixton Disorders." Cmnd 8427. London: HMSO.
Smith, D. J.
1976   *The Facts of Racial Disadvantage*. London: Political and Economic Planning.
Stoker, Gerry, and Tim Brindley
1985   "Asian Politics and Housing Renewal." *Policy and Politics* 13:3 (July 1985), 281–303.
Wolfe, Tim
1984   "Ethnic Minorities and Housing Action Areas." Dissertation, University of Nottingham.

7

Participation by Ethnic Minorities in Urban Renewal in the Netherlands

KAREN WUERTZ AND TON VAN DER PENNEN

Abstract. This chapter investigates the significance of social relationships in neighborhoods regarding decision-making processes. An outline of the history of the current renewal programs, in which the multicultural composition of the population has already played an important part, is followed by a brief discussion of the opportunities open to all residents to influence policy. Then attention is given to the ways in which migrants can represent their interests. In principle, there are three ways: (1) through participation in the general decision-making process; (2) through a neighborhood organization of their own; or (3) through internal networks for the rendering of assistance and service. The possibilities offered by and the inherent restrictions in these alternatives are illustrated.

INTRODUCTION

This chapter is based on the findings of four case studies of the participation of migrants in urban renewal decision making in three Dutch cities (Rotterdam, Dordrecht, and The Hague). In order to find explanations for the low degree of participation, as observed by officials, 105 residents in urban renewal areas were interviewed. Also key informants concerned with urban renewal policy were interviewed. The fieldwork was carried out between October 1984 and October 1985.

FACTORS LEADING TO URBAN RENEWAL

During the 1970s the beginnings of a change could be observed in the attitude of municipal government in the Netherlands to urban building and urban living. Prior to that time, urban development activities and the demolition of dwellings were carried out solely with an eye to the economic function of the inner city. The renewal plans mostly called for the construction of high-rise office buildings, luxury apartments, and major highways. Most of the money that financed this kind of urban renewal came from private developers. In many cities, significant displacement of the low-income residents of these areas was proposed and actually occurred. Large-scale urban expansion initiated by the central and local government was to solve their housing problem.

The concern of the municipal government for the problems of their residents increased only very gradually. The worsening economic outlook was in no small way responsible for this. Participation was structured and managed by the local government. Efficiency was the key. Citizen groups organized to protest against renewal plans and in some cases they made new plans or participated in the revision of the existing plans. In the early 1970s this resulted in a radical change in policy, a main feature of which was the improvement of neighborhoods and the renovation of residential areas. Thereafter, it did not take long before the new direction of the policy called "building for the neighborhood" was incorporated in most policy papers concerning urban renewal. It was recognized that the quality of the housing stock and also the quality of life was threatened, both in the physical sense and in the social sense. In this new form of urban renewal an important place was reserved for the participation by the people of these areas. During the planning process the citizens are involved in the decision making. The participants are provided with written and graphic information about the plans and alternatives, including costs, advantages, and disadvantages. They are assisted by their own housing and planning experts.

The development of urban renewal in Holland has similarities with that in the United States. Godschalk and Zeisel (1983) postulate an oscillation between centralization versus decentralization, standardization versus diversity, and government versus citizen control. The resulting long-term trend takes the form of a gradually changing curve, as shown in Figure 7.1. Despite similarities, there are important economic, political, and social differences between the Dutch and the U.S. experiences in providing housing and community development.

The level of government subsidies, and therefore involvement, is many times greater in the Netherlands than in the United States. The political philosophies of the two countries echo this difference between a commitment to the welfare state in the Netherlands and to the market economy in the United States. In Rotterdam for example, one of the cities investigated, the city government is the largest landlord, having acquired 50 percent of all the dwellings in renewal areas.

The deterioration of houses, which had originally been built in haste and were poorly constructed, was accelerated by lack of maintenance and real estate speculation. Also, the areas surrounding the houses no longer met present-day standards since there was a lack of parks and play areas, inadequate parking space, and lack of space for social activities owing to the high building density.

The social problems of these neighborhoods can in part be accounted for by the above-mentioned physical decay. There was a large turnover of residents, and the fast-changing composition of the population affected the social structure and the network of relationships in the neighborhoods. Many of the old residents, some of whom had been born in the area, felt this to be a very negative devel-

Figure 7.1
General Participation in the Urban Renewal Efforts of the United States and the Netherlands

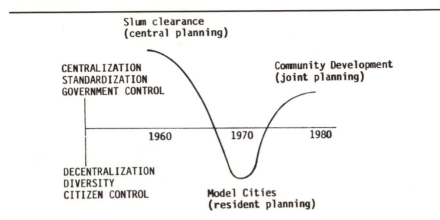

Source: Godschalk and Zeisel (1983). Reprinted by permission of the authors and the publisher.

opment. The age composition changed. A relatively high percentage of young, one-person households (the so-called starters), and a high percentage of the aged (the stayers) remained, while the younger families with children, those who could afford to, moved elsewhere. Simultaneously, the homes that had been vacated were taken over by the so-called socially weaker groups who could not easily be housed elsewhere. This heterogeneity of age, ethnic, and family composition and the arrival of "problem families" caused potential conflict situations because of different life-styles.

In the urban renewal areas migrants accounted on average for 30 percent of the total population, with higher concentrations (up to 90 percent) in some streets. This was found to be unacceptable, at first only from a policy point of view and by nonmigrants, but later also by the migrants themselves.

In these areas, which were originally built by speculators to poor standards, the roots of decay were already present. Because of the physical circumstances and relatively low rents, the areas started to attract the economically deprived and the composition of the population changed drastically. Inversely, because of the turnover of the population and the accompanying social disintegration, the involvement of the residents with their surroundings was reduced. Less effort was made to maintain the dwellings and the physical and social environment. Instead, efforts intensified to leave the area in search of better living conditions elsewhere. Residents born in those neighborhoods often attributed the decay to the incoming migrants, who were the most visible expression of change. Consequently it was not surprising that action committees of the nonmigrant residents voiced dissatisfaction in their efforts to achieve a different urban policy. As a result, all the policy papers concerning the areas of the study started to mention inner-city development as a possible means of changing the "unbalanced composition of the population."

Insofar as these policy papers have focused on the position of migrants in the urban renewal process, they concerned mainly the ethnic concentrations and the fear of racial tension. In other words, in spite of the limited active involvement of migrants in the actions for and participation in the urban renewal, their mere presence has been of importance in determining the content and shaping of the policy.

URBAN RENEWAL AS AN ORGANIZATIONAL PROBLEM

The principle of "building for the neighborhood" has implications in respect to management and organization. The preferred way to involve the residents in the making and execution of policy must therefore be formalized.

Urban renewal participation through the project group, as first developed in Rotterdam, has generally been adopted elsewhere. For each urban renewal area a project group has been formed. This group consists of representatives of the residents and appointed officials from the several municipal departments that are involved in urban renewal. They prepare the policy outline, the local allocation plans, the plans for renovation, demolition, and construction of new buildings, and they coordinate the implementation. They form an organization that works as a coalition model. The participating residents are proposed by the residents' organization(s) from the neighborhood concerned. They are assisted by technical advisors, community workers, and social workers, all paid by the government. The officials comprise the staff of the project development office and officials of the several municipal departments involved.

Before the plans are developed, general studies are made of the living conditions and the technical aspects, and the quality of the surroundings is assessed. Insight into the social aspects of the neighborhood is acquired through a survey of the population involved; quantitative data are collected on the socioeconomic position of the residents, the age distribution, size of household, number of persons per housing unit, housing costs, and so on.

Within the project group, teams are formed to develop plans for new houses, housing improvement, and such. The most crucial decisions are made in these planning teams; choices regarding new building or rehabilitation of existing houses, the extent of the renovation, the variation in housing types, the layout of the surroundings, and the composition of the population are made here in a consultation process.

The part the residents can play varies in the different phases of the process. In the first stage of the planning process, possibilities to affect the plans are greatest. However, our investigation shows that the residents who participate in this phase in the planning teams function essentially as a sounding board. The proposed measures and their interconnections are, at set times, referred back to the neighborhood at public hearings. These meetings are often of an informative nature; residents make remarks and suggestions, ask questions, and indicate their preference with regard to certain external aspects of their future housing. Arnstein (1969) developed the ladder of citizen participation to be able to judge opportunities people have to influence governmental planning. The participation structure created in urban renewal in Holland corresponds with one of the highest degrees of participation—degrees of citizen power as Arnstein called it. The role citizens play in the decision-making process corresponds with a lower degree called "tokenism" (consultation, information, placation). It should be clear that the nature of participation differs widely in respect to the planning object involved and the participation methods used. Therefore, it was important to investigate at which levels of the decision-making process migrant residents actually participate.

RESIDENT PARTICIPATION IN POLICY

Residents and Their Representation

As far as the attendance at public hearings, street-level meetings, block meetings, and the like is concerned, there is little discernible difference between migrants and nonmigrants. Key informants think that attendance could be improved in both categories of residents.

In the planning teams, migrant representation is lacking while nonmigrant residents do take part in the decision-making process. There are a variety of reasons for this. It is partly historical; the nonmigrants' action committees who were in favor of neighborhood improvement gradually became the official participants in the dialogue with the municipality. This institutionalization of the originally spontaneous resident opposition led to the resident organization becoming partly responsible for the participation process. This meant that the recruiting of migrant residents for active resident participation also became one of their tasks. They were, however, either unsuccessful or not sufficiently motivated. At the same time, the interests of the migrants were not as a matter of course represented by them. At different times during the process decisions were made that turned out to be disadvantageous to the migrants (see also the preceding chapter). Because the nonmigrant resident organizations had a one-sided influence on the decision-making process, the migrants did not succeed to identify with them as representatives of their interests. Table 7.1 illustrates the differences between the migrants and nonmigrants in their participation in the decision-making process in urban renewal.

Policy makers, however, assume a community of interest that undertakes collective political action. At the project group level, the ethnic heterogeneity of the population is regarded chiefly as an organizational problem of urban renewal. However, in practice the decision-making process often assumes the character of a conflict between parties concerned with the division and organization of urban space.

Table 7.1
Participation of Migrants versus Nonmigrants

	Non-migrants	Migrants
Hearings	+	+
Planning teams	+	-
Resident organizations	+	-

While policy makers and nonmigrants tackled this conflict through the available channels of participation, the migrants remained passive. The input of "the residents" in the decision-making process has, therefore, a specific group character that is passed over at the project group level. This has to do with what Offe (1972) as well as Beck (1976) have described as the structural legitimizing problem. The authorities must continually look for the necessary support from the residents in order to be able to execute their policy. Not only is it difficult to get a building program going under current conditions, also the legitimacy of the residents' representation can be in dispute. Therefore, as long as this approach remains challenged, the existing forms of legitimization are used, that is, the established resident organizations.

Residents' Conflict of Interests in the Decision-Making Process

Although conflicts of interests were mentioned by key informants in all interviews, a majority talked about this in an anecdotal way. Only a few recognized these conflicts as an important factor. The following incidents serve as illustrations of the importance of the conflicts of interests in decision making.

The first example is the choice made by a (nonmigrant) resident organization for demolition instead of renovation of the Molenwijk, The Hague. In spite of the reasonable quality of the houses, the action group that represented the residents chose for complete slum clearance and rebuilding of the neighborhood. One of the considerations was the expectation that after the rebuilding many migrants would not return to the neighborhood.

The second example is the manner in which the flexibility of a proposed variation in housing (sizes and types of dwellings) was managed. Informed by an inquiry among all the residents in an urban renewal area, a variation in housing types and rented level was proposed, also based on the income and housing situation of the migrants. In the Afrikaanderwijk, Rotterdam, the resident organization chose a low limit for the proposed number of large housing units. Because migrants tend to require large houses, only a number of them could be included in the project.

In a different renovation project in this neighborhood there lived few migrants. The other residents wished to maintain this composition. For this purpose they used seemingly neutral procedural arguments. They demanded temporary housing and retransfer of all residents simultaneously, instead of temporary individual housing all over town, for the duration of the building activities. In this way they could prevent housing units in the renovated complex being allocated to other people (that is, migrants) urgently in need of housing.

A final illustration concerns the choice for the utilization of a vacant bathhouse in Krispijn. A group of Moroccan residents asked the council in the city of Dordrecht to permit them to use this space as a mosque. There did not seem to be any opposition to this. However, when the neighborhood committee heard this, there was a feeling of having been slighted as official resident representation in the urban renewal consultation. The problem of the vacant bathhouse was brought up in the project group, which then had to make the decision. The neighborhood committee was in favor of demolition to create a play area. The officials were divided, and then the council had to implement the wishes of the majority. The desire of the Moroccans, who had taken the first initiative regarding this unoccupied space, was no longer discussed.

LIMITED LEVEL OF MIGRANT ORGANIZATION AT THE NEIGHBORHOOD LEVEL

In view of the problems experienced by migrants in the policy-making procedures, it should be possible for them to take part in the consultations through their own representative organization. However, this was not the case in the neighborhoods we studied.

Nevertheless, different elements in the research point to favorable conditions for the forming of neighborhood-oriented organizations. Because of the conflicts of interest between residents as well as the limited neighborhood integration, migrants have to rely upon themselves to look after their own interests.

Illustrative of this are migrant homeowners. (None of these respondents gave as a reason for purchase of their houses the desire to invest in housing. On the contrary, they had to buy qualitatively very poor houses for a high price.) To carry out the urban renewal program it was necessary for the local authorities to buy the old houses. In negotiations about the sales price of their dwellings, migrants often found themselves in a common position vis-à-vis the council.

Also, all three ethnic groups (Turkish, Moroccan, and Surinamese) had functional neighborhood relationships that could have developed into community action. Moreover, a great number of respondents had important emotional ties with their country and culture of origin.

Thus, from an objective point of view, there were many common interests on which a united front could have been based. Such common interests are, according to some authors, important elements in successful community organization by ethnic groups (Roosens 1982; Oepen 1982). Nevertheless, there was a lack of community organization by migrants. How can this be explained? Factors in the countries of origin as well as those in the context of the Netherlands played a part.

Factors in the Countries of Origin

First, the differences between the political culture in Dutch society and that in the countries of origin of the migrants played a role. It is considered characteristic for the policies of the welfare state that political pressure groups come into action when authorities do not safeguard the interests of the citizens sufficiently. The welfare state is, in a political-cultural sense, sometimes characterized as a democratic form of government that is extremely sensitive to pressure from the ''grass-roots level'' (van Doorn 1982).

One of the typical characteristics of the political culture in the countries of origin (especially the rural areas) is that political participation takes place to a large extent through informal channels, through persons with a strategic position in different networks. In the literature this personalistic approach to the protection of interests is referred to as patronage or political brokerage (Derveld 1981; Boissevain 1974). The migrants' relative unfamiliarity with forms of collective action and participation means that there is a great dependence on aid from friends, neighbors, and family. In the Netherlands this remains to some extent a factor. However, the length of residence in the Netherlands is also a significant influence. As time goes by, migrants use institutional channels to further their interests just as much as nonmigrants do, and they use their informal networks only for supplementary services.

Another factor related to the situation in the countries of origin concerns the nature of the interethnic relations there. Linguistic, religious, socioeconomic, and political differences have created great divisions. As a result, population groups were traditionally less activated by their deprived position in the community, but were mostly activated by common ethnic roots and blood or tribal relationships with, as the most important ties, language and religion. This also has its effects in the Netherlands. The ethnic-religious factors still prove to be a more important organizational principle than common material interests, although this has been changing rapidly in recent years.

Factors within the Context of the Netherlands

Various other factors explaining the low degree of migrant organization can be understood only by reference to the migrants' situation in the Netherlands. First, their minority status has a negative influence on their relationships. They are in a competitive position, both objectively and emotionally, in respect to scarce commodities such as jobs and housing, not only in regard to nonmigrant residents but equally (certainly emotionally) in regard to members of their own community. For most migrants, the reason for immigration was a desire to improve their social position. Therefore, the success or failure to achieve these aspirations is very significant. The psychological pressure and the partial estrangement from their own culture, necessary for social advancement, does not contribute to a solid foundation on which to establish a firm community. Besides this, one sees a process of fragmentation as a result of the magnitude and subjective experience of problems concerning income, jobs, return to the country of origin, education of the second generation, racism, and so on. Moreover, the internal dynamics of the migration process must not be forgotten. For the first generation the importance of the original cultural community diminishes slowly. For the second generation, cultural identity has a totally different meaning. Finally, it is less likely that the pooling of common interests will occur at a neighborhood level because the relationship networks within the migrant community do not exist at the neighborhood level but at the urban level. At the neighborhood level we observed an avoidance of contact with fellow countrymen because of the fear of being stigmatized and discriminated against by the original residents as a result of "forming cliques."

INFORMAL PATTERNS OF PROTECTION OF INTERESTS

In interviews with residents from Turkey, Morocco, and Surinam we inquired about the methods of protecting their own interests in their countries of origin and about their opinions on these. On the basis of insights from literature we assumed that their values concerning assistance would not correspond to the forms of participation offered by the local authorities.

It appears, however, that none of the respondents objected to protecting their interests by using the decision-making channels offered by the authorities. Many explained that informal aid and other forms of mutual assistance in obtaining housing were no longer necessary because of the good, and for everybody similarly available, official provisions. Many contrasted their experiences with professional aid services in the country of origin, involving corruption and nepotism, with the equality of opportunity in the Netherlands.

Of course, some commented that the ideology of equality is not always practiced. Discriminating regulations, attitudes, and treatment had also been encountered. Nevertheless, they concluded that, in comparison, the formal mediating channels for, for example, work and housing were much to be preferred to the extended family assistance and the aid of neighbors. These were chiefly regarded as a last resort owing to the lack of governmental provision and social legislation in the country of origin. The question of informal aid versus professional service led a number of respondents to reflect on the nature of the problems encountered in the Netherlands. They concluded that, after a longer length of residence, the traditional patterns of protection of interests were no longer adequate in dealing with the kinds of problems encountered in the new situation.

This does not negate that many had very positive memories of the neighborhood networks in the country of origin and of the mutual help that was inextricably bound up with it. In comparison with the neighborhood relationships that they had known there, they characterized their relationships with neighbors in their current living area as "distant and everyone for himself." Those who had been helped by Dutch neighbors, family, or compatriots were positive about their experiences but did not wish to be dependent on such relationships. A comment by Vestering (1983) is relevant here. She opposes the conclusion of Kaufman and Schat (1982) that problems in the contacts of migrants with official bodies may be traced to communication problems arising from conflicting norms and value patterns. She also rejects the suggested remedy: the migrants' adaptation to the (bureaucratic) norms of our society. With this the Western ways of furthering one's interests would implicitly be deemed superior to the migrants' internal networks for giving aid, which Vestering rejects as an "evolutionistic Europe-centered way of looking at things."

On the basis of our interviews with migrant residents, however, we must conclude that migrants wish to adapt themselves to the bureaucratic norms of our society and that they find the dominant Western bureaucratic structure for the protection of interests more adequate than traditional networks for giving aid. In contrast to the strategic significance given by some authors to ethnicity, in our research it was more a question of strategic adaptation. Adapting was seen as a necessity; in private life the original culture was preserved as much as possible.

CONCLUSIONS AND RECOMMENDATIONS

The decision-making process itself, paradoxically, confirms the often-heard complaint of the migrant population: "They" decide for us but without us. The organizations of nonmigrants residents and the supporting professionals do not sufficiently represent the interests of the migrant population. The viewpoints of the resident organizations are largely representative of nonmigrants. Tension between nonmigrants and migrants is latently present in all neighborhoods; it is not a pleasant living climate. Interviews with nonmigrants made clear that there is (still) no basis for a common stand on policy issues. One of the difficulties is the starting point of official policy, which assumes a community of interest and does not question the representativeness of the resident organizations. An alternative to the badly functioning bureaucratic participation structure (for the migrants) could be the use of informal aid patterns to solve migrant housing problems. In view of the present power relationships between nonmigrants and migrants, this is not desirable. The present situation of unevenly divided power would be confirmed. In the long run more could be expected from approaching the difficulties on two levels:

1. The tackling of the social problems must be initiated at the policy level. One should build for a multicultural neighborhood. This demands that at a policy level specific attention be given to the different interests of the residents and to the present power relationships between them. The usual approach to intercultural problems is too limited. The policy makers' emphasis on cultural factors originating in the country of origin hinders their understanding of social factors in the Dutch context and of changes associated with length of residence.

2. Self-organization of migrants must be at the neighborhood level. It is of utmost importance that migrants join all levels of the decision-making process and that purely individual involvement be replaced by common interests. Initiatives will have to be developed aimed at cadre-forming among the migrants, a paradox that might appear to hinder their participation and integration. Stimulating their identity development could contribute to greater social consciousness, a higher degree of organization, and less individualization. The ultimate goal should be a strengthening of the migrants' social position, so that they, as a group, become an important factor in the urban renewal process. Many minorities have followed this road to emancipation (compare Verwey-Jonkers 1983).

NOTE

This chapter is based on an empirical study: *Bouwen voor de kleurrijke buurt. Allochtonen en besluitvorming in de stadsvernieuwing.* 's-Gravenhage: VUGA, 1985.

REFERENCES

Arnstein
1969   "A Ladder of Citizen Participation." *Journal of the American Institute of Planners* 35, 216–24.
Beck, W.
1976   *Democratie in de wijken.* Amsterdam: Van Gennep.
Boissevain, J.
1974   *Friends of Friends: Networks, Manipulations and Coalitions.* Oxford: Blackwell.
Derveld. F.
1981   *Politieke mobilisatie en integratie van de Javanen in Suriname.* Leiden: Rijksuniversiteit Leiden.
Doorn, J. van
1982   "De verzorgingsstaat in de praktijk." In *De stagnerende verzorginsstaat,* edited by J. van Doorn and C. J. M. Schuyt. Meppel: Boom.
Godschalk, D. and J. Zeisel.
1983   In Coproducing Urban Renewal in the Netherlands." *Paternalism, Conflict and Coproduction,* edited by L. Susskind, and M. Eliot. New York: Plenum Press.

Kaufman, P., and R. Schat
1982   "Allochtonen: interne circuits van dienstverlening; over familie, ombudsmannen en informele leiders." *Tijdschrift voor agologie* 11, 373–83.
Oepen, M.
1982   "Interkulturele Kommunikation. Ihre Bedeutung für die Segregation and Integration von Immigranten." In *Migration; Texte über die Ursachen und Folgen der Migration*, edited by I. Aslan and D. Klitske, 11–18. Berlin: Verlag Express Edition GmbH.
Offe, C.
1972   *Demokratische Legitimation der Planung, Strukturprobleme des kapitalistischen Staates*. Frankfurt am Main: Suhrkamp.
Roosens, E.
1982   "Etnische groep en etnische identiteit. Symbolen of concepten?" In *Immigrant en samenleving*, edited by J. Amersfoort and H. Entzinger. Deventer: Van Loghum Slaterus.
Verwey-Jonkers, H.
1983   *Emancipatiebewegingen in Nederland*. Deventer: Van Loghum Slaterus.
Vestering, E.
1983   "Over Europacentrische betutteling. Een reactie op: Allochtonen: interne circuits van dienstverlening." *Tijdschrift voor Agologie* 12, 257–69.

PART III

SUBURBS AND PLANNED COMMUNITIES

It reasonably can be said that in the advanced nations of the world suburbanization has been *the* master urban trend of the twentieth century. While the growth of suburbs has very old historical roots, it has been mainly in the twentieth century that the centrifugal forces of urbanization have replaced the centripetal. Urban areas have grown faster than urban populations, leading to decreasing urban densities and the decentralization of urban living.

The chapters in this section discuss two of the major social consequences of this suburban trend: the local communities in which people increasingly live have become more privatized, and they have become more homogeneous in social class and racial terms. In Chapter 8, Popenoe discusses how suburbanization has led to a growing privatization of life. He suggests that this may have contributed to the growth of juvenile delinquency in suburban societies, and he points to specific suburban community characteristics that seem related to high rates of juvenile crime.

Fava, in Chapter 9, points out that even when suburban development takes the form of totally planned communities, as in Reston, Virginia, the suburban tendency toward demographic homogeneity is not very satisfactorily overcome. She analyzes the reasons for this. Nevertheless, she notes, because it had community diversity as a major planning goal, Reston has come closer to achieving community heterogeneity than most unplanned suburban developments.

8

Suburbanization, Privatization, and Juvenile Delinquency: Some Possible Relationships

DAVID POPENOE

Abstract. Urbanization has long been associated with the growth of crime. In the post-World War II years, a time when much urbanization took the form of suburban development, crime and juvenile delinquency rates have risen dramatically. Some possible relationships between the ecology and social character of suburban development and juvenile delinquency are explored, focusing especially on the social process of privatization. In many countries suburbanization has involved a retreat into private life and a withdrawal from public concerns. It is suggested that suburban privatization may be related to juvenile delinquency through the breakdown of informal social control mechanisms and family instability.

INTRODUCTION

One of the strongest statistical associations found by the social sciences is that between urbanization and crime. With great consistency in nearly all parts of the world, cities and metropolitan areas have had higher crime rates, especially for property crime and juvenile delinquency, than have small towns and rural areas. As one urban specialist put the matter (Light 1983, 375): "The worldwide association of crime and delinquency rates with big cities is so marked that some criminologists have regarded it as a law of nature." The characteristics of cities that are frequently singled out as being related to high crime rates include increased opportunity for theft; urban anonymity; weakened family, community, and religious bonds; the mixing of mutually alien populations; and a concentration of unattached young males (Wilson and Herrnstein 1985).

Advanced industrial nations have faced an especially sharp increase in crime since the end of World War II, a period during which much of urban growth in these nations took the form of suburbanization (Radzinowicz and King 1979; Gurr et al. 1977). In this period juvenile delinquency and property crime have come to plague suburban as well as urban life (Elliott et al. 1983). What is the general connection, if any, between suburban development and the growth of crime? In this chapter I shall focus on some possible ways in which the ecology and social character of suburban communities, particularly as mediated through the social process of privatization, may contribute to high rates of juvenile delinquency. I put forward these possible relationships tentatively, and for further discussion and research, in full realization that our knowledge of the causes of crime is still rudimentary.

What little we know about the causes of juvenile delinquency suggests that community and environmental factors pale in importance when compared to personal traits, family socialization, and probably school experiences (see, for example, Rutter and Giller 1984, Chapter 6; Wilson and Herrnstein 1985, Chapter 11; Murray 1983). Indeed, it is extremely easy to overstate the significance of community and environmental factors as causes of any form of human behavior. Sociologically, the kinds of housing, residential environments, and communities in which people live have never been shown to have the same causal importance as the personal attributes people are born with, the kinds of families they come from, the types of cultures they live in, and even how much money they earn.

Nevertheless, we do know from many years of research (as well as from common sense) that the type of community in which we live has *some* effects, especially when all the elements of a community are considered in combination (Krupat 1985; Michelson 1976). In addition, the community has indirect effects working through such community-based institutions as families and schools. For public policy purposes the importance of community effects is magnified by virtue of the fact that the community built environment is one of the most malleable factors in human societies: It both can be and is constructed and reconstructed in widely diverse shapes and sizes. Even an intangible trait like community cohesion is capable of being modified through social programs (Newman 1980; Podolefsky 1983). We are considering, then, a set of variables that lend themselves more readily than most to direct, collective intervention into human affairs.

SUBURBANIZATION IN PERSPECTIVE

To begin, let us put the phenomenon of suburbanization in perspective. Although suburbanization has been a feature of urban growth throughout world history, since World War II it has been the dominant form of urban development in advanced societies, leading to decreasing urban densities and the decentralization of urban living. The first suburbanites came from central cities, but they were soon followed by people moving directly from small towns and rural areas; today, the new suburbanite is as likely to come from another suburb. Demographically, a high percentage of persons in almost every advanced society, often the greatest percentage, lives today in metropolitan suburban communities that are neither rural, nor small town, nor urban (in the traditional meaning of "urban" as large, dense, and heterogeneous aggregations of people).

In social and ecological character, suburbs have typically represented a compromise between city and small town. The social idea behind the suburb was that a person could remain "urban," with close access to the central city, but at the same time live in a more human-scale environment with lower densities and better access to the countryside. This general idea has in fact been fairly well realized in practice in many nations, either with the single-family house on private lot of the United States and the nations of the British Commonwealth, or the low-rise apartments in park-like settings of northern Europe. In some nations suburbanites have been short changed, of course, ending up with neither city nor small town but rather a gigantic apartment building in what might be called the middle of nowhere, examples being the endless, monolithic suburban high-rise buildings of the East European nations (most of which, however, are not advanced industrial societies), the Grand Ensembles of Paris, and some of the massive housing projects around West German, English, and Dutch cities.

Yet it is hard to deny that, mainly through suburbanization, the citizens of industrial nations have become housed at a level of urban environmental quality never before achieved. Compared to what they might have had in the older city forms, suburban dwellers as a whole have more spacious housing in cleaner, less-noisy environments, with improved community facilities provided either privately, as emphasized in the "free-market" nations, or publicly in the more "collectivist" states. This high-quality level is of course related to the fact that the postwar suburban trend has been associated with unparalleled economic affluence and high standards of living.

In addition, suburbanization in advanced societies has enabled urban development to take place without many of the more serious social costs of, let us say, early Victorian cities or cities in much of the Third World today, where population densities have far outrun the capacity of cities to make reasonable adaptations (Stretton 1978; Berry 1981). Indeed, those cities that have done the most intelligent planning for suburban growth, notably the cities of northern Europe, appear to have the most successful metropolitan habitats from the point of view of livability and environmental amenity.

However, these dimensions of suburban success are being overshadowed today, again particularly in the United States, by the increasing crime and delinquency in suburban communities, by the continuing flight of people beyond the suburbs, and by a growing feeling of resentment among suburbanites at the social quality of their environments (Kowinski 1980). That most suburbs have in fact been more successful than the central cities in mitigating the problem of crime is attested to not only by abundant empirical data (for example, Davidson 1981; Herbert 1982) but also through people "voting with their feet." One of the reasons for the mass movement of people to the suburbs over the years has been the search for safety and personal security (Skogan and Maxfield 1981, Chapter 14), and very few persons have chosen to return to the city. Nevertheless, the suburbs have somehow not provided the immunities from crime and delinquency for which many people had hoped.

Much of the new suburban crime problem is not based on, nor are people's feelings of resentment largely directed at, the character of suburban communities.

These phenomena are more related to the fact that "big city problems" have at last spilled over into the suburbs. The makeup of suburban populations has changed, becoming more "urban" in character, and the suburbs have become increasingly vulnerable to the serious crime committed by city dwellers. Still, might there not be some intrinsic suburban community characteristics that have exacerbated, at the very least, the problem of suburban crime? The high rate of delinquency among suburban-born youth, for example, seems out of character with the economically and educationally privileged settings of most suburban communities.

THE STRUCTURE OF SUBURBAN COMMUNITIES

What are the intrinsic characteristics of suburban communities that put suburbs in a class apart from other community types, and that might have a significant impact on the lives of residents? Unfortunately for ease of discussion and research, actual suburbs come in all shapes and sizes. Some are really parts of the city; others are simply small towns that have become incorporated into a metropolitan area. But the prototypical suburb in advanced societies, I suggest, has the following fundamental characteristics: it is dependent, it is specialized, and it is homogeneous. In short, it is a very incomplete community; in many cases, a very large, incomplete community.

The suburb is almost by definition dependent on other communities to an extreme degree. It typically represents but one specialized piece of a comprehensive community (usually the metropolitan area as a whole): the residential piece. People who live there usually work elsewhere, they may shop elsewhere, and they probably even spend their recreation time elsewhere. Put another way, the usual suburban community is only a bedroom, with the living room located a long way off. Much of the life of the typical suburban dweller, especially during the day, takes place outside of the suburban environment, with the suburb being merely a nice place to come home to at night (Popenoe 1977).

Not only is the suburb but one dependent and specialized piece of a community, it is usually at the same time a very homogeneous piece, especially in the United States. This homogeneity can take the form of a single social class (or race), a single age grouping or stage of the life cycle, a single housing type, or some combination of these.

I suggest that a fundamental consequence of these intrinsic features of suburbs is that the development of a socially rich, residentially based, communal life is retarded. Such a communal life is one with dense social networks, vigorous local associations, and an active public life. A number of researchers (for example, Wellman 1979; Fischer 1982) have put forth the position in recent years, backed by extensive empirical research, that people in metropolitan areas have much richer social networks than previously had been thought. I do not wish to question directly this line of reasoning, but I must point out that these "rediscovered" metropolitan social networks are not confined to the local residential environment;

indeed, they span the metropolitan area as a whole, and in many cases go beyond it. While the social networks of suburbanites may be quite rich, therefore, their local communal life can be—and often is, I argue—quite poor.

SMALL TOWNS AND URBAN VILLAGES

Before discussing further the special character of suburban communities, and how it might relate to high rates of delinquency, it will help our understanding to look briefly at how suburban communities differ from some other main community types. Most discussions and analyses of suburbs have compared them to large, dense, and heterogeneous central city areas, which of course usually have higher crime rates. To better understand suburban delinquency, it is important to see how suburbs differ from those community types most closely associated with lower rates of crime and delinquency (Alder et al. 1980). The most important of these types is the traditional small town, where most people used to live.

What are the intrinsic community structures of the prototypical small town? In addition to being small it is a relatively comprehensive community, in the sense that most of life can be lived within it without having to go outside; it has a relatively high degree of political and economic independence or autonomy; it is rather stable in the sense of having low residential mobility and population turnover; it is fairly heterogeneous, at least in terms of age and stage of the life cycle; and it is a community whose people have a rich public life with strong feelings of community belonging and identity.

I realize that the character of the typical small town today may in fact be somewhat removed from this prototype. For example, many small towns are in large degree dictated to by outside political and especially economic forces and are far from being autonomous in any meaningful sense. In addition, many of the young, better educated, and more upwardly mobile citizens of small towns have left to go to metropolitan areas, often for economic reasons. These changes may help to explain why the difference between urban and small town rates of delinquency appears to be narrowing (for example, Erickson and Jensen 1977). Nevertheless, the typical suburb is a human settlement of quite a different order, as I have indicated above, one still further removed from this small town community prototype.

A second community type that makes a useful comparison with the suburb, because it ranks low in delinquency at least when compared to other city areas, is the central city counterpart of the traditional small town: the "urban village." An urban village is an area in the city that has maintained many of the essential features of small town life (Gans 1962; Suttles 1972). When transferred to an urban setting, the small town or village prototype necessarily becomes modified. The urban village is much less comprehensive and autonomous than the small town, yet it retains such characteristics as residential stability, age and life cycle heterogeneity, and most important a rich public life with strong feelings of community identity and belonging. In these ways it differs significantly from the suburb, a still a more truncated community form.

PRIVATIZATION

Returning to the suburbs, a useful way to look at suburbanization and metropolitan development as a whole is with the concept of *privatization*. I have fully discussed this concept elsewhere (Popenoe 1985). It refers to the growth of the private at the expense of the public, with public defined as "of, pertaining to, or affecting a population or community as a whole." The local residential environment of the prototypical suburb, I suggest, is a highly *privatized* environment; the suburban community is one in which public activities and sentiments have been curtailed, and the community as a whole is organized mainly to foster private pursuits.

At the end of the day, for example, when the mass of suburban residents return from their far-flung pursuits, rather than seek companionship or solace in the local community they typically lead a private, inwardly focused life, relatively unconcerned about neighbor or locality (Popenoe 1977). The result is that the "public life" of the suburb is often bleak and lifeless: Street life and public events are minimal. When compared to the urban village and even the compact small town, very little is going on outside of the suburban window. At the same time suburban community life is relatively anonymous: The highly dispersed social networks make it less likely that neighbor will know neighbor. This reduces the likelihood that community activities will develop. As one urban scholar has recently found, suburbanites have a strong sense of "placelessness." Compared to the residents of other community types, for many suburban residents the community per se has little meaning (Hummon 1986).

There are many exceptions to this portrayal: the new suburb with young families (Gans 1967), for example, or the suburb that is really a small town. Also, many of the suburbs in Switzerland, Japan, New Zealand, and Australia, and to a smaller extent England and Canada, seem to have less privatization than elsewhere because they have tried harder to maintain an urban village or small town character. But for many U.S. and northern European suburbs, comparisons made with small towns and urban villages in terms of the degree of privatization can be striking. Privatization and a weak public life characterize both the high-density suburbs made up of multifamily apartment buildings, as in many parts of northern Europe, and the very low-density suburbs of North America consisting of single-family housing. In the one case privatization is fostered by the anonymity associated with living in apartment buildings, and in the other it is enhanced by the inward-looking life-style shaped by the single-family house on a large private lot (Popenoe 1985).

Suburban homogeneity also is associated with a privatized life-style. Although homogeneity can enhance communal life in the short run when it leads to a sense of common interest (Newman 1980), as when families with children or persons of the same social class live together, it often has the opposite effect. A critical element in the formation of community cohesion, perhaps the most critical, is the length of residency (Kasarda and Janowitz 1974). (This element is already in short supply in many suburbs owing to the recency with which they have been built.) The homogeneous suburb, especially with respect to stage of the life cycle and housing type, forces people to leave the community entirely and start all over again somewhere else merely because their need for housing changes. The newly married couple must leave to find a small apartment, for example; the expanding family must leave to get more space; or the upwardly mobile person must leave for housing of higher status. This causes suburbs to be more transient than they otherwise might be, a trait that is further enhanced in suburbs where job opportunities are minimal.

In addition, privatization is fostered as suburbs grow in demographic scale, and many have surpassed the size of even moderate-sized towns. The effects of community scale on social life are complex and not fully understood, but in balance I think it is a reasonable proposition that increasing scale is associated with a withdrawal from public concerns and a retreat into private life (Milgram 1970; Fischer 1981).

Many other factors can make a contribution to the privatization of suburban life, of course, some of which relate only indirectly to characteristics of the community. These include the increase of women in the labor force (leading to empty homes during the day), the popularity of television (causing people to pursue leisure in private), and the commercial household services that increase with affluence (generating less need for neighborhood relations).

PRIVATIZATION AND JUVENILE DELINQUENCY

If suburbanization is interpreted as a process of community privatization, how might this be related to the growth of juvenile delinquency? A principal connecting link is that long-familiar concept of social control (Black 1984; Hirschi 1969). Social control refers to any social process that conditions or limits the actions of people to motivate them to conform to social norms. A fundamental problem in modern societies is a breakdown in *informal* social control mechanisms. When related to the growth of delinquency, this refers to a breakdown in the application of social sanctions informally through the actions of people with whom juveniles come into contact on a daily basis. Suburban privatization, in my opinion, is closely related to this breakdown of informal social control mechanisms.

Although the causes of delinquency are exceedingly complex, a general consensus appears to be emerging among delinquency theorists that two general social processes are almost always involved (for example, Shoemaker 1984). First, high rates of delinquency occur when there is a lack of social control by adults in the family, school, and community. It seems to be the case that juveniles are strongly motivated to obey the law in terms of how they perceive the negative reaction from people they know well, more than from any other single factor such as, for example, the chance of arrest (Hirschi 1969). Even when they are motivated to break the rules, as one sociologist put it, "they usually squelch those impulses so that they will maintain the respect of friends and relatives" (Tittle 1980). Second, high rates of delinquency occur when there is an increased influence of peers on adolescent behavior. This is closely associated with the first principle, because the influence of peers typically increases when the influence of adults decreases (thus leaving a kind of vacuum in social relationships).

Surveillance

The importance of informal social control for crime and delinquency has been looked at from two perspectives: in terms of how it effects the underlying causes of crime, such as through family functioning; and in terms of how it limits the opportunities to commit crime. The relation of community characteristics to juvenile delinquency has most often been viewed from the second of these perspectives: the effect on criminal opportunities (Clarke 1980). For example, if juveniles are to be negatively sanctioned in public areas prior to committing crimes (thus limiting their opportunities), their actions must first be observed either by persons known to them or by others acting, as it were, as the agents of such persons. Having been popularized through the classic book of Jane Jacobs, *The Death and Life of Great American Cities* (1961), and the work of Oscar Newman and his associates (discussed later), this phenomenon, known as "surveillance" or "neighborhood watchfulness," has often been analyzed and found lacking in many city neighborhoods and large apartment complexes.

The privatized suburb, I wish to argue, also lacks many of the elements necessary for the mechanisms of surveillance to be very effective. The inwardly focused orientation of much of suburban life means that few people are looking out their windows to survey the public scene, and few people are out walking the streets, especially in the automobile-oriented suburbs of the United States. Moreover, scattered, loose-knit social networks insure that there will be few persons present in the local environment who are known to the youth.

The motivation for widespread informal social control activities in public is related to a high level of neighborhood and community solidarity (Hartnagel 1979; Lewis and Salem 1985; Podolefsky 1983; Skogan and Maxfield 1981). Without a feeling of solidarity or cohesion among people who live near one another, it becomes less likely that strangers on the scene will act as informal social control agents, for example. This is the phenomenon that has become known as "bystander intervention" (Hackler et al. 1974). The loose-knit social networks of privatized suburbs (especially the larger suburbs), together with high rates of residential turnover, mean that a strong communal solidarity in suburbs is not likely to develop (Sampson et al. 1981), and informal social control mechanisms therefore remain weak. In a careful analysis of one American suburb it was found that informal social control was often marked by inaction, non-confrontation, and avoidance (Baumgartner 1984).

Peer Groups

Almost all studies of juvenile delinquency have concluded that delinquency is typically a group activity, accomplished not by the lone individual but by young people in groups, and that the influence of peers is of critical importance (Elliott et al. 1985; Erickson and Jensen 1977; Johnson 1979; Hindelang 1976; Schwendinger and Schwendinger 1985). This is especially true of so-called middle-class delinquency, the kind most commonly found in the suburbs (Richards et al. 1979; Wynne 1977). The anonymity of the suburb, together with its lack of daytime street life, can make it a fertile environment for the spawning of teen groupings in which the influence of peers becomes far more important than the influence of parents and other adult authority figures. In many suburbs, especially during the afternoons, the only age group out in the residential environment is teenagers. Parents and other adults are away (especially with a high percentage of women working), and young children are under somebody's care, but teenagers often have the freedom of the local area. Such factors may contribute to the fact that in advanced societies the age at which the highest number of crimes is committed is about 16.

Direct Effects of Physical Design

So far we have been discussing connections between community ecology and delinquency in which social structure plays a dominant role. But there are also connections based more strictly on the built environment that have been carefully researched and widely discussed. Triggered by the pioneering work of Oscar Newman (1972), studies have shown that the way buildings and their immediate surrounding environments are designed can measurably, though subtly, affect the level of social control in an area, and consequently the incidence of delinquency and crime (Poyner 1983; Rubenstein et al. 1980). Put another way, it has been shown that the physical design of buildings and adjacent properties can directly affect the degree of neighborhood privatization.

The research of Newman and his associates pointed to the effects of anonymity, the lack of surveillance, and the presence of alternative escape routes around housing projects as contributors to high crime rates. Features of buildings singled out as closely related to these traits were the overall size of the apartment development, the number of stories in the buildings, the number of people using a single entrance to a building, and the degree to which the grounds and common parts of the buildings are not shared and "defended" by individual households (Newman and Franck 1980). An additional finding was that a high density of children and youth in an area is a major factor in delinquency, as one might expect. Such density, too, can be directly affected by aspects of the built environment, like the mix of dwelling types and costs.

Most of this work on "defensible space" has dealt with the negative effects of high-rise apartment buildings—a building form that in the United States is found almost exclusively in central city areas. In Europe, however, high-rise apartment buildings are found as often in suburban areas, and it is in such areas that social control problems typically have been the most severe. Indeed, social conditions in some of the more massive developments in European suburbs have so deteriorated, leading to so much residential abandonment, that some of these developments have had to be demolished (as have some dense public housing projects in American cities). More demolitions are probably in the offing.

An early study in Glasgow (Jephcott 1971) pointed to the then emerging problems of high-rise buildings, especially for families with children. Since then, abundant European research has documented the many problems associated with this building form, so much so that there has been a widespread retreat from high-rise buildings in Europe (as well as in most other advanced societies). A recent British study (Coleman 1985) that analyzed 4,099 apartment buildings compared with 1,800 single-family houses concluded that the built environment elements most closely associated with high rates of such problems as vandalism, litter, and graffiti are dwellings per entrance (too many), dwellings per block, number of stories, overhead walkways, and spatial organization. This conclusion is strikingly similar to Oscar Newman's findings based on North American housing.

Delinquency and Suburban Family Life

Perhaps the most important effect of the community on juvenile delinquency, however, is that mediated through families. Family instability and inadequate parenting are factors for which strong and consistent associations with delinquent behavior have been found in a variety of cultural settings (for example, Gove and Crutchfield 1982; Hirschi 1983; West 1982). It seems likely that family functioning is strongly affected by the character of the surrounding environment, yet this is an area about which our knowledge is very limited (Johnstone 1980; Geismar and Wood 1985).

There is solid evidence to indicate that the kind of child rearing or parenting most likely to minimize juvenile delinquency is one that builds a strong attachment between parent and child (for example, Gove and Crutchfield 1982). Attachment, in turn, can be broken down into two components: love or affection, and discipline or control. Some studies have found that, of the two, lack of discipline is the more important factor in accounting for high delinquency rates (Hirschi 1983; H. Wilson 1980; Wilson and Herrnstein 1985, 237–39). (The kind of discipline meant is "authoritative" rather than "punitive.") While it may be that the privatization of communities in various ways can diminish the amount of love and affection that parents have for their children, the more likely relationship is that between privatization and the degree and kind of parental discipline that is used.

One way in which parental control can be weakened is through marital instability and/or marital breakup, if for no other reason than the "distractions" involved, or the fact that one person ends up having to do the child rearing normally done by two persons. There can be no doubt that maintaining a happy marriage and providing good parenting have become rather precarious activities in the modern era. The pull of individualism and the increased desire for self-expression, the tension, especially for women, between the world of work and the world of home and childcare, changing gender roles, and sexual permissiveness—all contribute to a cultural climate in which marriage vows are easily broken (or not bothered with in the first place), parents and children are pulling in different directions, and families are commonly split up. One of the most striking increases in recent decades is in the rate of divorce of families with children; children no longer seem to be the inhibitor of divorce that they once were (Cherlin 1977).

Although it may often be the case that children are better off in divorced than in very unhappy intact families, there is little research to suggest that divorce is beneficial for most children, quite the contrary (for example, Peres and Pasternack 1985). Certainly the child or teenager is seldom found who feels that his or her parents' divorce was a good thing (Mitchell 1985; Wallerstein and Kelly 1981). The evidence shows, in fact, that "broken homes" are particularly hard on boys, the gender at issue in the high rates of juvenile delinquency (Rankin 1983).

The consequences of increasingly privatized communities on family stability are not at all clear, but it is likely that recent community changes have had some effect. Having a happy marriage and successfully raising children can be extremely rewarding pursuits in the long run, which is why so many people continue to marry and to have children. But in the short run, success in marriage and child rearing is highly problematic, involving a tremendous number of day-to-day hurdles that must be overcome. The probability seems high that it is easier to overcome these hurdles when one is working cooperatively in the presence of others in a similar situation than it is when working alone. Put another way, successful family life depends heavily on a social and cultural climate in which norms of familism are emphasized, and in which people are working cooperatively to that end.

Family life is an extremely *localized* activity. It takes place for the most part in and around a home, and nowhere else. It is the relationships within that home that are important—for example, the evening meal together. In addition, especially for children, the quality of life in the surrounding neighborhood has a major significance. It may be that in the metropolitan areas of advanced societies we have what one urbanist several decades ago called "community without propinquity" (Webber 1970), but this is without much benefit for family life. The successful family depends heavily on "community *with* propinquity." Specifically, the family depends on a local community that not only is cooperatively organized to assist with the care of children, but also one where there is a cultural climate in which the social norms of familism and good parenting are continually reinforced. In social control terms, successful familism, like success in anything else, depends heavily on the presence of sanctions that motivate people to conform to its norms.

As communities in advanced societies become more privatized, it seems likely that such sanctions are increasingly in short supply. An example of this is the apparently growing loneliness of the stay-at-home parent. Although it may once have been believed that the suburbs are ideally designed to promote family life, the suburban parent today can often be a lonely figure, as frequently is noted by people in the women's movement. While it has been fairly well established that suburbs, especially low-density suburbs, have real disadvantages for working women owing to a lack of jobs, transportation, and child-care facilities (for example, Hayden 1984), these communities may also have drawbacks for the stay-at-home parent. What is lacking in the suburban environment for anyone who must stay there throughout much of the day to care for children (and this includes many working women, for at least a portion of their lives when the children are young, plus a small but growing number of men) is a richness of neighborhood and local community life that makes staying at home a rewarding activity. It is one thing to stay at home when the family is the center of work life, as in preindustrial times, or when the local environment is the center of public life, as in the small town and urban village; it is quite another thing to stay at home when the local environment is generally bereft of life, as is often the case in the contemporary suburb.

One empirical measure of this situation would be a growing disinvestment of time spent by parents in family activities, especially time spent with children. Most important, if the delinquency studies are to be believed, is the time spent on directing and monitoring children's activities and, if necessary, providing punishment. There is some evidence that the time spent by parents on such activities has, in fact, been dropping (Uhlenberg and Eggebeen 1986).

This only touches on the possible ways in which the character of suburban communities, as it affects the functioning of families, can impact on the problem of delinquency. Surely this is an area where additional social research could make a useful contribution.

DISCUSSION AND CONCLUDING REMARKS

The significance of community characteristics for juvenile delinquency has been pointed up on an international scale in recent years by the experience of two advanced societies noteworthy in the annals of delinquency: Japan and Switzerland. Both countries are highly affluent and highly urbanized, but both have extraordinarily low rates of juvenile crime (and crime in general) (Adler 1983). While the reasons for this have much to do with the nature of family life and culture in each nation, also commonly singled out as an important factor is the character of each nation's community life.

Both countries have found a way to preserve "village life" within the neighborhoods of city or suburb. For Japan, a society with "a history that glorifies samurai violence, a rather permissive pattern of child rearing, the absence of deep religious convictions, and the remarkably low ratio of police officers to citizens," urban dwellers are strongly subject to the informal social controls of family and neighbors making them "extremely sensitive to the good opinion of others" (J. Q. Wilson 1985, 12; Vogel 1979). Similarly for Switzerland, strong local communities have been maintained within metropolitan aggregations and the operation of village-like social controls remains very much in place (Clinard 1978; Segalman 1986). In addition, Switzerland seems more successful than most other advanced nations in maintaining the viability of small towns. While the Japanese and Swiss cultures can not be duplicated elsewhere, this is less true for the community structures found in these two nations.

Some readers may be wincing at the thought that I seem to be implicitly favoring a return to the "coercive, parochial, ignorant, stultifying" small town or urban village of an earlier era. And some surely feel that a little crime and family breakdown is a small price to pay for such human virtues as the creativity and intellectual achievement, the personal freedom, and the economic opportunity, to say nothing of the liberation of women, that are associated with life away from small-town-like environments. I am well aware of the negative side of excessive communal solidarity, but in the circumstances of advanced industrial societies that hardly seems a danger. The problem is how to preserve what little community solidarity we have left. Modern societies have unleashed a pervading privatism and individualism, and perhaps also a new freedom from social responsibilities, that can ultimately be corrosive to the social order. In the United States, there are some signs that the corrosion has already begun to cut deeply into the social fabric (for example, Bellah et al. 1985).

It is of interest to note that suburban residents themselves appear to sense the inherent social defects of suburban communities; indeed many could even be said to be living in suburban areas against their will. A recent poll in the United States, for example, where more than two-thirds of the population live in or very near urban areas, found that nearly half of the population, if given the chance, would move to places of 10,000 people or less. Only 25 percent chose the suburb as their habitat of choice (*New York Times*, March 24, 1985). Other studies have shown that community satisfaction varies negatively with size of place (Marans and Rodgers 1975). In many European countries I do not believe the popular sentiment is very different. In several advanced nations today, in fact, such sentiment has led to a decentralization of the urban population to a degree not anticipated by most analysts.

Does this longing for smaller places represent nothing more than nostalgia for a past that can never return? I do not think so. Certainly in North America, but also in two other countries that I know well, Sweden and the United Kingdom, the popular judgment runs something like this: We want to live in smaller places to avoid such urban problems as crime, traffic congestion, and noise; because life there is less competitive, more relaxed, more personal, more balanced; and because in the small town one is closer to the countryside. If jobs were available there, many people would gladly move to smaller, less troubled places. In other words, there is a popular realization that the suburban community has not been able to live up to its promise.

Because of advanced technologies the small towns of the contemporary period need not have many of the disadvantages of the small towns of the past. Without wishing to give an undue emphasis to the role of technology in shaping our lives, I think it is nevertheless the case that the mass media, mass transportation, and now the personal computer have in some measure reduced the intellectual and cultural costs of small town life. The cultural flourishing of urbanism can be piped into small towns today almost as easily and quickly as it can be transmitted to urban neighborhoods. This is also true of much formerly urban employment, which finds itself today functioning quite well in decentralized settings. In short, in the small towns of the future we may be able to have both an intimate, human scale plus many of the opportunities of urban life packaged together in a manner heretofore thought impossible to achieve.

Of course not everyone feels a desire to live in small towns. The desire is strongest among the "middle mass" of people, especially middle-aged family heads, the elderly, and almost certainly I think, if they were able to express an opinion, young children. But many teenagers and young, single adults and the cosmopolitan upper middle class in general, especially the group that has come to be known in the United States as Yuppies, much prefer the opportunity, variety, and dynamism of big city life and are quite willing to overlook its drawbacks. Also, there is some sentiment in both Europe and the United States among people in very low-density or outlying suburban settings, especially women, to prefer residential environments closer to the city center (Rothblatt and Garr 1986). My guess is that these groups are seeking more of the characteristics of the urban village. At the same time it should be stressed that not everything about small town life is admired, even by those who choose to live there. The parochialism and narrow-mindedness, the lack of "opportunity," and the general ennui and boredom are frequently singled out for criticism.

In the final analysis, the economic feasibility in advanced societies of a mass exodus of people from metropolitan areas to small towns is limited at best. If the line of reasoning in this chapter is on target, however, in our metropolitan housing, planning, and urban development programs we might be well advised to give greater recognition to the social costs of breaking up the sinews of human communities and scattering them about the urban landscape. To diminish the amount of crime and delinquency, as well as to achieve a variety of other worthwhile human goals, it seems important to build new suburbs—and rebuild existing ones as time goes on—to be more comprehensive, self-contained, and socially rich environments; places where, even in the metropolitan context, local community life can flourish.

NOTE

This chapter is based, in part, on my paper entitled "Suburbanization and Social Control: The Role of Housing and the Built Environment," delivered as a keynote address to the International Conference on Housing sponsored by the Ad Hoc Committee on Housing and the Built Environment of the International Sociological Association, the Dutch Sociological and Anthropological Association, and the Gestructureerde Samenwerking, Amsterdam, June 3, 1985. It also extends the discussion of privatization made in my recent book, *Private Pleasure, Public Plight: American Metropolitan Community Life in Comparative Perspective* (New Brunswick, NJ: Transaction Books, 1985).

REFERENCES

Adler, Freda
1983   *Nations Not Obsessed with Crime.* Littleton, CO: Fred B. Rothman.
Alder, Christine, Gordon Bazemore, and Kenneth Polk
1980   "Delinquency in Nonmetropolitan Areas." In *Critical Issues in Juvenile Delinquency*, edited by David Shichor and Delos H. Kelly, 45–61. Lexington, MA: Lexington Books.
Baumgartner, M. P.
1984   "Social Control in Suburbia." In: *Toward a General Theory of Social Control*, edited by D. Black. New York: Academic Press.
Bellah, Robert N., R. Madsen, W. M. Sullivan, A. Swidler, and S. M. Tipton
1985   *Habits of the Heart: Individualism and Commitment in American Life.* Berkeley: University of California Press.
Berry, Brian J. L.
1981   *Comparative Urbanization.* New York: St. Martin's Press.
Black, Donald (ed.)
1984   *Toward a General Theory of Social Control.* New York: Academic Press.
Cherlin, Andrew
1977   "The Effect of Children on Marital Dissolution." *Demography* 14, 265–72.
Clarke, R. V. G.
1980   "Situational Crime Prevention: Theory and Practice." *British Journal of Criminology* 20, no. 2, 136–47.
Clinard, Marshall B.
1978   *Cities with Little Crime: The Case of Switzerland.* Cambridge: Cambridge University Press.
Coleman, Alice
1985   *Utopia on Trial: Vision and Reality in Planned Housing.* London: Hilary Shipman.
Davidson, R. N.
1981   *Crime and Environment.* New York: St. Martin's Press.

Elliott, Delbert S., S. S. Ageton, D. Huizinga, B. A. Knowles, and R. J. Canter
1983   *The Prevalence and Incidence of Delinquent Behavior: 1976–80.* Boulder, CO: Behavioral Research Institute.
Elliott, Delbert S., David Huizinga, and Suzanne S. Ageton
1985   *Explaining Delinquency and Drug Use.* Beverly Hills, CA: Sage.
Erickson, M., and G. F. Jensen
1977   "Delinquency Is Still Group Behavior! Toward Revitalizing the Group Premise in the Sociology of Deviance." *Journal of Criminal Law and Criminology* 68, 262–73.
Fischer, Claude S.
1981   "Public and Private Worlds of City Life." *American Sociological Review* 46, 306–16.
1982   *To Dwell Among Friends.* Chicago: University of Chicago Press.
Gans, Herbert J.
1962   *The Urban Villagers.* Glencoe, IL: The Free Press.
1967   *The Levittowners.* New York: Pantheon.
Geismar, Ludwig L., and K. M. Wood
1985   *Family and Delinquency: Resocializing the Young Offender.* New York: Human Sciences Press.
Gove, Walter, and R. Crutchfield
1982   "The Family and Delinquency." *The Sociological Quarterly* 23, 301–19.
Gurr, T. R., P. N. Grabosky, and R. C. Hula
1977   *The Politics of Crime and Conflict: A Comparative History of Four Cities.* Beverly Hills, CA: Sage.
Hackler, James C., Kwai-Yui Ho, and Carol U. Ross
1974   "The Willingness to Intervene: Differing Community Characteristics." *Social Problems* 21, 328–44.
Hartnagel, Timothy F.
1979   "The Perception and Fear of Crime: Implications for Neighborhood Cohesion, Social Activity and Community Affect." *Social Forces* 58, 176–93.
Hayden, Dolores
1984   *Redesigning the American Dream: The Future of Housing, Work and Family Life.* New York: W. W. Norton.
Herbert, David
1982   *The Geography of Urban Crime.* London: Longman.
Hindelang, M. J.
1976   "With a Little Help from Their Friends: Group Participation in Reported Delinquent Behavior." *British Journal of Criminology* 16, 109–25.
Hirschi, Travis
1969   *Causes of Delinquency.* Berkeley: University of California Press.
1983   "Crime and the Family." In *Crime and Public Policy,* edited by James Q. Wilson, San Francisco: ICS Press.
Hummon, David M.
1986   "City Mouse, Country Mouse: The Persistence of Community Identity." *Qualitative Sociology* 9, no. 1, 3–25.
Jacobs, Jane
1961   *The Death and Life of Great American Cities.* New York: Random House.

Jephcott, Pearl
1971   *Homes in High Flats.* Edinburgh: Oliver and Boyd.
Johnson, Richard E.
1979   *Juvenile Delinquency and its Origins.* Cambridge: Cambridge University Press.
Johnstone, John W. C.
1980   "Delinquency and the Changing American Family." In *Critical Issues in Juvenile Delinquency,* edited by David Shichor and Delos H. Kelly, 83–97. Lexington, MA: Lexington Books.
Kasarda, Jack D., and M. Janowitz
1974   "Community Attachment in Mass Society." *American Sociological Review* 39, 328–39.
Kowinski, William S.
1980   "Suburbia: End of the Golden Age." *New York Times,* March 6.
Krupat, Edward
1985   *The Urban Environment and Its Effects.* Cambridge: Cambridge University Press.
Lewis, Dan A., and Greta W. Salem
1985   *Fear of Crime.* New Brunswick, NJ: Transaction Books.
Light, Ivan
1983   *Cities in World Perspective.* New York: Macmillan.
Marans, Robert W., and Willard Rodgers
1975   "Toward an Understanding of Community Satisfaction." In *Metropolitan America in Contemporary Perspective,* edited by A. H. Hawley and V. P. Rock, Chapter 7. New York: Halsted/Wiley.
Michelson, William H.
1976   *Man and His Urban Environment.* Reading, MA: Addison-Wesley.
Milgram, Stanley
1970   "The Experience of Living in Cities." *Science* 167, 1461–68.
Mitchell, Ann
1985   *Children in the Middle: Living Through Divorce.* London: Tavistock.
Murray, Charles A.
1983   "The Physical Environment and Community Control of Crime." In *Crime and Public Policy,* edited by James Q. Wilson, 107–22. San Francisco: ICS Press.
Newman, Oscar
1972   *Defensible Space.* New York: Macmillan.
1980   *Community of Interest.* Garden City, NY: Anchor Press.
Newman, Oscar, and Karen Franck
1980   *Factors Influencing Crime and Instability in Urban Housing Developments.* New York: Institute for Community Design Analysis.
Peres, Yochanan, and Rachel Pasternack
1985   "The Importance of Marriage for Socialization." In *Contemporary Marriage,* edited by Kingsley Davis, 157–78. New York: Russell Sage Foundation.
Podolefsky, Aaron
1983   *Case Studies in Community Crime Prevention.* Springfield, IL: Charles C. Thomas.
Popenoe, David
1977   *The Suburban Environment: Sweden and the United States.* Chicago: University of Chicago Press.

136   David Popenoe

1985   *Private Pleasure, Public Plight: American Metropolitan Community Life in Comparative Perspective.* New Brunswick, NJ: Transaction Books.

Poyner, Barry

1983   *Design Against Crime: Beyond Defensible Space.* London: Butterworths.

Radzinowicz, Leon, and Joan King

1979   *The Growth of Crime: The International Experience.* London: Penguin Books.

Rankin, Joseph H.

1983   "The Family Context of Delinquency." *Social Problems* 30, 466–79.

Richards, P., R. A. Berk, and B. Forster

1979   *Delinquency as Play. Delinquency in a Middle Class Suburb.* Cambridge, MA: Ballinger.

Rothblatt, Donald N., and Daniel J. Garr

1986   *Suburbia: An International Assessment.* New York: St. Martin's Press.

Rubenstein, H., C. Murray, T. Motoyama, and W. V. Rouse

1980   *The Link Between Crime and the Built Environment: The Current State of Knowledge.* Washington, DC: National Institute of Justice.

Rutter, Michael, and Henri Giller

1984   *Juvenile Delinquency: Trends and Prospects.* New York: Guilford

Sampson, R. J., T. C. Castellano, and J. H. Laub

1981   *Juvenile Criminal Behavior and Its Relation to Neighborhood Characteristics.* Washington, DC: Office of Juvenile Justice and Delinquency Prevention.

Schwendinger, Herman, and Julia S. Schwendinger

1985   *Adolescent Subcultures and Delinquency.* New York: Praeger.

Segalman, Ralph

1986   *The Swiss Way of Welfare.* New York: Praeger.

Shoemaker, Donald J.

1984   *Theories of Delinquency.* New York: Oxford.

Skogan, Wesley G., and Michael G. Maxfield

1981   *Coping with Crime: Individual and Neighborhood Reactions.* Beverly Hills, CA: Sage.

Stretton, Hugh

1978   *Urban Planning in Rich and Poor Countries.* Oxford: Oxford University Press.

Suttles, Gerald D.

1972   *The Social Construction of Communities.* Chicago: University of Chicago Press.

Tittle, Charles R.

1980   *Sanctions and Social Deviance: The Question of Deterrence.* New York: Praeger.

Uhlenberg, Peter, and David Eggebeen

1986   "The Declining Well-being of American Adolescents." *The Public Interest* 82, 25–38.

Vogel, Ezra F.

1979   *Japan as Number One: Lessons for America.* Cambridge, MA: Harvard University Press.

Wallerstein, Judith S., and J. B. Kelly

1981   *Surviving the Breakup.* New York: Basic Books.

Webber, Melvin

1970   "Order in Diversity: Community without Propinquity." In *Neighborhood, City and Metropolis*, edited by R. Gutman and D. Popenoe. New York: Random House.

Wellman, Barry
1979   "The Community Question." *The American Journal of Sociology* 84, 1201–31.
West, D. J.
1982   *Delinquency: Its Roots, Careers and Prospects*. Cambridge, MA: Harvard University Press.
Wilson, H.
1980   "Parental Supervision: A Neglected Aspect of Delinquency." *British Journal of Criminology* 20, 203–35.
Wilson, James Q.
1985   "The Rediscovery of Character: Private Virtue and Public Policy." *The Public Interest* 81, 3–16.
Wilson, James Q., and R. J. Herrnstein
1985   *Crime and Human Nature*. New York: Simon and Schuster.
Wynne, Edward A.
1977   *Growing Up Suburban*. Austin: University of Texas.

9

Diversity in New Communities: A Case Study of Reston, Virginia, at Age 20

SYLVIA F. FAVA

Abstract. The goal of achieving residential diversity—especially in economic mix and in racial composition—is examined for Reston, Virginia, the planned new community 20 years "old" in 1985. Reston has higher proportions of the poor and of blacks than most suburbs in its metropolitan area. The limits of diversity are set by microhomogeneity, by suburban attitudes to large cities, by the need for federal financial support for below-market housing, and by the fact that propinquity does not necessarily lead to interaction. Because of its convenient location Reston is becoming a high-tech satellite town with many jobs but an increasingly inadequate range of housing to accommodate diverse residents.

INTRODUCTION

Many nations around the world have built or are building planned new cities. In the United Kingdom the first wave of New Towns built immediately after World War II was designed to "decant" the population of London while also replenishing the housing stock destroyed in wartime air raids. The Brazilians built Brasilia as a new federal capital and to draw population and development to the vast interior. The Israelis constructed new towns on the periphery of their nation for defense and to absorb immigrants. In Japan, Tsukuba City, north of Tokyo, is nearing completion as the site of Tsukuba University and of laboratories and research facilities aimed at injecting more flexibility and creativity into Japanese higher education and, it is hoped, to achieve scientific breakthroughs. India constructed Chandigarh in the early 1950s as the capital of the Punjab region, which had lost its former capital to Pakistan in the postindependence division of territory. Mexico hopes to build new cities throughout Mexico to encourage regional development and especially to relieve congestion in Mexico City. In the Soviet Union, Akademgorodok, south of Novosibirsk, was built as a science town. Saudi Arabia is building two completely new industrial cities— Jubail on the Gulf and Yanbu on the Red Sea.

The United States also built new towns for many of the same reasons as other nations. Thus, Washington, D.C., was built as a planned new capital for a then-young nation. Cities were plotted out in the West to extend the frontier, some of them originating as forts for protection against the Indians. Later there were cities of science and technology, such as Los Alamos, New Mexico, and Oak Ridge, Tennessee. But in the United States, especially in the mid-twentieth century, the goals of building cities have more often been social. The most important goal has been to build housing to build community, that is, to build housing that is not only attractive and affordable and considerate of the natural setting, but to build housing that will facilitate interaction and a sense of belonging. To build such a sense of community among peoples of diverse economic, ethnic, racial, and family backgrounds is a high ideal of American democracy. The Garden Cities movement, transplanted to the United States from England in the 1920s; the towns such as Radburn, New Jersey, constructed under the movement's precepts; the Greenbelt towns built in the 1930s; and the federal new communities legislation of the late 1960s and early 1970s—all reflect the social benefits we hope for from housing, especially large-scale planned housing developments that also include the planning for jobs, services, and infrastructure.

RESTON: BACKGROUND

Reston, Virginia, a privately developed new town, was founded in the same period as the federal government sought to spur the development of large new communities under federal aegis. The federal vehicles were the 1966 Demonstration Cities and Metropolitan Development Act, Title IV of the 1968 Housing and Urban Development Act, and, especially, Title VII of the 1970 Housing and Urban Development Act. Ultimately 13 new communities were designated to receive loan guarantees by the federal government, guarantees that were intended to see the developments through the long costly period of land purchase, building infrastructure, housing, and commercial establishments, and attracting industry, business, and residents. All of the new communities, with the exception of The Woodlands, Texas, defaulted on their guaranteed debentures, and in 1983 the federal government terminated the new communities program (U.S. Department of Housing and Urban Development 1983, i-ii). Because the scenario for federally assisted new communities was never "played out" it is impossible to assess how they might have achieved one of their goals—the diversity of residential population.

Reston, 20 years "old" in 1984–86, provides an opportunity to assess on a longer-term basis the possibilities of achieving diversity in large planned communities. This is particularly important in the 1980s when the federal government has eliminated provision for almost all subsidized housing and is taking a less aggressive stance in interpreting and enforcing civil rights legislation. Robert E. Simon, whose initials form the name of Reston, purchased 7,400 acres in western Fairfax County in the early 1960s and began building the first large present-day planned community in the United States. Reston, about 18 miles west of Washington, D.C., had its first commercial and residential tenants in late 1964 but was officially dedicated in May 1966. Reston grew more slowly than expected and had only 2,500 residents by the end of 1967, grew to 20,000 residents by 1976, (Urban Land Institute 1976, 195), to 37,000 by 1984, with a projected population of 60,000–70,000 in the 1990s. In 1985 Reston had public schools, including a high school, a variety of religious institutions, movie houses, restaurants, a theater, a hotel, many recreational facilities, four village centers for shopping, and more than 70 office and industrial facilities (*Reston Neighborhoods* 1985, back cover). Money troubles piled up for Simon (as they had for the federally assisted new communities) and his direct control ended in 1967 when Gulf Oil, a major lender to the Reston venture, took over financial and managerial matters through its subsidiary, Gulf-Reston. In 1978 Gulf sold the undeveloped commercial and residential acreage of Reston to Mobil, which now is developing it through the Reston Land Corporation; Gulf sold the developed properties to another firm in 1980.

Reston set itself the goals of diversity in land use, in population characteristics (socioeconomic levels and race), and in housing. Four of the eight goals that Robert E. Simon enunciated early on, goals that still guide Reston's development today, resonate with the aim of being *inclusive*, with creating a *community of diversity*.

- To build a community where people may live, work, play, and have the widest possible opportunity to realize their full potential.
- To build a community where barriers created by race, income, geography, education, and age are removed.
- To build the fullest possible range of housing types for the company janitor, the company president, the elderly widow, and the young bachelor.
- To make it possible for people to become rooted in their community, to identify and feel part of it by providing housing for different needs and incomes so that one may find the kind of housing one needs when one is 20, 40, or 65 without leaving one's neighborhood (Urban Land Institute 1976, 195–96).

RESTON: A DIVERSE SUBURB

How has Reston done? How diverse is the population? Has the diversity been accompanied by interaction and a sense of community? These *are* separate questions—because diversity does not necessarily lead to interaction or a sense of community—and will be addressed later. First we must ask what are we comparing Reston to? What is the yardstick of diversity by which Reston measures up or falls short? Do we compare Reston to cities, or suburbs? In my view Reston is a suburb, albeit a more diverse one than most suburbs in its metropolitan area, and probably in the United States.

Reston's diversity is best assessed in the context of the metropolitan area of which it is a part: the Washington, D.C.-Maryland-Virginia Metropolitan Statistical Area. As defined by the Office of Management and Budget in 1983, using 1980 census data, this metropolitan area contained 3.25 million people, spread over five counties in Maryland, and five in Virginia, as well as the District of Columbia. (The 1983 definition added three counties—Calvert and Frederick in Maryland and Stafford in Virginia—to the earlier seven-county metropolitan definition.) Most Americans (75 percent in 1980) live in metropolitan areas, that is, large core cities surrounded by suburban counties that are economically and socially interdependent with the core city. The lessons of what Reston has and has not accomplished in the way of diversity are certainly broadly relevant for the United States. Metropolitan areas in the United States are highly segregated by race and income: the poor and the minorities concentrated in the core city, surrounded by affluent white suburbs. Table 9.1 illustrates that the metropolitan core city, the District of Columbia, has much higher proportions of blacks and families below the poverty line than either the United States as a whole or suburban Fairfax County. The table also compares Reston with Fairfax County and with the District of Columbia. Such three-way comparisons are virtually never made in either the *Reston Times* (the Reston newspaper) or in the profiles distributed by the Reston Land Corporation or Reston developers. The comparisons are only between Reston and Fairfax County; the references to Washington, D.C., deal almost exclusively with how easy it is to get there. Reston is identified with suburban Fairfax County, not urban Washington, D.C.

Washington, D.C., like many other metropolitan centers, lost population between 1970 and 1980; it lost over 15 percent of its population in the decade, while suburban Fairfax County gained 31 percent and Reston a spectacular 536 percent. The population of Washington, D.C., is older, blacker, poorer, and less-well-educated than either Fairfax or Reston. As noted, such contrasts are typical for American core cities and suburbs. More than 11 percent of Washington's people are over 65, but in recently settled suburban Fairfax only 4.5 percent, and in even more recently settled Reston only 3.5 percent. Out of every 100 Washingtonians, 70 are black, but only about 6 of every 100 residents of Fairfax County, and 10 of every 100 residents of Reston. Some 15 percent of Washington's families have incomes below the poverty level, but only 3 percent of Fairfax families and 5 percent of Reston's families. Roughly 67 percent of adult Washingtonians are high school graduates, but almost 90 percent of Fairfax adults and over 90 percent of Restonians. In sum, Reston, like Fairfax County, is an affluent suburb. But Reston is something more and that something is important. Reston has a greater proportion of blacks and of poor people than Fairfax. Both of these types of diversity have resulted from the deliberate policies of the past 20 years; they did not simply happen.

Reston was founded as part of the private-sector response to what Raymond Burby and Shirley Weiss (1976, 39–40) have called the "suburban critique"—the many-faceted criticism: aesthetic, ecological, governmental, and social—of the unplanned suburbs that mushroomed after World War II. The new communities legislation of the late 1960s and early 1970s was the public-sector

Table 9.1
Population and Housing Characteristics, 1980

	U.S.	District of Columbia	Fairfax County	Reston
Population change, 1970–1980	11.5%	− 15.6%	31.4%	536.2%
Black	11.7%	70.2%	5.87%	9.9%
Spanish Origin	6.5%	2.78%	3.35%	2.3%
Age 65+	11.3%	11.6%	4.5%	3.5%
Housing Structures built in 1939 or earlier	25.8%	39.1%	2.5%	......
Median value of Owner-occupied units	$47,300	$70,000	$95,200	$92,500
Median gross rent of rental units	$243	$226	$352	$360
12 yrs. school completed (persons 25 yrs.)	66.5%	67.1%	88.5%	92.5%
Median household income (1979)	$16,841	$16,211	$30,011	$28,406
Per capita income	$7,298	$8,960	$14,730	$11,575
Families below Poverty line	9.6%	15.1%	3.0%	5.1%

Source: U.S. Bureau of the Census, *County and City Data Book*, 10th ed. (Washington, DC: U.S. Government Printing Office, 1983), Tables A, B, and D.

response. Reston has been successful in showing how planning, and a social conscience, can produce beautiful, environmentally sensitive suburbs that have some economic and social diversity. Reston illustrates that diversity is possible to a limited degree in affluent, upper-middle class suburbs. The question is what are the limits.

THE LIMITS OF DIVERSITY

Microhomogeneity

One set of limits concerns the internal structure of diversity, that is, how physically close people are willing to live with those who differ from them in socioeconomic class, race, age, or life-style. Herbert Gans recommended to James Rouse, the developer of Columbia, Maryland (another privately developed new community begun only a year or two later than Reston), that some local internal homogeneity would lead to more stable overall diversity in Columbia. Specifically, Gans recommended "block" homogeneity ("block" in a single-family house area was defined as the four to six houses on either side of a given house) (Gans 1968, 189–90). Gans's basic point, derived from his study of suburban Levittown, New Jersey, is that Americans have "an inability to deal with pluralism . . . they cannot handle conflict because they cannot accept pluralism" (Gans 1982, 414). If a people are to identify with, "belong" to, and interact in a local neighborhood, there must be some similarities, some common bonds other than location. Building a community of diversity is then to some extent a contradiction, and can be accomplished only with the retention of some internal homogeneity. Brian Heraud's examination of the "social balance" of British new towns concluded similarly that in each town as a whole, there was a considerable degree of class diversity but individual neighborhoods within them had taken on distinctive characteristics (Heraud 1968, 33–58). Heraud, too, notes the contradictions between planning for diversity and planning for social interaction.

Reston's internal structure shows some socioeconomic, racial, and life-style separation. The Dulles Access Road divides Reston into "the two Restons": the wealthier portion south of the road with residents who tend to work further away from Reston, while those north of the road are less affluent and work in or close to Reston (*Reston Times*, February 28, 1985, 1). There are seven villages in Reston and each contains a range of single-family homes, townhouses, and, sometimes, rental apartments. There is no residential racial segregation in Reston, except for that associated with the location of two low-income subsidized housing apartment complexes in the same section of Reston.

The limits of diversity result, also, in my view, from two other sets of factors: first, the views of the American public about their cities; second, the proper division of responsibility between public and private sectors in our governmental system.

Attitudes Toward the City in the Suburban Era

The views of the American public about their cities indicate a love-hate relationship in which suburban living enables the middle class to have its cake and eat it too. The conventional wisdom in social science has been that Americans are antiurban, but this simplifies a complex set of opinions. The people of the United States are ambivalent about their cities, especially their large cities. They value cities highly as commercial, recreational, and intellectual centers, but have a low regard for cities as places to live. This duality was evident in a survey of a national representative sample of American adults conducted in 1978 for the Department of Housing and Urban Development (HUD) by the Louis Harris organization (Louis Harris and Associates 1978). Only 16 percent of the respondents said that the large city (250,000 +) would be their first preference for a place to live. The city is associated with crime and other problems and was regarded as "the worst place to raise children" by 82 percent of the sample. On the other hand, big majorities viewed the large city as having the best employment opportunities, the best shopping, the best health care facilities, the best plays and cultural activities, the best restaurants, and the best selection of movies. There is support for saying that Americans believe cities are "nice places to visit—and work in—but not to live in," especially for family life and raising children.

For many Americans, living in the suburban commuting range of large cities combines the best of both worlds: close to the attractions of large cities, but insulated from perceived urban problems. Restonians have taken this option, but have elected to include some urban economic and racial diversity. The mix is inherently limited, however. The cost of private housing limits the number of low-income people, and since proportionately more blacks than whites are low-income, the number of blacks is also limited. Economic and social integration in Reston are not cosmetic—and they are to be applauded loudly—but they are indirectly controlled by the larger realities of American society.

The attitudes of Americans toward *living* in large cities—and a willingness to address the problems of the poor and the black who are disproportionately concentrated in cities—are likely to become more negative. My own recent research deals with the "suburban generation," the people born after World War II who have lived all their lives in increasingly autonomous and self-sufficient suburbs (Fava and DeSena 1983). The suburban generation will loom ever-larger in the United States, since by 1980, 44 percent of all Americans lived in suburbs, a larger percentage than in any other kind of place. My studies have suggested that the "suburban generation"—who are under 40 since they were born after World War II—are often afraid of the city, do not know how to handle themselves with strangers in dense urban public places, seldom visit the core cities of their metropolitan area (except for stellar attractions), and tend to regard the problems of the poor and minorities as urban problems, that is, not their suburban concern.

Most members of the suburban generation are not likely to want to create an echo of urban diversity in their suburbs by deliberately planning for the poor and minorities. A provocative study by Zane Miller (1981) of the suburb of Forest Park, Ohio, from 1935 to 1976 contends that the concerns of the residents and the definition of community became increasingly less metropolitan and less civic, focusing now on ''inward-turning individuals.'' He documents how this shift altered the residents' approach to racial integration. Reston and other suburbs that are more racially integrated than the suburbs around them may, in fact, be helping to reduce integration in the surrounding suburbs. In updating his study of Levittown, New Jersey (now renamed Willingboro), Gans noted that by 1980 Willingboro's population was 38 percent black, in contrast to 11 percent in 1970. Gans (1982, xiv) commented that

Willingboro resembles other suburban new towns built during the 1960s in this respect: Columbia, Maryland; Reston, Virginia; and Park Forest South, Illinois, are also racially integrated. Undoubtedly the size and visibility of these new towns virtually required that they be open to black residents, which then made it even easier for smaller communities and subdivisions to remain invisible, and therefore all-white. South Jersey suburbia is highly segregated and I was told that black families were both attracted by and steered into Willingboro.

Role of the Federal Government

My final limiting point is the responsibility of private as opposed to public sectors. Private developers cannot resolve income inequality in American society, nor should that be their task. Providing affordable housing for all groups is a national government responsibility, explicitly stated in the Housing Act of 1949: ''The Congress hereby declares that the general welfare and security of the Nation and the health and living standards of its people require . . . the realization as soon as feasible of a decent home and a suitable living environment for every American.'' Government implementation of housing affordability in terms of various forms of subsidies has waxed and waned over the years. When, as is the case currently, government leaves housing construction as much as possible in the private sector, the result is to squeeze poor and moderate income groups out of the housing market because developers cannot afford to build for them. The current situation in Reston illustrates the process.

THE PRICE OF SUCCESS: RESTON THE HIGH-TECH SATELLITE TOWN

In the absence of federal subsidies and support for low- and moderate-income housing, Reston's opportunity for economic diversity is severely diminished. Reston is also the victim of its own success in attracting jobs and affluent residents. Reston was named in 1975 by the *Ladies' Home Journal* as one of the 15 most outstanding places to live in America (Urban Land Institute 1976,

195). The Residential Planned Community zoning passed by Fairfax County for Reston in 1962 enabled Reston to have very innovative planning that preserved the natural environment and mixed a wide variety of residential types with business, industry, shopping, schools, and outdoor recreational and leisure facilities (Urban Land Institute 1976, 196–97). Individual architecture is also very attractive, having won several awards, and is part of a total effect—the smallest details are considered and planned for in Reston. The result is a place of striking beauty and many amenities.

With the completion of the long-awaited Dulles Access Road to Reston in 1984, Reston is only a 10-minute drive to the Dulles airport and a 20-minute drive to downtown Washington, D.C. The combination of convenience, a large pool of educated labor, and the quality of life that Reston offers produced a "boom" of corporate headquarters and high-tech industry. Reston is now "one of the fastest-growing centers of high technology on the East Coast"; in fact "so big is the business boom that there are more jobs in Reston (22,000) than households (15,000)" (Grubisich and McCandless 1985, 13).

What is happening in Reston housing in the mid–1980s is twofold. On the one hand an influx of young, affluent professionals drawn by local high-tech industries is creating a market for higher-priced homes than the "old Reston." According to the *Reston Times* (February 28, 1985) the "new Restonians," especially south of the Dulles Access Road, have a median household income of over $38,000 and live in homes with an average value of over $106,000; the "old Restonians" have a median household income of $31,400 and live in homes valued at $93,000, on average. Simultaneously, federal subsidies for apartment construction have been discontinued and local substitutes are difficult to obtain. The result is a very low rental vacancy rate and higher rents at the very time that higher single-family prices have driven more Restonians into the rental market. The *Reston Times* has been headlining the dire consequences of these trends: "You've Got to be Lucky to have an Apartment in Reston," "Rents are Increasing Faster than Rate of Inflation," "Area Lost Apartments though Population Soared," "Tax-Exempt Financing Critical to Apartments" (April 18, 1985); "Apartment Shopping's Frightening Reality" (April 25, 1985); and they are right. It will be harder and harder to maintain an economic mix in Reston as one's financial situation changes. A group of concerned Restonians was formed in 1983 to address the issue of housing for low- and moderate-income people but has made little headway (Reston Interfaith Housing Corporation 1984).

Reston is on its way to becoming a high-income, high-tech satellite town like Fairfield, Stamford, or Greenwich, Connecticut, where many of the workers attracted by the jobs find they cannot afford to live. The *Washington Post* (June 17, 1984) reports that many workers at clerical-level jobs paying $12,000-$16,000 a year in the new Reston firms are settling in the Sterling area because Reston does not have enough moderately priced housing for them. Established Reston residents are also affected—the chairperson of the 1984 Reston festival, a secretary who worked in Washington, found it necessary to leave Reston because she could no longer find an affordable place to live (Grubisich and McCandless 1985, 98). The maintenance of housing diversity is a general problem in large planned suburbs that have attracted jobs and upscale home buyers. Columbia, Maryland, established with the same goals of economic mix as Reston, found by the 1980s that the "Columbia Dream" was "flawed by the fact that the children . . . raised here cannot buy a home in their hometown" (Columbia Forum 1982, 25). Irvine, California, another privately developed new community, did not have social goals of economic diversity, but did originally include some moderate-priced housing, that before long had to be dispensed by lotteries; recent attempts to improve opportunities for "low-end" housing offer houses starting at $90,000 (Hill 1986, 18).

Even if the mechanisms were available to build housing for low- and moderate-income groups, the more profoundly disturbing question is whether Restonians still have the will to implement them. After Gulf-Reston took over the management of Reston in 1967 it had to be sued by the Washington Metropolitan Housing Authority and the Housing Opportunities Council before the corporation agreed to provide additional subsidized housing units for workers at the U.S. Geological Survey headquarters that had relocated to Reston. The Housing Committee of the Reston Community Association was active in these efforts.

Members of the Housing Committee of the Reston Community Association also felt that they had had a tremendous influence on Gulf-Reston, Inc. The tendency without their input would have been to address the needs of upper-income residents only and to ignore the needs of those priced out of the private housing market. Simon had sold these early "pioneers" on the idea of low- and moderate-income housing (Smookler 1976, 91–93).

In contrast, the *Washington Post* (June 17, 1984, A6) reported that in 1984 the Artery organization was encountering opposition from prospective renters in the Waterside apartments in Reston who objected to the fact that 20 percent of the units had to be set aside for low- and moderate-income households as a condition of the tax-exempt financing provided by the Fairfax County Redevelopment and Housing Authority. This is of particular interest since the cheapest apartment in Waterside will rent for $400 (*Reston Times*, April 18, 1985, A12).

There is a general feeling in Reston in the mid–1980s that there is "decreasing support among residents for more assisted housing" (Grubisich and McCandless 1985, 98). The media have also picked up the theme that Reston is more conservative and less socially conscious (*Washington Post*, June 17, 1984, A6). One of the few empirical studies suggests that the change may be considerably more complex. In 1983 Polly Bart conducted a questionnaire survey of Columbia, Maryland, residents among three groups whose degree of community participation suggested that they would differ in regard to their commitment to the goals of a "balanced community" (Bart 1984). The responses among the three groups were not statistically different, nor was length of residence in Columbia. Bart's results indicate there has been no significant decline in commitment to the integrative goals of Columbia. However, her research also indicates that the commitment had been made effective by permanent residents who were active leaders in Columbia. The "pool" of these potential leaders may be declining, she notes, as attitudes toward volunteer work change and as more women join the labor force. Of particular interest are the signs of "burnout" among formerly active high-status women, a major source of past community leadership. Bart concludes that it is as important to examine the context of community participation as to determine whether residents believe in social goals.

DIVERSITY AND COMMUNITY

Economic Integration and Community

What happens to moderate-income and especially low-income people who *do* live in Reston? Reston's goal has been to build not just housing but to build community. If the less affluent are not to be mere tokens, how are they served by Reston's facilities and how are they meshed into daily life? How do the poor become part of the community? Reston is upper-middle class in its expensive recreation, trendy shops, and time-consuming organization meetings. Does Reston provide jobs for unskilled workers? Is there frequent and reliable public transportation? Are there stores that carry less-expensive cuts of meat, discount-priced day-old bakery products, generic-brand canned goods, and bulk-priced staples? Is it easy to use food stamps? Are there inexpensive clothing stores? How are the community recreational fees of low-income residents financed? To what extent has the concentration of low-income housing within particular areas of Reston been ameliorated? To what extent are the poor of Reston also elderly (a strategy often used to achieve economic integration)? All of these questions are variations on the question of whether low-income groups are socially marginal in Reston or are part of the community.

In Columbia, Maryland, the dynamics of economic integration have been studied in some depth. Neil Sandberg studied six families placed in the Underhill housing project; although these families were not the very poor they were on welfare (Sandberg 1978). Transfer to Columbia uprooted them from their support network and "their coercive placement among neighbors they do not choose leaves welfare recipients profoundly ambivalent about their commitment to local community life" (Sandberg 1978, 220). Consequently they participate only hesitantly or when pressed. Sandberg suggests that the major problem is the welfare bureaucracy that demoralizes the poor, stating that "the same people, unaware of their welfare status, might make for better neighbors" (Sandberg 1978, 220). Lynne Burkhart's ethnographic study of Columbia based on four years of residence as a participant-observer indicates a complex, shifting, overlapping set of alliances on the basis of economic class, race, age, religion, and marital status in which the local neighborhood within Columbia is relatively unimportant (Burkhart 1981). She suggests the alliances are concerned fundamentally with power—

which groups have access to what resources in Columbia—and are mediated by a set of verbal symbols in which class confrontation often fronts for race. She concludes that

these negotiations, while employing only the idiom of class, represent indirect power struggles between blacks and whites as well as poor and nonpoor. It is important that we understand these power struggles as positive signs of social change if the moves to end racial and socio-economic discrimination in our society are to continue (Burkhart 1981, 153).

Not surprisingly, but significantly, both these studies of Columbia link economic and racial integration to the larger realities of American society.

Racial Integration and Community

We have already indicated that in terms of the percentage of black residents Reston does better than suburban Fairfax County in which it is located. Blacks in Reston cover a range of income groups, as does the white population. Patricia Blackwell, head of the NAACP in Northern Virginia, and an 11-year Reston resident, was quoted in the *Washington Post* (June 17, 1984) as saying of Reston that there is very little overt racism and that what exists "is very well masked." There is no racial steering in Reston, and Reston also stands in marked contrast to the harassment, violence, and houseburnings that still occur when blacks move into some suburbs (Witherspoon 1985, 37–44).

Reston is racially open but the message is conveyed very indirectly, almost subliminally. In the developers' materials there are no statistics on blacks, only an occasional picture of a black resident, and, all-important, a few advertisements featuring black realtors. Significantly, in the current restatement of Simon's goals by the Reston Land Corporation there is no mention at all of race, although a "variety of income levels" is mentioned. The emphasis instead is on "full use of leisure time," "recreational and cultural facilities," and "beauty—structural and natural" (Reston Land Corporation 1985). Word-of-mouth and knowledge of the Reston commitment to integration are probably the major methods of recruiting black homebuyers—and warning off whites who will not live in integrated areas. The important thing, studies have shown, is that the policy be known and adhered to. The policy is still in effect, but it is no longer trumpeted.

The success of racial integration is Reston must be measured not only by numbers but also by the extent to which blacks have been able to build community in Reston, both within and across racial lines. Black residential preferences may be related to their desire to construct social communities. Thus, relatively few blacks—1 to 4 percent in national surveys—want to live in "mostly white" areas (Fava 1974). In the Louis Harris survey for HUD noted earlier it was pointed out that only 16 percent of Americans chose the large city as their first residential preference. However, 38 percent of the blacks have the city as their first choice, as contrasted to only 13 percent of the whites and 32 percent of the Hispanics. This may reflect a genuine preference for big city living among blacks, a recognition of the racial housing market, or a desire to live among larger numbers of blacks so that black institutions, such as churches, social clubs, and political power bases, can be maintained.

The dynamics of racial integration and community building in Reston and in Columbia, Maryland, were studied in the middle 1970s by the sociologist Peggy Wireman. She concluded that in both Reston and Columbia there was limited social interaction between races and an extensive system of all-black organizations. "There are alumni branches of fraternities and sororities and a number of all-black couples' clubs, women's clubs, and men's clubs, as well as a local chapter of Jack and Jill" (Wireman 1984, 107). Wireman notes that "blacks in Reston were more vocal than in Columbia at an early point in the town's development about their desire to obtain community recognition of their black identity and to deal with racial issues." The organization Black Focus was formed and sponsors an annual Black Arts Festival and other events emphasizing black culture. Eighty percent of black families in Reston were estimated to belong to Black Focus, which Wireman holds was formed "to give black families black support—a kind of extended family" (Wireman 1984, 108).

Gender and Community

An aspect of diversity that has received attention only in the past decade is the diversity in female gender roles. Low-density suburbs of single-family homes segregated from nonresidential activities provide a setting suitable only for the traditional housewife-mother role (Fava 1980). However, women have been entering the paid labor force to the extent that in March 1984 six out of ten mothers with children under 18 were also working outside the home. The divorce rate has also increased and so has women's life expectancy, both trends leaving more women alone for many of their adult years.

Accessible work places, shopping, child care, medical, recreational, and other facilities are crucial for women because they reduce time pressures, enabling women to integrate their various roles. Higher densities and built environments combining residential and nonresidential functions provide a greater availability of services and activities close to home. These characteristics had been found mainly in cities and therefore it had been thought that cities allowed women more role diversity because they could move readily from one activity to another. However, the mixed-use pattern in Reston, locating residences within short distances of shopping, jobs, and support services, makes it easy for women to combine their contemporary multiple roles, although Reston was not designed with this in mind. Both Reston and Columbia were designed with the "model" of home-bound women whose regular orbit would be the local neighborhood. A study of women in Columbia in the mid–1970s found they did not want to be confined to the local neighborhood but wanted it to offer educational opportunities (for themselves), child care, communal facilities for cooking, and other housekeeping activities, and so on, that would make it simpler for them to prepare for and carry out their nonhome, nonlocal roles (Stuart 1974). What has happened in Reston, and probably Columbia, is that the growth of population and the continued addition of jobs and facilities have reached a "critical mass" in these new towns, offering women the setting they need for multiple roles (Fava 1985).

The critical dimensions for women are availability of jobs close to home *and* career ladders in the work place; a variety of housing types and price ranges; many services including child care and medical care in the local neighborhood; easy availability of many people for companionship and emotional support; and transportation systems other than the private automobile. All of these are part of the Reston dream—and much of the reality.

IN CONCLUSION

Is the glass of diversity in Reston half-empty or half-full? The glass is half-full in measuring Reston against the greater economic and racial homogeneity of conventional suburbs. It is half-empty in measuring Reston against the range of inequality in the United States, inequities that depend on national policy changes. Without federal subsidies and other support for low- and moderate-income housing, only very small amounts of housing for these groups can be added to the existing stock in Reston. Federal programs for *realistic* job-training and welfare restructuring are also important.

Racial integration in Reston is well-established but only upper-middle-income blacks (and whites) can afford to move there now. Racial integration does not necessarily carry with it interracial social life. Achievement of that goal hinges not only on national policy (that could only help in making more housing available for low-income blacks and whites) but on long-range historical changes in race relations in the United States.

NOTE

An earlier version of this chapter was presented at the Reston 20th Anniversary Symposium, Reston, Virginia, May 9, 1985.

REFERENCES

Bart, Polly
1984   "New Town to Young City: Goals and Commitment in Columbia, Maryland."
        Unpublished manuscript.
Burby, Raymond, and Shirley F. Weiss
1976   *New Communities, USA*. Lexington, MA: Lexington Books.
Burkhart, Lynne
1981   *Old Values in a New Town: The Politics of Race and Class in Columbia, Maryland.*
        New York: Praeger.

Columbia Forum 1982
1982   "A Day of Work, An Evening of Fun." Columbia, MD: mimeo.
Fava, Sylvia F.
1974   "Blacks in American New Towns: Problems and Prospects." *Sociological Symposium* 12, 111–34.
1980   "Women's Place in the New Suburbia." In *New Space for Women*, edited by G. Wekerle, 129–49. Boulder, CO: Westview.
1985   "Gender and Residential Preferences in the Suburban Era: A New Look?" *Sociological Focus* 18, 109–17.
Fava, Sylvia F., and Judith DeSena
1983   "The Chosen Apple: Young Suburban Migrants." In *The Apple Sliced: Sociological Studies of New York City*, edited by Vernon Boggs, G. Handel, and S. Fava, 305–22. South Hadley, MA: Bergin and Garvey.
Gans, Herbert
1968   "Planning for the Everyday Life and Problems of Suburban and New Town Residents." In *People and Plans*, edited by H. Gans, 183–201. New York: Basic Books.
1982   *The Levittowners*. With a new preface by the author. New York: Columbia University Press. Originally published in 1967.
Grubisich, Tom, and Peter McCandless
1985   *Reston: The First Twenty Years*. Reston, VA: Reston Publishing Co.
Heraud, Brian
1968   "Social Class and the New Towns." *Urban Studies* 5, 33–58.
Hill, Gladwin
1986   "Big But not Bold: Irvine Today." *Planning* (American Planning Association) 51, 16–20.
Louis Harris Associates for the Department of Housing and Urban Development
1978   *A Survey of Citizens' Views and Concerns about Urban Life: Final Report*. Washington, D.C.: U.S. Government Printing Office.
Miller, Zane L.
1981   *Suburb: Neighborhood and Community in Forest Park, Ohio, 1935–1976*. Knoxville: University of Tennessee Press.
Reston Interfaith Housing Corporation
1984   "Affordable Housing for Low and Moderate Income Families in Reston." Reston, VA: mimeo.
Reston Land Corporation
1985   "Reston's Goals," mimeo sheet.
Reston Neighborhoods
1985   "Facts and Figures." Reston, VA: Reston Visitors Center distribution.
Reston Times
1985   "The Two Restons," February 28.
       "You've Got to be Lucky to Have an Apartment in Reston," April 18.
       "Rents are Increasing Faster than Rate of Inflation," April 18.
       "Area Lost Apartments though Population Soared," April 18.
       "Tax-Exempt Financing Critical to Apartments," April 18.
       "Apartment Shopping's Frightening Reality," April 25.
Sandberg, Neil
1978   *Stairwell 7: Family Life in the Welfare State*. Beverly Hills, CA: Sage.

Smookler, Helene
1976   *Economic Integration in New Communities*. Cambridge, MA: Ballinger.
Stuart, Mary
1974   "A Study of Women's Needs in Columbia." Columbia, MD: Columbia Association, mimeo.
Urban Land Institute
1976   "Washington, D.C. Metropolitan Area . . . Today." Washington, D.C.: ULI Spring 1976 Meeting Project Brochure.
U.S. Department of Housing and Urban Development, Division of Policy Studies
1983   "An Evaluation of the Federal New Communities Program." Washington, DC: mimeo.
Washington Post
1984   "Time Hedges Billion Dollar Bet at Reston," Sunday, June 17.
Wireman, Peggy
1984   *Urban Neighborhoods, Networks, and Families*. Lexington, MA: D. C. Heath.
Witherspoon, Roger, with S. Lee Hilliard
1985   "Off Limits: the Dilemma of Moving into Suburbia." *Black Enterprise* 15, 37–42.

PART IV

ASPECTS OF PLANNING AND DESIGN

Recent history of the built environment contains numerous vivid illustrations of mismatches between people's needs and preferences as they exist in actual fact and as they are found in the minds of design professionals. The award-winning Pruitt-Igoe public housing project in St. Louis, dynamited 18 years after the first residents moved in, is perhaps the most infamous example in the United States, but every country has its white elephant.

Chapter 11 by Simon and Wekerle provides another, albeit less dramatic, example of differential priorities of residents and planners. The planners' attempt to recreate a traditional neighborhood in Toronto under a new set of much stricter constraints led to a number of design compromises, most notably miniaturization of outdoor spaces, which was found to conflict with functional usage by the residents.

The account by Van Kempen in Chapter 12 of the demise of the Bijl-mermeer high-rise estate in Amsterdam not only points to the sociobehavioral effects that living in such an environment may have on its inhabitants, but it also clarifies how the broader economic context, as formed in this case by the regional housing market and governmental subsidy policies, may interact with the physical environment to produce given effects. Van Kempen also identifies a number of factors having to do with physical design as well as social organization that may alleviate negative effects.

Franck's Chapter 10 makes clear that even designs that at one point in time were seen as congruent with the needs of at least a substantial majority of the population, may become a poor fit as these needs undergo changes. The single-family detached house, while still prominent in the American Dream, is no longer the predominant housing choice it once was. In part, this is because of economic factors that have put this housing type out of reach for households who may still aspire to it. However, a segment of the population has emerged that includes a number of life-styles better accom-modated by dwelling types other than the single-family home. Franck surveys a number of such alternatives as various forms of shared housing, smaller dwellings, and units that can be adapted by users to fit their particular requirements.

Certainly, the case for a broader spectrum of housing types, reflective of the broader array of life-styles that has emerged, is a timely one. Considerations bearing on this matter relate not only to concerns of physical design, but also to issues of tenure and management and to political and economic interests. In addition to the chapters that follow, Part V of this book offers relevant discussion in this connection.

10

Shared Spaces, Small Spaces, and Spaces That Change: Examples of Housing Innovation in the United States

KAREN A. FRANCK

Abstract. This chapter identifies five central characteristics of the ideal of the American single-family house that deter the development of alternative forms of housing, despite the rising costs of housing and the recent changes in household composition. Three types of alternative housing that have recently appeared are described: (1) shared housing, including renovated residential hotels, "mingle" units designed for two unrelated adults, and "quad" housing designed for four unrelated adults; (2) housing consisting of smaller sized but complete dwelling units, including "limited living units"; and (3) housing where dwellings are planned for expansion or contraction, including elder cottages placed on the lots of existing single-family houses. Specific examples of each of these types are presented. The chapter concludes with a discussion of the legal and social barriers that these and other types of alternative housing face in the United States in the form of zoning ordinances, building codes, and underlying values that esteem the nuclear family as the ideal household and that favor the social and spatial separation and self-sufficiency of all households.

INTRODUCTION

In the United States, despite the rising costs of housing and the inability of many people to afford to buy a house, the ideal of the single-family detached house in a suburban location still holds great sway. Five characteristics are central to this ideal:

1. that the house be spatially private and self-sufficient so that no interior or exterior spaces or facilities be shared with other households;

2. that it be inhabited only by members of a single nuclear family with children, or by a couple;

3. that the unit be physically detached from other houses, preferably with enough space so that one can walk around it;

4. that it be spacious enough and designed in such a way so as to contain a wide range of discrete rooms with assigned functions that remain fixed;

5. that it be owner-occupied.

Not only is this ideal actually realized, since most American housing does meet many of these criteria, but the ideal is also often enforced by law. In many communities comprised of single-family homes, local zoning ordinances forbid rental housing and require that houses be detached, that they be located on lots of a minimum size, that they contain a minimum amount of floor space, and that they be inhabited by no more than a specific, small number of people who are related to each other by blood or marriage.

Additional enforcement of the ideal that is more indirect but nonetheless powerful comes in the form of home mortgages and construction loans. Banks will refuse to finance the construction or purchase of a home with innovations they believe will make it of questionable resale value. Other innovations of a physical or a social nature are discouraged or even prohibited by local building codes that may treat those innovations as "substandard housing." Zoning ordinances, bank financing policies, federal subsidy policies, and building codes all serve to ensure the continuation of the ideal home either in its complete detached form or modified in attached houses and apartments. Yet the desirability of that ideal and its appropriateness are increasingly questionable.

Its desirability can be questioned on the basis of affordability. The costs of construction, land, and maintenance (including heating and property taxes) could all be reduced by building other types of housing. More interesting perhaps is the appropriateness of this dwelling type for many contemporary American households. Both the characteristics of the detached house itself and of the larger suburban community where it is typically located do not meet the needs of many of these households: of one-parent families, young singles, elderly, and employed mothers with young children (Hayden 1984). The American single-family detached house in a suburban location was originally intended for the household composed of a working father, a homemaking mother, and young, dependent children. It is not clear that the prototype single-family house was ideal even for this configuration (Franck 1985b), but the proportion of households of this type is decreasing as more mothers are employed, as more families are headed by single parents, and as fewer families have any children at all. In 1970, 28.2 percent of all married women living with their husbands who had children under six were employed (U.S. Bureau of the Census 1973). This proportion increased to 43.9 percent in 1980 (U.S. Bureau of the Census 1983). For those with children between the ages of 6 and 17 only, the proportion increased from 47.1 to 60.1 percent. The proportion of family households headed by single parents increased from 13 percent in 1970 to 26 percent in 1984 and the proportion of family households with no children increased from 44 to 50 percent (U.S. Bureau of the Census 1985).

There has also been an increase in "nonfamily households," that is, in the proportion of households comprised of people living alone or with others to whom they are not related. In 1984 a full 23 percent of all American households consisted of people living by themselves and another 4 percent of people living with unrelated others, up from 17 percent and 1 percent in 1970 (U.S. Bureau of the Census 1985). As a society we have not developed images of the desirable or appropriate living arrangements for one-person or for one-parent households. Indeed, we tend to assume that they should and want to live in the same arrangements as traditional family households—that is, completely independently of other households in dwellings that concretize and enforce that independence and self-sufficiency. Granted the dwellings may be smaller, but few facilities or spaces are to be shared with other dwellings.

One way to accommodate the increasing diversity of household types, and to confront the uncertainty of what the future composition of households may be, would be to design and build dwelling units where the configurations of functions and spaces could easily be changed and where the overall size of the dwelling could be increased or decreased. This, however, is not being done in the United States and partly contradicts another characteristic of the ideal American house— that it contain discrete rooms with fixed functions. In the 1950s single-family housing in suburban subdivisions was often designed and built with future expansion of the dwellings in mind. A one- or two-bedroom house was arranged in such a way on a lot large enough to allow for the future addition of two bedrooms and other rooms (Gellen 1985). Yet the assignment of functions to spaces in the original house was expected to remain the same.

It is surprising that despite the rising costs of housing and the continuing changes in household composition, there has been relatively little innovation in the physical or social characteristics of housing in the United States. Innovations are discouraged both by the power of the traditional image of the single-family house and by the ways in which that ideal, or modified versions, is enforced by banks, federal subsidies, zoning ordinances, and building codes. Some possible innovations include shared housing, smaller sized dwelling units, and dwellings designed to be changed as the household's needs change. Each of these types of innovation is discussed in turn.

SHARED SPACES

The characteristics of the ideal American house that seem the least susceptible to change are the dwelling's social and spatial privacy and self-sufficiency—that it will be inhabited only by members of a single family and, whenever possible, no spaces or facilities will be shared with other households. This ideal of privacy and self-sufficiency developed relatively recently in the United States. The Colonial household often contained a mixture of family members, boarders, servants, and apprentices, as well as poor people or juveniles whose board was paid by the town government (Model and Hareven 1978). By the nineteenth century, the function of the household for sheltering the poor and homeless was transferred to institutions. The phenomenon of boarders in private homes continued right up into the 1930s, although beginning in the late nineteenth century the practice of boarding was decried by reformers for contributing to the deterioration of the family and the decay of morals (Model and Hareven 1978; Kobrin 1978). The middle-class definition of privacy grew stricter and, with growing economic prosperity and various technolocial developments including the trolley and then automobiles, could be realized first by the middle class starting in the late nineteenth century and then by the working class particularly after World War II (Jackson 1985).

In addition to boarding in private homes, single women and men in the nineteenth century could live in buildings designed and built for them with shared amenities such as dining halls, lounges, reading rooms, and housekeeping services (Mostoller 1985). Over the course of the late nineteenth and early twentieth centuries additional building types developed that were appropriate for single people: the apartment hotel, owner-occupied rooming houses, and single-room-occupancy hotels. Gradually, however, it became economically possible for many single people to occupy their own complete dwelling units; more of such units were built in the form of small apartments without shared facilities, and the construction of housing designed specifically for single people declined even as the number of single-person households increased (Franck 1985b). Apartment hotels and single-room-occupancy hotels (SROs) went into a serious social and physical decline, especially after World War II. In some cities they have been converted to luxury housing and in other cities they have been replaced by expensive hotels for transients. The possibility of finding shared accommodations outside cities decreased as single-family-home neighborhoods outlawed boarding and restricted the number of nonrelated people who could share a house.

Rising housing costs and economic hardships experienced by the elderly, young single people, single parents, and homeowners, as well as the tremendous increase in homelessness in the United States, seem to be making the sharing of housing more acceptable, but primarily for economic, not social, reasons. Three examples of shared housing are presented here: renovated SRO hotels, the quad, and the mingles house. Unlike the ideal single-family house, each of these examples was designed to be inhabited by unrelated adults.

Single-Room-Occupancy Hotels

The destruction or conversion of SRO hotels has produced a serious loss of low-cost housing stock in urban areas and has helped precipitate the homelessness of urban populations (Hopper and Hamberg 1984). In some cities—including San Francisco, Portland, Oregon, and Seattle—municipal governments and local community groups have taken various steps to stem this loss and to renovate the remaining hotels while also preserving them as low-cost housing. One unusual case of a renovated SRO hotel is the Apex Belltown Cooperative in Seattle. So far, it is the only SRO limited equity cooperative in the United States. The group of people who worked long and hard to purchase and renovate the Apex decided that both the SRO building type and its life-style should be kept but that it should be cooperatively owned by the residents (Collins 1985). This means that the original small single rooms have been kept; bathrooms, kitchens, and living spaces are shared; and the residents hold shares in the building's ownership.

Today the Apex has 21 rooms on each of two floors above a furniture store and a parking garage. The rooms are 130, 280, and 440 square feet. Co-op shareholders make down payments of $1,100 and have monthly carrying costs of $161 to $331. To live there one must be an artist either in terms of substantial income earned or time commitment. Eighty percent of the residents must earn an annual income of less than $18,000. The ages of the residents range from 20 to 50. Two-thirds of them are women; most are white but there are a few Asians. Five residents share a kitchen and living/dining space; these are warm and inviting spaces. There are four bathrooms on each floor for which residents did colorful tile work. Residents assign and carry out maintenance chores themselves. Currently they are trying to adjust to other residents' housekeeping habits and to raise money to continue work on the building. Even though their commitment and energy are considerable, problems continue to arise, particularly in the joint use of kitchens.

As a rehabilitated SRO the Apex is rare in several ways. By virtue of the ownership system and the residents' assumption of maintenance duties, the Apex requires a legal and social commitment to sharing. The residents are also relatively skilled, able people who do not have the problems of alcoholism, homelessness, mental disturbance, or extreme poverty common to residents of other SROs. Their skills and the absence of these problems should ensure some degree of success in sharing without the support and guidance from outside parties such as a management staff or a local community group. In other SROs, where commitment to sharing is not legally required and where residents do have a range of problems, the absence of a strong commitment to interactive living can be counteracted by strong management and maintenance services. Common use of spaces in these buildings can take place without a high degree of social interaction among residents as long as these services are provided. These same services, as well as counseling, can also provide the support and supervision needed in SROs occupied by residents with problems of alcoholism or mental disturbances. In Portland, Denver, Seattle, and San Francisco, renovated hotels with these services provide a beneficial way of life that we need to recognize. One example of such a hotel is the Civic Center Residence (CCR) in San Francisco.

The CCR is owned and managed by the Tenderloin Neighborhood Housing Corporation and was purchased with funds from the city and from the Franciscans. Formerly a women's residence owned and very strictly managed by the Salvation Army, it now houses a very heterogeneous population of 200 residents. Many of the original residents continue to live there; one is in her eighties. Other residents include about 10 single parents with small children, some elderly men and women, several displaced homemakers, a large number of young and middle-aged mentally disturbed persons, and some foreign students. Priority is given to low-income people and people with disabilities, but there are no strict admission requirements. The CCR also takes in travelers who are visiting San Francisco.

A considerable amount of counseling with the residents is done by the staff, including the live-in manager. Altogether there are 17 staff members, including desk clerks, kitchen staff, and maintenance people. Fourteen of them live in the building. Holidays, birthdays, and other special occasions are celebrated with enthusiasm. The manager's goal is to create "an extended family environment," which she succeeds in doing with those who are interested in participating. The CCR serves two meals each day. The rent is $336 to $386 a month, including meals. Housekeeping services and linen are provided. The building is an imposing eight-story structure with 224 rooms, three lounges on the first floor, a laundry room, a music room, and a canteen in the basement. There is also a special lounge for children, a lounge for adults only, and a roof deck.

Renovated SROs provide economic advantages that are important in a period when many people are homeless. SROs provide locational advantages as well, allowing people to live downtown within walking distance of public transportation, facilities, services, and possibly friends and familiar haunts. They allow the elderly to remain independent but with the presence, support, and services provided by both staff and other residents. This is also true for the mentally disturbed or for alcoholics. SROs provide a chance for people to share activities or to remain aloof. Some house people of an amazing range of ages and lifestyles and thereby help bring those people in contact with one another.

Quads

The purely economic benefit of sharing a kitchen and a bath is recognized and realized in commercial housing for students in Eugene, Oregon, and in other locations on the West Coast. Called a "quad" because four people share kitchen and bath, this type of rental housing is also inhabited by single working people or the elderly. The four bedrooms, each with a half bath and ranging from 130 to 190 square feet, are grouped around a central kitchen/dining room and full bath. Outdoor corridors, much like a motel, allow each bedroom to have its own entrance to the outdoors, giving maximum privacy for coming and going. In one example in Eugene a live-in manager functions much like a housemother, interviewing new residents and placing them with others of similar habits. Rent is $159 a month for the smaller rooms. The manager has found it better to restrict residency to students because of their common life-style; the habits of working people tend to conflict with those of students.

Mingles House

The "mingles" house is another variation of sharing that originated primarily in its financial advantages. A house or apartment is bought jointly and the mortgage held jointly by two unrelated single people who find primarily an economic advantage in this sharing of costs (Irwin 1984). Since both owners live there, common spaces are shared as well. To meet the needs of this potential market, developers have been building tract housing with "mingles" floor plans. These contain two equal "master" bedrooms, each with bath. The most successful plans separate the two bedrooms for maximum privacy and provide common spaces that are designed to allow the two residents to use them jointly or separately but simultaneously. In new tract housing in California, this floor plan is routinely included and constitutes from 10 to 30 percent of all units. One example is Tierra Vista in Seranno Highlands between San Diego and Los Angeles. Two equal and full-fledged bedroom suites are separated by a shared living/dining space. Each bedroom also has an entrance to the patio. The dining space is somewhat separated from the living space but not enough to constitute a completely separate socializing area. The units cost between $110,000 and $112,000.

The SRO and the quad have social and physical configurations considerably different from those of the ideal American house: Several people who did not know each other previously are expected to share both bathroom and kitchen. The mingles house, however, is occupied by people who did know each other previously, well enough to share a mortgage, and each has his or her own bathroom. While the composition of the mingles household is different from that of a nuclear family, the physical configuration of the house is only slightly different—providing two master bedroom suites instead of one—but this small difference is significant. Because residents are independent adults, rather than members of a nuclear family, the design of the mingles house attempts to maximize the equality, privacy, and independence of its occupants. In contrast, the traditional single-family house encourages togetherness of members in social spaces, pairs the parents in a single bedroom and bath, and provides smaller bedrooms and often shared bathrooms for children. Privacy of the single "master" suite is maximized, whereas privacy of the subsidiary bedrooms is not a concern. Since they are intended for single occupancy by children, the subsidiary bedrooms are also smaller than the "master" suite. Because of these design characteristics, the single master suite plan is inappropriate for several types of households where equality and privacy of all members is a concern. Thus the mingles plan is suitable for mingles as well as for grown siblings, a single parent with a grown child, or a couple who wish to sleep separately.

SMALL SPACES

The most widespread recent modification in American dwellings is probably their decreasing size and, relatedly, their increasing density and the increasing proportion of attached units (Mosena 1984). According to Mosena, the average new single-family detached house progressed from 983 square feet in 1950 to 1,760 in 1979 to 1,500 in 1983. He estimates an average of 1,200 square feet in 1990. Others have predicted that the average new home in the year 2000 could easily be 1,000 to 1,200 square feet (White 1983). As mentioned, house size is often controlled by local zoning ordinances. Often these ordinances must be changed to allow the building of smaller houses. In a study released by the American Planning Association in 1982, 171 of the 451 communities that responded to the survey reported that they had revised zoning codes within the previous five years to increase allowable densities and to decrease minimum square footage in single-family house districts (Mosena 1984:11).

With higher land and construction costs in the West, it is not surprising that California is pioneering in smaller dwellings. San Francisco recently amended its zoning ordinance to allow "minicondos" of 300 square feet. In several outlying communities a British development firm, Barratt, has been building housing that includes a unit called the "studio solo" of 350 square feet costing $40,000 in Upland, near Los Angeles. Barratt advertises this as a "unique home for the individual, an attractive, efficient living space at an affordable price." The apartment is fully furnished but the unit is laid out in such a way that few alternative furniture arrangements are possible.

Boulder, Colorado, has revised its building code to allow and regulate the construction of apartments as small as 400 square feet, which have the unfortunate name of "limited living units." This dwelling type is popular with developers who are able to build two limited living units for every standard dwelling unit allowed by code. The apartments are often rented by University of Colorado students or bought by their parents who then have simultaneously provided for their children's housing and made an investment. In some cases, such as Canyon Crest, the floor plan of 450 square feet includes a separate bedroom but the plan is cumbersome and allows few alternative furniture arrangements. Other plans provide a loft as well as a bedroom but then each individual space is quite small, if not cramped, allowing little, if any, possibility for change.

In some cases, a house will be reduced in size but the symbolism of being detached will be retained. Donald MacDonald, developer and architect, claims his garden houses in San Francisco are detached because the units do not share a wall. Since this is not visible except to a very discerning eye, the meaning is questionable. The houses are nonetheless interesting. They are small—two-story 800-square-foot boxes (20 by 20) built in transitional neighborhoods, costing from $115,000 to $190,000. Two bedrooms and one bath are on the first floor and a large, high ceilinged living/dining and kitchen space constitutes the second floor. Garages and backyards are also provided. The building was treated as an "armature in which screens, decks or planters could be bolted. The owner could create his own exterior design at relatively little extra expense" (MacDonald 1984:22). In this example, the large open space on the second floor does provide a certain amount of flexibility.

As dwelling spaces become smaller, good design of the spaces *and* the furniture becomes more important. Building industry publications such as *Builder* magazine give design guidelines for "downsizing" (Updegrave 1984). Suggestions include: cathedral ceilings, nooks, fewer walls, and enclosed patios. They do not, however, analyze the best dimensions of a space for alternative furniture arrangements or for alternative uses. Nor do they suggest flexibility in the assigned functions of different spaces or of different pieces of furniture. Moreover, it is not apparent that developers building units at 350 or 450 square feet are taking the suggestions to heart. These developers seem simply to be reducing the size of the traditional set of spaces and eliminating some pieces of furniture, which is essentially miniaturizing. There is no analysis of the space's configuration and its functions and, correspondingly, no flexibility is designed into either.

Michael Mostoller (1984) has pursued these very tasks in his design analysis of the optimum dimensions and furniture requirements of a room in a SRO hotel where almost all living functions, other than cooking and bathing, take place in a single room usually not more than 120 square feet and often 100 square feet or less. After studying a variety of possible shapes and dimensions, Mostoller proposes the long room (8 by 16 feet) as having the best zoning (back, middle, and front spaces), the best rotational possibilities for furniture, and the greatest variety of possible furniture arrangements. He concludes that the long dimension "organizes furniture into coherent functional and visual entities" and increases the sense of scale. Each of six pieces of furniture is analyzed and eventually designed in terms of the range of purposes it can fulfill.

Simply reducing the size of a particular type of space without analyzing how the original size supported particular functions that may be jeopardized by the reduction in size is also a problem in the design of outdoor residential space as described by Wekerle and Simon in Chapter 11 in this volume. By simply miniaturizing the dwelling, inside or outside, without providing possibilities for later expansion, developers are also assuming that the functions of the now smaller spaces and the total size of the unit will remain fixed. If the inhabitant's needs or resources change, he or she is expected to move, not to modify in any significant way the dwelling itself.

The theme of separateness and self-sufficiency is also maintained in the miniaturization process: the apartments may be 450 square feet in Canyon Crest in Boulder but the only facilities shared are a laundry room and a hot tub. There ostensibly could be a large kitchen/living area for entertaining, a rentable guest room, or other facilities, but there are not. Each household and each dwelling unit has its own bathroom, kitchen, and living space even if, as is often the case in small units, it is occupied by only one person.

SPACES THAT CHANGE

The characteristic of the ideal American house that appears to be least desirable for all concerned is the relative permanence of the configuration of rooms and of the functions of those rooms. Even in those cases where expansion was explicitly intended, as in Levittown, New York, the functions of the original rooms were expected to remain the same. In 1949 at least expansion of the dwelling was intended and planned, whereas today there seems to be less recognition among developers of residents' need to expand or contract the dwelling. Indeed, tract housing is often designed for a particular group of households defined by their stage in the family life cycle—first-time home buyers, those with growing families, and "empty nesters." Now the assumption is that as household size changes, households will move. This assumption and the inability to expand the dwelling are particularly strong in the design of high-density, attached housing, although even in those cases expansion or contraction of units would be possible. Some exceptions to this assumption are described below.

Although the building of accessory or secondary dwelling units within an existing single-family house was not intended in the original design of the house, the phenomenon is widespread enough in the United States to merit discussion as a "space that changes." Philip Hare (1981) estimates that there are 2.5 million such units nationwide, most of them being illegal under local zoning ordinances that restrict dwellings to single-family houses only. In recognition of the need for more housing, for smaller units, for housing for elderly relatives of home-owners, for lower cost housing, and for income to home owners, many municipalities have adopted ordinances to legalize and to control accessory apartments.

The accessory apartment ordinances adopted make some important restrictions. Often the second unit must be subordinate to the main unit, which is achieved by limiting its size. Often the unit must be completely within the existing structure and must not change the external appearance. Sometimes occupancy requirements are set up: that the tenant be a relative of the owner or that the tenant be elderly. To prevent builders from constructing homes intended for later conversion, conversions are sometimes restricted to houses of a certain age or more (Hare 1981). These restrictions demonstrate that municipalities often wish to maintain the social and physical character of single-family neighborhoods and that, while accessory apartments will be *tolerated*, they are not to cause any significant changes in the community. Moreover, the intended growth of a *new* home through eventual conversion is discouraged, if not prohibited. Yet it is this very planned expansion/contraction of dwellings that seems important for a household's adaptation to changing circumstances.

One invention that recognizes this need, specifically for an accessory unit that can easily be installed and removed, is the elder cottage. First invented in Australia, an American elder cottage has been developed in Lancaster, Pennsylvania, by builder Ed Guion. It is a small manufactured house of 288 or 524 square feet that can be placed on the lot of an existing single-family house and hooked up to the utilities and sewage system of that house. It contains kitchen, bath, living room, and one or two bedrooms. Intended originally for an elderly relative of the occupants of the house whose lot it shares, the cottage can easily be removed when that relative finds other accommodations or dies.

Architect Donald MacDonald has also recognized the need for expansion and contraction of the dwelling and is planning condominium dwellings that will consist of two units, which can be consolidated into one dwelling when the household is large and returned to two when the household contracts. Architect Edmund Berger has developed the "grow home" in San Pablo outside San Francisco (Anton 1983). The basic unit is 700 square feet on one level, consisting of living room, kitchen, one bedroom, one bath, a laundry room, and a two-car garage, selling for $59,950. This unit can be expanded by adding a second floor or by adding rooms to the back of the unit. The intention is to make the expansion as easy as possible. Contraction, however, in the form of converting rooms to a separate apartment, has not been considered.

A final example of a house whose interior can easily be changed is Ted Smith's Blendo project in San Diego. The living/dining space and the kitchen of this single-family house are separated by a set of ceiling-high pieces of furniture— two cupboards with shelving on both sides and several lattice screens. These are essentially movable walls so that the spatial configuration of the common spaces can easily be modified, allowing for a large country kitchen, a smaller kitchen, or one spacious living/cooking and dining space. Upstairs is one fixed bedroom and a large open space with its own bath. This space can be two bedrooms and storage, two smaller bedrooms and a play space, or one large bedroom. It could also be a loft space, large and open, possibly for an artist's studio.

These examples of dwellings intended to grow or change seem limited in number and imagination. Examples in Europe are more numerous and more experimental. Several of these examples follow the theoretical work and design principles developed by John Habraken and his colleagues at the Stichting Architecten Research (SAR) at the Technical University of Eindhoven in Holland (Habraken 1972; Carp 1984; van der Werf, 1984; Maurios 1984). Central to these projects is Habraken's belief that is should be possible for residents to design and alter their dwellings independently of each other. The projects built allow for a great variety of room configurations and functions, which the residents themselves choose, and allow future alterations in the dwellings including expansion in some cases. Both the possibility for variety and the opportunity for tenants to design and alter their own units are principles espoused by John Turner (1976), whose speciality is self-help housing. Apparently in the United States the characteristics of the ideal house and other barriers to innovation prevent the realization of these principles and seriously inhibit the possibilities inherent in the idea of a "space that changes."

CONCLUSIONS

The central characteristics of the ideal American house reflect social values that esteem the nuclear family as the ideal household, the spatial and social separation between households, and the spatial segregation of residential from work or commercial activities (Hayden 1984; Franck 1985a). Much of the housing that presently exists in the United States possesses many of the characteristics of the ideal house, and zoning regulations, building codes, and mortgage financing practices help ensure that new housing will continue to have them. The social values underlying the ideal also guide the decisions designers and housing developers make about appropriate design, even when legal or financial constraints are not an issue. This complex and intertwined array of social, legal, and design factors presents formidable barriers to social and physical innovations in housing.

Small living spaces and living spaces that can easily be changed in size or configuration are innovations that do not threaten the two leading characteristics of the ideal house—spatial privacy and self-sufficiency of the dwelling and its habitation by a single household of related persons. They are contrary to the ideal characteristics of spaciousness and fixed functions of spaces. Moreover, a full realization of the potential for variety and change in spaces and functions requires that people have a notion of the alternative arrangements they might like. Often users do not have such ideas and, in fact, prefer conventional arrangements. This has been true in some of the housing experiments stimulated by Habraken's principles (Maurios 1984). It is possible, however, that people's preferences for conventional arrangements are determined in part by their lack of exposure to alternatives. Once more alternatives are available and experienced, preferences could change. Developers and bankers are unwilling to build alternatives for fear they will not sell, or in the case of single-home mortgages, will not be resold. The position of housing as a commodity with great importance placed on its market value becomes yet another barrier to innovation.

Zoning ordinances present additional obstacles to building small spaces and spaces that change. While municipalities are gradually amending ordinances to allow smaller dwellings (Mosena 1984), it is not certain how far they are willing to go, particularly in communities that exclude multifamily housing altogether. Often the implicit reasoning behind restrictions on house size is that smaller houses will reduce the market value of existing homes; the commodity aspects of housing again present a barrier to innovation.

Zoning ordinances are an outstanding hindrance to accessory apartments and thereby to Guion's elder cottages and other types of single-family homes that can be converted easily to two-family homes. Gellen (1985) points out that accessory apartments present two types of potential problems: those arising from increasing the population density and those arising from changing the type of occupant and the life-style in single-family neighborhoods. These two types of problems are confused in ordinances that exclude accessory apartments ostensibly to control density but implicitly to control type of occupant and life-style. While recent court rulings acknowledge the distinction between controlling density and controlling life-style, they have confirmed that life-style regulation can take precedence over density control. Gellen is nonetheless optimistic that accessory apartments will become increasingly acceptable in legal terms.

These same ordinances in single-family neighborhoods exclude the sharing of a house by more than a minimum number of unrelated adults in order to protect a conventional "family" life-style in the community. Even more powerful than the ordinance is the underlying social value—that the appropriate living arrangement for all types of households is a self-sufficient, spatially private dwelling inhabited by a single household of related persons and, if necessary, by a single person. Of all the characteristics of the ideal American house, this is perhaps the most deeply imbedded and has led to the ultimate privatization of the American landscape—one person living alone in a complete dwelling or even in a complete single-family house (Popenoe 1985; Franck 1985a). A tradition of collective living has helped generate the new communal public housing in Sweden described by Woodward in Chapter 13 in this volume. The absence of this or any comparable tradition in the United States makes the development of various forms of sharing difficult except when the economic incentives are great enough, as in the mingles house or quad housing, or when the need for shelter is severe enough, as in the recent renovation of SROs. Possible social benefits of sharing are not widely recognized in the United States, even though they might be considerable as in SROs with comprehensive management and support services. As Edwards et al. (1987) suggest, house sharing is still seen as a social problem, not a social solution.

Even when the social benefits of sharing are recognized, building codes can present yet another obstacle. In many American cities building codes consider the small size of SRO rooms and the absence of private baths and kitchens to be characteristics of substandard housing. Consequently, the city of Portland, Oregon, had great difficulty persuading the U.S. Department of Housing and Urban Development that Section 8 moderate rehabilitation funds should be used to finance the renovation of SRO hotels. In order to do so and to initiate an SRO demonstration program, Portland amended its building code to include requirements that renovated SRO housing must meet. These include a minimum size for rooms (100 square feet), cooking facilities, and one bathroom for every 12 rooms. The Settlement Housing Fund in New York City has been working for several years to introduce standards for a new type of housing unit into the city's building code. Called the "mini-dwelling unit," these rooms would contain a pullman kitchen and would share community spaces and bathroom facilities for every four rooms (Fox 1985). In the absence of such standards, the subsidizing of the renovations of SRO hotels in New York City has been very difficult (Baxter 1984).

Other forms of shared housing can also be encouraged or discouraged by building codes. In some municipalities, such as Brookline, Massachusetts, the definition and requirements for a "lodging house" are very useful for the renovation of a single-family house to be shared by several people, whereas in Philadelphia the absence of any comparable building type in the city's code forces the design of shared housing to conform to the fire code requirements for apartment houses, which can be costly and make the house appear unduly institutional. Shared living arrangements may also be prevented or discouraged by other types of laws, such as state laws that prohibit a man and a woman who are not married from occupying the same dwelling.

The variety of household types in the United States and the economic necessity for developing housing alternatives are increasing, yet the image of the ideal house remains unchanged and zoning ordinances and building codes continue to enforce that ideal. The innovations described here and those outlined in other recent publications (National Trust for Historic Preservation 1981: Lawton and Hoover 1981; Streib et al. 1984; Hayden 1984; Birch 1985; Gellen 1985; Sprague 1986) indicate that alternatives to the single-family house are being explored in the United States. Further exploration of alternatives through design and research is needed along with examination of the policy changes that are required to allow the implementation of those alternatives. While the image of the ideal house and its power probably cannot be changed simply through research or design exploration, more frequent demonstration of alternatives may begin to modify that image. It is certainly worth trying.

NOTE

The research described in this chapter was supported by a grant from the National Science Foundation (CEE-830721-B). I am grateful to Maria D'Isasi, Christine Balint, and Stephanie Kidd, my research assistants, for their contributions to this project. Further information about the research is available from the author.

REFERENCES

Anton, Frank
1983   "Homes Buyers Can Afford and Expand." *Builder* March, 66–68.
Baxter, Ellen
1984   *Interim Progress Report: The Development of a Community Based Housing Model for Homeless Single Adults*. Report to the Ittleson Foundation, New York.
Birch, Eugenie Ladner (ed.)
1985   *The Unsheltered Woman*. New Brunswick, NJ: Center for Urban Policy Research.
Carp, John
1984   "Twenty Years of SAR." In *The Scope of Social Architecture*, edited by C. Richard Hatch, 22–27. New York: Van Nostrand Reinhold.
Collins, Alf
1985   "Artists Coop." *Arts and Architecture* Winter, 56–69.
Edwards, Patricia, John M. Edwards, and Judith A. Jones
1987   "Shared Housing as a Policy Alternative." In *Housing Markets and Policies Under Conditions of Fiscal Austerity*, edited by Willem Van Vliet—. Westport, Conn.: Greenwood Press.
Fox, Clara
1985   "Shared Housing." In *The Unsheltered Woman*, edited by Eugenie L. Birch. New Brunswick, NJ: Center for Urban Policy Research.
Franck, Karen A.
1985a   "Together or Apart: Sharing and the American Household." Paper presented at the Annual Meeting of the Association of Collegiate Schools of Architecture, Vancouver, March.

1985b "Social Construction of the Physical Environment: The Case of Gender." *Sociological Focus* 18, 143–60.

Gellen, Martin

1985 *Accessory Apartments in Single Family Housing*. New Brunswick, NJ: Center for Urban Policy Research.

Habraken, N. J.

1972 *Supports: An Alternative to Mass Housing*. New York: Praeger.

Hare, Patrick H.

1981 *Accessory Apartments: Using Surplus Space in Single Family Houses*. Chicago: American Planning Association.

Hayden, Dolores

1984 *Redesigning the American Dream*. New York: W. W. Norton.

Hopper, Kim, and Jill Hamberg

1984 *The Making of America's Homeless*. New York: Community Service Society.

Irwin, Robert

1984 *Mingles: A Home Buying Guide for Unmarried Couples*. New York: McGraw Hill.

Jackson, Kenneth T.

1985 *Crabgrass Frontier*. New York: Oxford University Press.

Kobrin, Frances E.

1978 "The Fall in Household Size and the Rise of the Primary Individual in the U.S." In *The American Family in Social-Historical Perspective*, edited by M. Gordon, 69–81. New York: St. Martin's Press.

Lawton, M. Powell, and Sally Hoover (eds.)

1981 *Community Choices for Older Americans*. New York: Springer.

MacDonald, Donald

1984 "Affordable Housing." *San Francisco Bay Architects' Review* Spring, 21–23.

Maurios, Georges

1984 "The Limits of Flexibility." In *The Scope of Social Architecture*, edited by C. Richard Hatch, 64–75. New York: Van Nostrand Reinhold.

Model, John, and Tamara K. Hareven

1978 "Urbanization and the Malleable Household." In *The American Family in Social-Historical Perspective*, edited by M. Gordon, 51–67. New York: St. Martin's Press.

Mosena, David R.

1984 "Downsizing Gracefully." *Planning* January, 9–13.

Mostoller, Michael

1984 *Preliminary Designs for Rooms and Furniture*. Report for Design Development Grant, National Endowment for the Arts. Newark, NJ: New Jersey Institute of Technology.

1985 "A Single Room." In *The Unsheltered Woman*, edited by Eugenie Ladner Birch, 191–216. New Brunswick, NJ: Center for Urban Policy Research.

National Trust for Historic Preservation

1981 *Rehabilitating Residential Hotels*. Washington, DC: National Trust for Historic Preservation.

Popenoe, David

1985 *Private Pleasure, Public Flight*. New Brunswick, NJ: Transaction.

Sprague, Joan
1986   *A Manual on Transitional Housing*. Boston: Women's Institute for Housing and
       Economic Development.
Streib, Gordon, F. Folts, Edward and Mary Anne Hilker
1984   *Old Homes—New Families*. New York: Columbia University Press.
Turner, John F. C.
1976   *Housing by People*. New York: Pantheon.
Updegrave, Walter L.
1984   "Goodbye to the Detached House?" *Builder* January, 198–202.
U.S. Bureau of the Census
1973   *Characteristics of the Population: U.S. Summary*, Vol. 1, Part 1. Washington,
       DC: U.S. Department of Commerce.
1983   *Characteristics of the Population: General Social and Economic Characteristics*.
       Vol. 1, Chapter C. Washington, DC: U.S. Department of Commerce.
1985   *Current Population Reports, Series P–20, #388: Household and Family Char-
       acteristics March 1984*. Washington, DC: U.S. Department of Commerce.
van der Werf, Frans
1984   "A Vital Balance." In *The Scope of Social Architecture*, edited by C. Richard
       Hatch, 28–37. New York: Van Nostrand Reinhold.
White, Betty Jo
1983   "The Future of the American Housing Dream." *Journal of Home Economics*
       Summer, 21–28.

11

Planning with Scarce Resources: The Miniaturization of an Urban Neighborhood

JOAN C. SIMON AND GERDA R. WEKERLE

Abstract. Toronto planners rejected the planning principles used in the 1950s and 1960s to create medium-density urban housing projects because they believed that these developments did not meet the needs of the inhabitants. This chapter examines the urban design approach used in Toronto in an 850-unit new urban neighborhood. The planners' intentions are compared to the reactions of people living in the new project. The planners undertook no systematic research to ascertain the characteristics of the future residents, nor was social research used to establish a knowledge base for design decisions.

INTRODUCTION

During the 1970s in Toronto, Canada, as in many developed societies, concern about the quality of life in the city resulted in a renewed focus upon the viability and habitability of the individual building blocks—the urban neighborhoods. Residents, government policy makers, social scientists, architects, and planners turned their attention to conserving and rehabilitating existing residential areas and to creating new neighborhoods within the city that were distinct in form and character from suburban areas. This chapter deals with the development of a 850-unit enclave in Toronto known as Frankel/Lambert. The aims and aspirations of the planners are compared to the reactions of the people who moved into this planned community (Simon and Wekerle 1985).

BACKGROUND

Although Canadian cities never lost their viability as residential areas, by the late 1960s government officials, as well as citizen groups, were becoming disturbed by the changes they saw occurring in municipal land use patterns due to the continuing high rates of urbanization. The substantial resources flowing into housing, especially for low-income groups, urban renewal, and highway construction were often seen as contributing to the social and environmental stresses in established neighborhoods. The number of neighborhood-based citizen groups speaking out about local planning issues multiplied and in Toronto these organizations found that they were in sharp conflict with the municipal politicians and planners. Residents began to campaign against the construction of high-rise buildings and urban expressways and to demand that their views be incorporated into the city's plan for their neighborhoods. These citizen groups were instrumental in the 1972 election of a "reform" City Council in Toronto.

The newly elected mayor and his reform caucus created a municipal housing policy that had dual aims: to preserve the existing neighborhoods and to encourage the development of new housing for low- and moderate-income families (City of Toronto Housing Working Group 1973). Toronto officials decided to make extensive use of the Canadian federal government housing programs in order to assume a leading role in producing housing and in transforming underused industrial lands into residential areas.

Although the issue had economic and social dimensions, questions concerning the physical form of the proposed city housing developments dominated discussions. The existing models of government-sponsored housing built during the 1950s and 1960s were denounced for creating ghettos of poverty in environments noted for their sterility. Local residents opposed high-rise apartment buildings because they were out of scale with their houses, caused traffic congestion, and increased parking problems (Simon 1982). The new teams of municipal planners agreed that high-rise buildings were undesirable, but their objections focused primarily on the development pattern of superblocks with tower buildings sited well back from the traditional street building line (compare Chapter 12 of this volume). This type of urban design was seen as disrupting the urban "fabric" and as having a negative impact upon "street life." The nineteenth- and early twentieth-century development pattern of two- and three-story houses built on narrow lots along a gridiron street pattern was acclaimed as a physical design that had produced socially healthy communities (Zeidler Partnership 1975). In an attempt to replicate the social dynamics found in established neighborhoods, the municipal planners decided that new developments in Toronto should emulate this traditional physical pattern (City of Toronto Housing Department 1976).

In order to implement the municipal housing policy, two large projects were initiated in which the city acted as a developer. The major undertaking, commencing in 1974, was the creation of the 3,542-unit St. Lawrence Neighborhood on 22.22 hectares of unused industrial land almost immediately adjacent to the downtown commercial core. Two years later, the city was able to purchase a 9.27-hectare industrial site, which was also for redevelopment into a residential area. This second new neighborhood of 850 units, called Frankel/Lambert, is six kilometers from the city center.

The development strategy was to have the newly created city housing department assume overall responsibility for the coordination of the projects. Financing for land assembly and site improvements primarily came from Canada Mortgage and Housing Corporation, the federal government crown agency responsible for housing policy and programs. The city established the site planning guidelines and the development control instruments. Within this overall framework, parcels were developed by a variety of builders acting on behalf of special user groups, including the elderly, ethnic groups, and women. Maximum use was made of the federal nonprofit, cooperative, and assisted home ownership programs to create a stock of new moderate-cost housing (Simon and Wekerle 1986).

PLANNING ISSUES

Toronto's housing department staff were determined to create "neighborhoods," not "projects"(Worland 1983). However, the particular characteristics of the site required that a number of factors had to be juggled in the transition from policy statement to actual development. The site is bounded by arterial roads, industry, and a railroad line heavily used by freight trains. It was considered desirable to attempt to integrate the new development with a small enclave of existing housing on "traditional streets." The City Council was just as committed to preserving existing neighborhoods as it was to creating new ones.

Because planners adopted two mutually contradictory goals—re-creating the form of the traditional Toronto neighborhood of ground-related dwellings and, at the same time, achieving relatively high densities to produce housing that low- and moderate-income families could afford—the outdoor spatial elements were miniaturized (Simon and Wekerle 1985, 5).

The planners saw the traditional street design as having three critical elements: low scale, small buildings, and ground-related dwellings. They placed a very high priority on creating lively streets. The planners' concept of the linkage between physical form and social characteristics of the neighborhood is set out in the planning documents:

To achieve the successful physical and social character of existing Toronto neighborhoods through the creation of a variety of building types and designs within a basic street pattern, the new neighborhood should be as low as possible in scale and individual buildings should be kept small, encouraging a sense of community. Housing should be grade related, where possible, to support an active street life (Littlewood 1977, 8).

Land costs coupled with affordability issues resulted in the economic requirement to build at a density approximately twice that of the traditional housing on the adjacent streets.

Constraints imposed by the planners on all three dimensions of the potential development envelope—height, width, and depth—resulted in rooms built to minimum dimensions and the virtual disappearance of front- and backyards. In addition, open space uses also came under severe pressure because of the need to accommodate the automobile. Parking was a major open-space use in 1980 Toronto neighborhoods. Not only was it too expensive to locate parking underground or even to deck over the cars, ground-level parking was preferred by the planners. Parking was prohibited in front of the units. As a consequence, more ground-level space was devoted to lanes accessing the rear parking areas. Street and sidewalk dimensions are also slightly narrower than current municipal engineering standards. Little communal or public open space was provided to compensate for loss of private gardens.

The imposed design determinants created a new 1970s project vernacular, which, in its own way, is as distinctive as that of the 1960s or 1920s. Small developers generated a limited range of design solutions, but the fixed parameters discouraged the variety of expression that might have been expected. The characteristics of the new vernacular are low-rise buildings composed of narrow-fronted dwelling units; dense coverage of the site; very small areas of private and public open space; streets lined with buildings; streets organized on a grid pattern to create small blocks; pedestrian movement systems paralleling traffic routes. What distinguishes the 1980s development pattern from the 1880s is the miniaturization of the urban spaces. Some postmodern urban designers have argued that the miniaturized elements retain their symbolic attributes and that these are more important to consumers than functional factors. The research described here was undertaken to ascertain how the users responded to the reduced space standards.

RESEARCH BACKGROUND

A variety of research methods was used to gain an understanding of the evolution of the development strategy and design decisions and to investigate the residents' reactions to living with the physical outcomes of those decisions.

Officials' and consultants' priorities in planning Frankel/Lambert were studied by reviewing planning documents, minutes of meetings, newspaper clippings, and by interviews with the significant actors, including planners, city councillors, and representatives of the established adjacent neighborhood.

Because of the construction schedule, the 1981 census provided information only about the inhabitants of the first 53 percent of the family housing units. These data were supplemented by replies from a mail survey of all the family housing units conducted by the City of Toronto Housing Department in July 1983. Only 220 (38 percent) of the households responded; therefore, the information on the demographic characteristics is fragmentary.

Residents' satisfaction with living in Frankel/Lambert was determined using a procedure known as the "trade-off game." A gaming technique was employed because of its ability to simulate problem solving in a real-life situation (Sanoff 1979). The game consisted of 30 cards representing factors that planners, architects, and landscape architects had juggled in designing Frankel/Lambert. Factors ranged from housing costs to children's play spaces and public transportation availability. Residents began by arranging the cards in order of importance to them as residents living in the community. Then they noted each factor according to their experiences of living in Frankel/Lambert. The five-point rating scale was printed on each card. Residents were then asked which factors they would like to improve. In order to improve the quality of one factor, they had to "trade-off" a quality in another factor. For example, to improve soundproofing between units by three points, three points had to be taken from other factors. Most studies of residential satisfaction focus solely on rating of attributes and ignore the compromises that occur during the development process in order to realize the project. Meetings were held with volunteer subjects from each building project to explore reactions to living in the neighborhood.

Outdoor activities in gardens, parks, sidewalks, and parking areas were systematically mapped during two time periods, one in the summer and the other in the winter.

WHO ARE THE RESIDENTS OF FRANKEL/LAMBERT?

The development strategy was to create a housing stock that would attract residents to Frankel/Lambert whose demographic characteristics closely resembled those of the population living in the adjacent established neighborhood.

Excluding the senior citizens' project, the new housing drew a predominantly young adult population and, although there are fewer households with children, there is a high percentage of single-parent families. The median income was above the city average, but 25 percent earned less than the median city income. This is roughly equivalent to the population of the units that are given a rent supplement to make them affordable to low-income tenants.

The 1981 census revealed major demographic shifts in the population of the City of Toronto during the period 1971–81 that have implications for housing and community services. Demographic changes include a changing age structure due to the decline of the school-age population and an increase in the number of seniors; smaller size households with single persons the fastest growing household form; a greater diversity of household types with the growth of nonfamily and lone-parent families. Similar trends that affect the consumption of housing are reported in the United States by Franck in Chapter 10 in this volume.

There are fewer children, a lower level of home ownership, and more families for whom English is their first language than in the traditional neighborhood. The actual social mix of Frankel/Lambert goes beyond the range of stages of life cycle, life-styles, ethnic cultures, and socioeconomic characteristics anticipated during the planning process. Therefore, facilities would have to respond both to the range of specialized needs while, at the same time, creating a common focus. Opportunities for interaction that would cross group boundaries were not provided.

THE MINIATURIZED URBAN NEIGHBORHOOD

Frankel/Lambert retains traces of elements found in neighborhoods built before World War II. However, the residents perceive that they are living in a new type of urban neighborhood. This distinctively new urban form elicits behavioral responses and habitability problems unforeseen by the planners.

Previous postoccupancy evaluations of residential environments have often noted that professionals involved in development value different aspects of the environment than do the eventual residents (Cooper 1975; Darke 1984a). We asked nine architects and planners involved in this planning and design process to rank the same set of variables, using the same ''trade-off'' instrument we had presented to residents. They were told to try to recall the priority of these factors in their own decision making during the site planning process.

The only variable on which both residents and professionals totally agreed was that housing costs were the most important factor. Table 11.1 compares the 10 neighborhood characteristics deemed most important by residents and architects/planners.

Residents identified as the following important factors that could be called core planning issues ignored by the planners: safety, public transportation, access to shopping, and traffic safety aspects of the larger community environment.

The planners' concern for creating affordable housing linked with other self-imposed design constraints made the provision of their second priority, personal outdoor living space, problematic. One of the major program requirements for the individual projects was that housing should appear to conform to traditional house forms. This was interpreted as being as similar as possible to the single-family house with a frontyard, porch, door on the street, and backyard even though most of the units were, in fact, stacked townhouses.

FRONTYARDS

The planners' design concept for personal outdoor living space in front of the dwelling was predicated on the desirability of encouraging traditional social relationships that are facilitated by access to the dwellings and maintenance of frontyards. However, the site of the actual frontyards and porches limits the potential for street-related activities to develop at Frankel/Lambert.

Jan Gehl, a Danish architect/planner who studied street activity in many cities around the world, including Waterloo and Toronto, found that ''lively residential streets are those where the people meet and easily enjoy leisure and chores outdoors. To a large extent, this may depend on the design of the interface between public street and private house'' (Gehl 1980, 52).

Gehl distinguishes between three basic types of activities that take place in the residential street space. Necessary pedestrian activities, such as walking to work, school, and shops occur year round, regardless of the climatic conditions or the quality of the physical and social environment. Freedom-of-choice activities (strolling, sitting, talking, playing) are influenced by the individual's desire to participate. Therefore, the convenience, comfort, interest, and safety provided by streetscape design are critical to the promotion of these activities. The third type, maintenance activities—washing the car, shoveling snow, tending to the

Table 11.1
Frankel/Lambert Residents' and Architect/Planners' Development Factor Priorities

Residents N = 32	Architects /Planners N = 9
1. Housing Costs	1. Housing Costs
2. Safe neighborhood	2. Personal Outdoor Living Space Attached to your unit
3. Space in the Dwelling	3. Personal Parking
4. Personal Ourdoor Living Space Attached to your Unit	4. Children's Playspace Associated with your building
5. TTC Service	5. * Access to School * Protection from Outside Noises
6. Soundproofing Between Units	6. Neighbourliness
7. Access to Shopping	7. Space in the Dwelling
8. Protection from Outside Noises	8. * Access to Workplace
9. Traffic Safety	9. * Number of People in the neighborhood
10. Neighbourliness	10. Outdoor Space in the Whole neighborhood

*Like numbers indicate equal rank.
Source: Simon/Wekerle Tradeoff Game

garden, or sweeping the porch—are very important in generating social interaction because they provide a reason for being outside, increasing the opportunity
for casual conversation (Gehl 1980).

Observation studies showed that the major use of the new Frankel/Lambert
street space was for necessary activities, particularly by children going to and
from school and by adults going to and from work.

There is a dramatic difference in opportunities for "staying," "playing," and
"doing" provided by the existing streets and by the new streetscape. The design
constraints resulted in spaces in front of the dwellings that provide only very
limited opportunities for freedom-of-choice activities. A number of frontyards
are not larger than 1.5 meters by 2.7 meters.

Frontyards also act as a buffer between the street and the house, reducing
visual or aural intrusions. The abbreviated dimensions of the streetscape spaces
disturbed the subtle balance of transition from public sidewalk space to private
dwelling space. On the neighboring traditional streets people sitting on their
front porch are approximately six meters from the sidewalk. The semipublic
frontyard provides an insulating distance that corresponds to Edward T. Hall's
public distance. In his explanation of the distances North Americans use to make
different sorts of relationships comfortable, Hall (1969) says that 3.6 meters is
the minimum distance necessary to be "outside the circle of involvement." It
seems reasonable to assume that persons relaxing on their front porch do not
want to feel obligated to acknowledge every passerby. Residents' negative reaction is confirmed by their response to the statement, "The houses should be
further away from the street," in the City Housing Department survey: 55 percent
agreed that setbacks should be greater (21 percent disagreed). (See Figure 11.1.)

The miniaturization and, in some cases, elimination, of this buffer element
may explain the concern of some residents about public safety, even though the
police consider Frankel/Lambert to be a safe neighborhood (see Figure 11.2).
Newman (1981, 197–99) has demonstrated the importance of transitional spaces
defined by low fences, shrubs, and such, on controlling behavior of outsiders
and increasing safety.

Many neighboring frontyards are not separated by fencing. Worn grass and
tread-upon landscaping provide silent testimony of territorial encroachments.
Some residents have dealt with these intrusions by erecting minuscule fences
around their patch of front lawn; others do not even consider this area to be
private open space as evidenced by the many front lawns overgrown with weeds
and serving merely to store garbage.

Besides serving as a buffer between private and public open space and defining
territory, the frontyard serves an important status function. Cooper (1975, 11)
notes that "keeping up the front lawn, regarded as important in preserving the
property values, also is important in creating and maintaining status in the eyes
of one's neighbors, and in putting one's mark on an environment which is
otherwise monotonous and stereotyped."

At Frankel/Lambert, the upkeep or lack of upkeep of the front lawn becomes

Figure 11.1

The traditional neighborhood the planners hoped to replicate provides front-door areas that clearly define personal space and opportunities for personalization. Garden maintenance gives purpose to outdoor activities and facilitates informal neighborly contacts.

a source of conflict between different groups of residents. Many of the negative comments made by one group about another during the resident group meetings revolved around the lack of upkeep of the front lawns. Home owners in particular were critical of the lack of upkeep of the lawns by co-op and tenant groups. They complained that nonowners do not maintain their property and this depresses owners' property values.

For some home owners, the lack of upkeep of the front lawns was an indicator that the neighborhood was going downhill. This may also be indicative of the differences between individual and group maintenance of property and the lack of community standards for upkeep. The small scale of the front lawns may deter residents from doing much in the way of upkeep. Some residents were reluctant to invest time and energy in a minuscule frontyard; they could not justify the outlay of money for a hose, lawnmower, and fertilizer for a tiny square of sod. In the cooperatives the mechanism exists for communal ownership of these items, which may explain the more extensive planting of flowers in front of cooperative units than in front of rental units. The city-owned buildings were perceived to be the most poorly maintained and these tenants were less likely to have personalized their garden spaces with flowers, and so on.

PORCH AND FRONT DOOR

The design guidelines prepared by the city for Frankel/Lambert insisted that as many units as possible should be designed to have a front door opening directly toward the street, rather than into a courtyard or corridor. This requirement derived from the nostalgia for the traditional street combined with findings from a research project by the Metropolitan Toronto Social Planning Council that reported that most families with children living in apartment buildings would prefer to live in houses (Social Planning Council 1973).

In the small group meetings, respondents indicated their strong approval of buildings designed so that units have a front door facing the street. Seventy-five percent of participants supported this solution with comments such as "provides privacy" and "access for the disabled." However, reservations were shown in the following comments: "It provides privacy and convenience but at too high a cost" (in terms of compromising other planning factors), "Nice, but I'd be willing to trade it off" (for other amenities).

Many traditional Toronto houses have front porches that serve several functions: they provide protection from the rain and snow, places to sit out, a space to personalize, and possible play settings for small children. Most porches at Frankel/Lambert are very small or nonexistent. Protection is negligible and there is seldom room for a chair for sitting out. Observations recorded virtually no use of the front porch or entry space for sitting out activities.

BACKYARD

In their desire to provide residents with the traditional Toronto environment—a ground-level backyard, the site planners disallowed other solutions, except in the project constructed last, which has large second-floor decks over the parking. Observations revealed that these deck areas were the most extensively used private open spaces in the new community. This may be because they are larger than many of the ground-level backyards and their elevated position may be perceived as more private.

Residents identified only the space at the rear of their units as private open space. The provision of this personal outdoor living space ranked fourth in residents' design priorities (see Table 11.1). Yet residents' evaluation of Frankel/Lambert is mixed: almost one-third feel that their own personal outdoor living space is poor or below average; another third feel it is average; and about one-fifth evaluate it as either good or excellent.

In the small group meetings, participants were asked how they used their private open space. Half used the space for socializing or relaxing; less than one-third gardened; somewhat less than one-fifth used it for eating out. Others mentioned that backyards served as storage space or a place to keep their pet. Some people whose private open space was in front of their unit or conventional balcony complained that they had no outdoor space at all.

From observations at the site, we noted that the private outdoor open spaces provided only limited opportunities for residents to engage in those activities commonly associated with backyard space (see Figure 11.3). First, the space is just too small to accommodate a picnic table and chairs so that a small group of people can sit out and socialize; the spaces are too small to accommodate a swing set; they are too small to string a line to hang out washing. The small dimensions of the backyard also make it difficult to control visual and auditory contact. Residents whose yards abutted communal parking areas were particularly disturbed by pedestrians and by children playing in the parking areas. The clearest definition of territoriality was created by the high-level deck scheme. Also the deck clearly identifies the ground-level parking underneath as being for the exclusive use of the resident (see Figure 11.4).

PARKING

The traditional Toronto neighborhood was built before cars became a residential planning problem. In some older neighborhoods overnight resident parking on the street is allowed by special permit; in other areas parking is allowed on paved "frontyards." A few deep blocks do have garages accessed off rear lanes. At Frankel/Lambert major decisions affecting the form of housing followed from the requirement to provide parking attached to each development, which had to be accessed from a rear lane. This rear-lane parking solution proved to

Figure 11.2

Frankel/Lambert, built at twice the density of the adjacent established area, has resulted in miniaturized public and private open space. The entrances to the six units in this building lack territorial definition. Only the lower units have ''frontyard'' space, and this is below grade, receives little sunlight, and is seldom used.

Figure 11.3

The miniaturized backyards produce conflicts of use.

Figure 11.4

The elevated decks, which were opposed by the planners, provide the largest areas of personal open space on the site, which observation studies showed to be the most intensely used "backyards" in the new neighborhood. The clear identification of the parking space with the unit eliminates parking conflicts and provides an outdoor storage space for bulky possessions.

Figure 11.5

The requirement to have parking at the rear of the units resulted in back lanes dominated by parking and miniaturized backyards. Conflicts arise because assigned and paid-for parking spaces are used by others.

be costly in terms of land use, installation, and maintenance, and was inconvenient to use (see Figure 11.5).

During the planning process several assumptions were made about parking that have not been borne out in practice. With respect to parking requirements, the planners treated Frankel/Lambert as if it were an inner-city neighborhood on the assumption that car ownership would be lower than normal because the area was considered to be well served by public transit. Other assumptions were made about the relationship between tenure and automobile ownership. Only the home ownership units were allocated one parking spot per dwelling unit (which is the standard City of Toronto parking requirement); however co-op and nonprofit projects were permitted to reduce the number of required spaces by nearly 50 percent. The reduction was based on the assumption that these residents would have lower incomes than the home owners and, therefore, would be less likely to own cars.

However, 76 percent of the households at Frankel/Lambert own an automobile. This is in contrast to half the residents in the comparable core area St. Lawrence neighborhood who own an automobile. As a consequence, the off-street parking provision was not sufficient to accommodate the residents' cars. The shortfall in parking spaces has now been provided by allowing on-street permit parking— the "traditional" solution the planners had initially disallowed.

Dissatisfaction with parking remains high because of the inability to establish clear territorial rights to paid-for parking spaces. Also, access to many units is inconvenient from the off-street parking areas at the rear of the houses, because back patio doors cannot be unlocked from the outside. As a consequence, many residents have to walk around the block to enter their unit by the front door, even though their car is parked adjacent to their backyard.

PUBLIC OPEN SPACE

Although the planners placed children's play space associated with the building fourth on their priority list and outdoor space in the neighborhood tenth, these aspects were neglected in the actual development. Only three projects (all co-ops) provide play space for young children. Backyards are usually too small for children's play or active recreation by any age group, and the space traditionally provided on porches and in frontyards has been eliminated. Observations recorded few instances of play in the immediate vicinity of the front of the house.

Three new public open spaces were created: a school yard and two parks. The school yard is a barren patch of land defined by a chain link fence that keeps people out. One of the parks is so devoid of landscape features that residents do not even perceive it to be a park. The third space is well liked and heavily used but caters only to the needs of small children. The lack of places for teens to gather is a source of dissatisfaction and is seen as contributing to vandalism. There is no provision for the recreation needs of adults or senior citizens.

CONCLUSIONS

Frankel/Lambert accomplished many of its objectives: a new in-city housing area was built on a site where industrial activities had conflicted with the adjacent residential environment. the diversity of residents and their needs for locally based services went significantly beyond the planners' image of the types of families for whom they were building. This parallels the findings of Darke's (1984b) study of six London public housing projects that the architects of these projects had "generalized, imprecise and stereotyped" images of traditional nuclear families.

While avoiding the 1960s monolithic project appearance, the planning created a new 1970s project vernacular. The residents did not think that the housing resembled the older homes in the area and, indeed, did not believe that there was any reason that the new dwellings should resemble the old ones. This type of difference between architects' and tenants' perceptions of facade details was also noted by Cooper (1975) and Darke (1984a).

The new project vernacular squeezed the external spaces in the area to below federal government minimum standards. The city had obtained this reduction because it had successfully argued that the minimum standards had been written for suburban development. Yet, in fact, the older adjacent residential area con- formed to the standards. The new area, built at twice the density of the existing community, provides few communal amenities; however, the demographic pro- file of the user group indicates a diversity of spatial needs. The young, elderly, single-parent, and low-income residents have limited mobility and discretionary income; therefore, they are dependent upon the immediate environment resources.

One of the outcomes of the tight dimensioning of outdoor space is the pri- vatization of activities within the house. With a bare minimum of private outdoor space, limited communal space, and unattractive or overused public outdoor spaces, families must turn inward and try to meet most of their needs within the dwelling unit.

In trying to approximate a house-like environment and avoid institutional arrangements, elements that have been traditionally shared in medium-density housing were privatized. For example, the requirement that dwelling units have doors at grade meant that shared corridors were eliminated in favor of narrow, steep individual staircases to the upper-stacked units. In some small apartment buildings, the corridor works positively to provide a communal space for chil- dren's play and to facilitate contacts among residents. The tight interior dwelling spaces that resulted from cost limitations could create heavier demands on outdoor spaces, especially for children's play, than in the traditional residential neigh- borhoods, but the public and commercial spaces that might compensate for lack of private space are absent.

The emphasis on the privatization of functions within the individual dwelling unit is reminiscent of the planning philosophy apparent in suburban single-family neighborhoods where it is expected that each household will meet its basic needs for activities, such as recreation and socializing, within the framework of the private dwelling unit. When there are large lot sizes and generous internal spaces this may be possible. When privatization is combined with miniaturization, as at Frankel/Lambert, environmental stresses are created.

The density of development at Frankel/Lambert requires that the limited amount of open space be carefully designed. Faced with analogous space limitations, planners in The Netherlands, Sweden, West Germany, and Britain have adopted planning strategies that mix cars and pedestrians safely and attractively (Royal Dutch Touring Club 1980). Known as "woonerfs" on the continent and as "mixer courts" in Britain, they have proved popular as devices to better accommodate cars but to give people precedence over vehicular traffic in both new and older medium-density housing areas. One major British developer reports that houses on mixer courts are more attractive to home buyers than those on traditional streets (Marcus and Sarkissian 1986, 117).

In the design of the Frankel/Lambert neighborhood, the developer faced a basic conflict between building at the densities required to produce affordable housing and building a form of development that might be considered comparable to the housing forms found in the "traditional Toronto neighborhood." As both of these objectives are essentially irreconcilable, the Frankel/Lambert neighborhood ended up with a semblance of the traditional form but with front- and backyards miniaturized so that they no longer support the traditional social functions. Building at the densities needed to produce moderate-cost housing required a total rethinking of the site design. Alternative site layouts would have reduced the amount of space consumed by streets, and parking areas could have designed to eliminate the need for rear lanes. Nonfamily housing could have been allowed to exceed the four-story height limitations, freeing land for recreational activities.

In the development of the site plan, no sociologists or behavioral scientists were used to shed light on the needs and priorities of future residents. Moreover, none of the planning documents for Frankel/Lambert indicate any familiarity with the environmental behavior literature. Personal assumptions about resident characteristics and needs formed the basis for design decisions. Darke (1984b) found that British architects placed a similar reliance on their own personal experience when designing council housing, even though they had little direct knowledge of this tenant group. Relevant behavioral literature continues to be ignored when developing publicly funded housing developments.

REFERENCES

City of Toronto Housing Department
1976   *St. Lawrence Preliminary Site Plan*. City of Toronto.
City of Toronto Housing Working Group
1973   *Living Room: An Approach to Home Banking and Land Banking*. City of Toronto.

Cooper, Clare
1975   *Easter Hill Village*. New York: Macmillan.
Darke, J.
1984a "Requirements in Public-sector Housing: 1. Architects' Assumptions about the Users." *Environment and Planning B* 11, 389–404.
1984b "Architects and User Requirements in Public-sector Housing: 2. The Sources for Architects' Assumptions." *Environment and Planning B* 11, 405–16.
1984c "Architects and User Requirements in Public-sector Housing: 3. Towards an Adequate Understanding of User Requirements in Housing." *Environment and Planning B* 11, 417–33.
Gehl, Jan
1980   "The Residential Street Environment." *Built Environment* 6, 51–61.
Hall, Edward T.
1969   *The Hidden Dimension*. Garden City, NY: Doubleday.
Littlewood, Alan
1977   *Frankel/Lambert Status Report*. City of Toronto Housing Department.
Marcus, Clare Cooper, and Wendy Sarkissian
1986   *Housing As If People Mattered*. Berkeley: University of California Press.
Newman, Oscar
1981   *Community of Interest*. Garden City, NY: Anchor Press/Doubleday.
Royal Dutch Touring Club
1980   *Woonerf*. Trettagne: Ministerie van Veykeer en Waterstaat.
Sanoff, Henry
1979   *Design Games: Playing for Keeps with Personal and Environmental Decisions*. Los Altos, CA: Kaufmann.
Simon, Joan
1982   "Toronto: A Good Place to Live." *Urban Design International* 3, 430–3.
Simon, Joan, and Gerda Wekerle
1985   *Frankel/Lambert: Creating a New Toronto Neighborhood*. Ottawa: Canada Mortgage and Housing Corporation.
1986   "Development of the New Urban Neighborhood." *Plan Canada* 26, no. 2, 46–51.
Social Planning Council of Metropolitan Toronto
1973   *Families in High Flats*. Toronto: Social Planning Council.
Worland, Wilfred
1983   *Frankel/Lambert Report*. City of Toronto Housing Department.
Zeidler Partnership
1975   *St. Lawrence: Design Guidelines*. City of Toronto Planning Board.

12

High-Rise Estates and the Concentration of Poverty

EVA VAN KEMPEN

Abstract. High-rise estates occupy a prominent place among postwar housing disasters. In the Netherlands, the Bijlmermeer is representative of the high-rise problem. This chapter deals with the social downgrading process of the Bijlmermeer estate in Amsterdam. It is argued that this downgrading process does not occur autonomously or in isolation. External developments in the local and national setting, a persistent low appreciation in the Netherlands for high-rise living, and certain features inherent in high-rise design and high-rise living combined to produce a rapid process of social decay.

INTRODUCTION

In the Netherlands, high-rise neighborhoods have recently begun to attract public interest as vast problem areas. This interest might initially have been focused on the often poor technical construction of the buildings, but the deterioration of the social climate in the high-rise estates has since come to be viewed as much more of a menace. Vandalism, public nuisances, and the lack of social control have affected the living conditions in the estates. Vacancies, rent arrears, and a high turnover rate have undermined the financial position of the housing associations.

These negative developments in Dutch high-rise estates are not isolated cases. Among the spectacular public housing disasters in the United States and England, those at high-rise estates are notorious. The "Piggeries," a nickname for some near-derelict apartment buildings in Liverpool, were sold to a developer for next to nothing, and the Pruitt-Igoe project in St. Louis was blown up only 18 years after completion, an example that by now is not an exception any more (Dunleavy 1981; Ravetz 1985). The literature cites the excessively large concentration of problem families in badly designed and poorly maintained high-rise buildings as the cause of the deterioration (Bourne 1981; Rainwater 1966; Yancey 1971).

In the Netherlands, the Bijlmermeer in Amsterdam has come to be the prime example of the high-rise problems. As a place to live, Bijlmermeer has a very poor reputation indeed, and in the past few years the vacancy rate has constantly been above 20 percent. Until recently, partial demolition as a possible solution to the problem was taboo in the Netherlands, but it is coming to be a more and more widely discussed possibility. This chapter deals with the downgrading process in the Bijlmermeer and the factors impinging on this process. But first it is necessary to describe briefly the position of high-rise estates in the Dutch housing market.

HIGH-RISE ESTATES IN THE DUTCH HOUSING MARKET

Traditionally the Dutch are not very familiar with high-rise living. Before World War II, multifamily housing scarcely existed outside the big cities in the west of the Netherlands. "Real" high-rise buildings with six stories or more were constructed in Amsterdam and Rotterdam in the 1930s, but only as an experiment (Bock 1981; Dettingmeyer 1982). High-rise construction did not develop into a large-scale enterprise until the 1960s. More than 60 percent of the approximately 350,000 high-rise apartments (about 10 percent of the housing stock in the Netherlands) were built in a relatively short period between 1964 and 1974 (Rossum et al. 1981). Also, in England a high-rise housing boom took place in the same period (Cooney 1974; Dunleavy 1981).

From the outset the position of high-rise apartments in the housing market has been a marginal one. Even during the high-rise boom, people still did not want to live in apartment buildings, as housing satisfaction research has shown (Priemus 1984; *Waardering* 1970). This observation throws light on the downgrading process of high-rise housing estates, as does the influential concept of "filtering" in housing theory, based on the idea that new dwellings are to be preferred to older ones because they are up to current standards and are not worn out (due to a normal aging process). New construction would provoke a movement from older to newer dwellings, the new housing being reserved, because of its higher price, for the middle and higher income groups. The housing left vacant by these groups is for the lower income groups. Essentially the filtering concept is a normative concept that supposes that households improve their living conditions by way of the filtering process, regardless of the location, type, and price of new construction (Bourne 1981, 183). This view of market mechanisms influenced national and local policies in the 1960s. In Amsterdam, it even served to justify the plan when the proposed rent levels in Bijlmermeer became too high. However, the view did not correspond very well with the reality of a regulated housing market as found in the Netherlands. In at least three respects, high-rise housing deviates from the ideal sketched above:

1. The already existing and continuing low appreciation of high-rise living
2. The disturbed price-quality relation. The rent level of one-family houses, built at the same time and the same location, was often equal to or even lower than the rent level in high-rise apartment buildings

3. The disturbed competition with older dwellings as a consequence of the regulated housing market

These deviating aspects suggest that, from the outset, high-rise housing was very susceptible to deterioration and to changing conditions in the housing market. In this chapter, this statement will be substantiated by the history of the Bijlmermeer.

BIJLMERMEER

Bijlmermeer in Amsterdam is exceptional among the estates built at the time of the high-rise boom, not only because of its huge scale (more than 13,000 dwellings) and its high percentage of high-rise housing (90 percent), but also because of the experimental nature of the district. Architects and planners worked together to create "the city of the future." The principles on which this city of the future was based, however, were very academic. A rigorously applied seg-regation of functions and traffic types and the notion of the vertical garden city constituted the basis of the plan. The gross density is low—40 dwellings per hectare. In this sense, the Bijlmermeer project can be viewed as a direct heir to the ideas of the Congrès International d'Architects Modernes and Le Corbusier. In addition, the collectivity of urban living was to be expressed in the plan. Amenities such as communal rooms and indoor streets on the first floor along the full length of the buildings were to compensate for high-rise living and to stimulate social life (Du Laing 1973; McClintock 1971). Despite its honeycomb pattern of 10-story buildings, containing sometimes more than 500 dwellings each (see Figure 12.1), Bijlmermeer seemed very suitable for family living because about 60 percent of the apartments have three or more bedrooms. The management of these huge honeycombs was organized in a rather peculiar way. In accordance with common practice, the local government distributed the apart-ments among the existing housing associations in Amsterdam. The result was a scattered pattern of properties. In some cases, one building was managed by three different corporations.

THE HISTORY OF OCCUPANCY

In its simplest form, the life cycle of a neighborhood consists of three stages. In stage 1, the neighborhood is occupied and develops a distinct social character. In stage 2, the neighborhood stabilizes and gets a viable character. The turnover rate is low. In stage 3, mobility grows. As a consequence, the social composition of the population changes. A spiral development sets in, which ultimately leads to a concentration of the poor and to vacancy and abandonment.

The time it takes to pass through these three stages is different in each neigh-borhood. It is conceivable that some neighborhoods never reach stage 3 because of interventions or revaluation. Much, however, depends on the conditions of

Figure 12.1

The building "Grubbehoeve." Subway in foreground.

the local housing market and on the particular housing types. The turnover rate in apartments has been found to be much higher than in one-family houses. In Oudorperpolder, a housing estate in the town of Alkmaar built at the end of the 1960s and consisting of different housing types, the mean turnover rate in the high-rise buildings was nearly 23 percent as compared to a rate of only 1 percent in the adjacent row houses (Herber 1984). Other case studies, in the Netherlands as well as elsewhere, have obtained similar findings (Murie et al. 1976; Priemus 1984; Ravetz 1971). A high turnover rate is also accompanied by a social downgrading of the population (Guffens et al. 1969; Priemus 1984). Several questions now arise. Is it possible to observe the three stages in the high-rise estates? If so, what kinds of differences in the rate and nature of the downgrading process emerge?

Stage 1 in Bijlmermeer began with the welcome of the first tenant under extensive press coverage in November 1968, two years after the cornerstone was laid. In the following six years, about 13,000 high-rise apartments were completed in projects of 1,100 to 1,800 apartments each. Initially, it was not very hard to rent the apartments. There were few vacancies. However, the people for whom Bijlmermeer was designed, the residents of the "Western garden cities," were not interested. By the mid–1970s, only 17 percent of the new tenants had left a home elsewhere in Amsterdam. Because of its huge scale and massive character, the Bijlmermeer area already had a rather unattractive image in Amsterdam (Wielemaker-Dijkhuis and de Jonge 1972).

Paradoxically, the high occupancy rate in the first years was partly due to the high rents. Because of its high rent level, Bijlmermeer was not incorporated into the regular housing distribution system. As a result, the housing associations could allocate the apartments themselves and determine their own rules for assessing the housing needs of applicants. A new demand was revealed: households that did not conform to the allocation criteria of the local authorities and had had little chance of finding a decent home before, in spite of reasonable incomes.

There were no great differences in income and social position between the first residents of Bijlmermeer and the residents of other postwar neighborhoods in Amsterdam (Bureau van Statistiek 1971; Ferf-van den Brueke and Melger 1974). In other respects, the differences were significant. Singles (about 40 percent of the population in 1970), recently married couples, couples living together, and foreigners (including Surinamese residents, a rapidly growing immigrant group from the Caribbean), were concentrated in the Bijlmermeer. Household density was relatively low (2.2 versus 2.9 in Amsterdam and a planned rate of 3.4).

The bulk of the construction work had not been completed by 1970. Local government wondered how large and how permanent this new demand would be (Gemeentelijke 1970). There was indeed some reason for concern. The Bijlmermeer was not well integrated in the Amsterdam housing market. In- and out-migration was relatively high (see Figure 12.3). The local authorities had little say in the allocation of the apartments in Bijlmermeer. When the housing associations had to cope with relatively high vacancy rates in 1973, the smaller ones were faced with financial problems and relaxed their application criteria. As a result, the proportion of the young, singles, and Surinamese immigrants in the Bijlmermeer steadily increased (Figure 12.2). In 1974, more than 33 percent of the Bijlmermeer population were in their twenties as compared to 16 percent in 1968. The figures for Amsterdam as a whole were 19 percent and 16 percent, respectively.

A second consequence of the less stringent criteria was a growing differentiation among the buildings, noticeable in the composition of the population and in the incidence of social problems.

One building in particular, Gliphoeve I, has been singled out in this report as an illustration of the differentiation process. To a considerable extent, the history of this building has determined the image that outsiders hold of the Bijlmermeer. Moreover, the occupancy history of another building included in our study, Gliphoeve II, was greatly influenced by the living conditions in Gliphoeve I. Gliphoeve II was one functional unit with Gliphoeve I; they share a parking lot and entrance.

Gliphoeve I was managed by a small association with a weak financial position and very little know-how. The building was completed at the time when vacancies in Bijlmermeer were increasing. Confronted with a high vacancy rate, the housing association relaxed its allocation criteria. On grounds of nondiscrimination, the Surinamese immigrants, most of whom had been living in crowded hostels in the inner city, were accepted as tenants without the usual restrictions. Within a few years, Gliphoeve I turned into a ghetto: in 1975, 90 percent of the tenants were of Surinamese origin (Biervliet 1976). As a consequence, the vacancy rate increased in Gliphoeve II, which was managed by another association with a stricter allocation policy. In June 1974, Surinamese tenants from Gliphoeve I squatted 100 vacant apartments in Gliphoeve II. This set off a white exodus, although Gliphoeve II never became overwhelmingly black. Because of overcrowding, vandalism, and drug abuse, living conditions deteriorated (Diepen and de Bruyn-Muller 1976).

The management policy and the time of appearance on the housing market played an important part in the social differentiation among the buildings. Without the ongoing large-scale completion of housing, the differentiation process would presumably not have had the same impact. Internal migration in the Bijlmermeer was already considerable in the first years of its occupancy (Figure 12.3). A comparison of the former place of residence of the first tenants of two buildings, Gliphoeve II and Develstein, built in 1973 and 1974, respectively, shows that 13 percent of the first tenants of Gliphoeve II and 17 percent of the first tenants of Develstein came from the Bijlmermeer area. A more detailed look at the former place of residence of tenants who transferred internally reveals a movement from distressed to less troubled and newly built high-rise buildings.

Figure 12.2
The Surinamese Population in Amsterdam on January 1, 1975 (Percentage of Total Population)

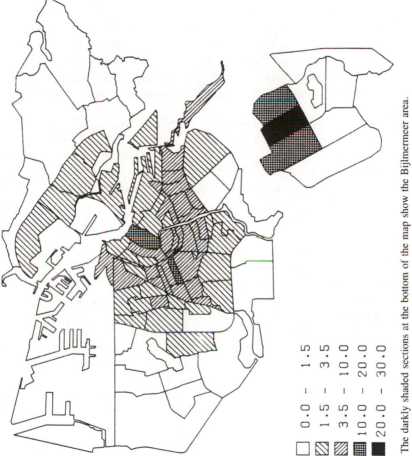

0.0 – 1.5

1.5 – 3.5

3.5 – 10.0

10.0 – 20.0

20.0 – 30.0

The darkly shaded sections at the bottom of the map show the Bijlmermeer area.
Source: Bestuursinformatie Afdeling Statistiek 1970–85.

In the case of Gliphoeve II, 53 percent of those tenants had lived in Gliphoeve I before; in the case of Develstein, 36 percent had lived in Gliphoeve II before.

Stage 2. In the years following the completion of the major construction work, the migration rate in Bijlmermeer diminished (Figure 12.3). We might view this as a sign that Bijlmermeer was entering the second—stabilization—stage of its development. Public interest and government concern also diminished in this period. Nevertheless, the shortness of this period of diminishing migration rates points up other factors.

In those years, housing production in Amsterdam decreased dramatically (Figure 12.4). In 1978 and 1979, the housing stock of Amsterdam even declined in absolute terms. The housing production in nearby new towns, linked to the Amsterdam housing market area, did not compensate for this stagnant production. The tight housing market was apparently the cause of the declining migration rates. Also in the city of Alkmaar, a decreasing turnover rate in the high-rise buildings was accompanied by a drastic drop in housing production (Herber 1984).

In spite of fluctuations in the turnover rates, high mobility was a fundamental feature of the high-rise estate, even in stage 2. Taking into account the problems of this period—overcrowding, clandestine subletting, vandalism, and a growing crime rate—we can hardly characterize Bijlmermeer as a stabilizing community.

Stage 3. The high migration rate from 1980 onward thoroughly changed the social nature of Bijlmermeer. In an expanding housing market, the severe overcrowding in Gliphoeve and some other buildings was alleviated by legalizing the clandestine tenants and giving them priority in the allocation of vacant apartments in their own or neighboring buildings. This measure eliminated one problem, but gave rise to another: the segregation between buildings became more pronounced. We compared the social characteristics of the people who moved into and out of several buildings in Bijlmermeer with bad (Gliphoeve II) and good (Gooioord) reputations.[1] In these years, vacancies increased even though distribution of dwellings in the Bijlmermeer still fell under the jurisdiction of the municipal housing authority.[2] The relative inaccessibility of Bijlmermeer was reflected in the composition of the population that settled there during this period. An overwhelming majority of the tenants came from the Bijlmermeer itself and from the rest of Amsterdam. Single people, couples living together, single-parent families, and foreigners (43 percent of the tenants in the buildings studied) were increasing in number in most of the buildings. In 1982, 60 percent of the new tenants in an average building like Develstein were of foreign origin, as compared to 18 percent of the prior tenants. A universal phenomenon was the lower social status of the newcomers. One-third lived on welfare or unemployment benefits (Table 12.1).

Compared to other housing estates built in the 1960s, it was not primarily the difference in social status that was apparent. Also in Banne Buiksloot, a low-rise housing estate in the north of Amsterdam, a large share of the tenants was on welfare. There was no great difference in income level either. Differences

Figure 12.3
Residential Mobility in Bijlmermeer and Amsterdam

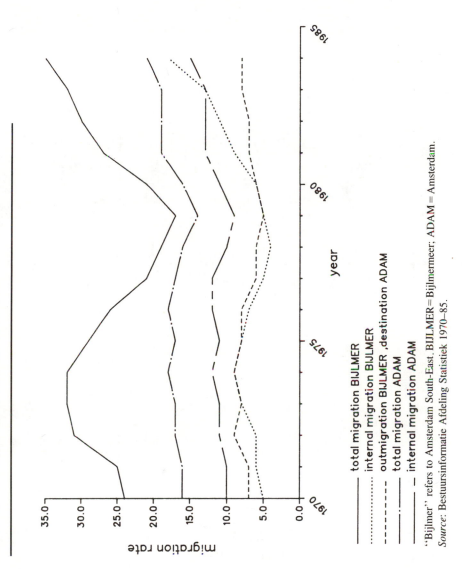

total migration BIJLMER
internal migration BIJLMER
outmigration BIJLMER ,destination ADAM
total migration ADAM
internal migration ADAM

"Bijlmer" refers to Amsterdam South-East. BIJLMER=Bijlmermeer; ADAM=Amsterdam.
Source: Bestuursinformatie Afdeling Statistiek 1970–85.

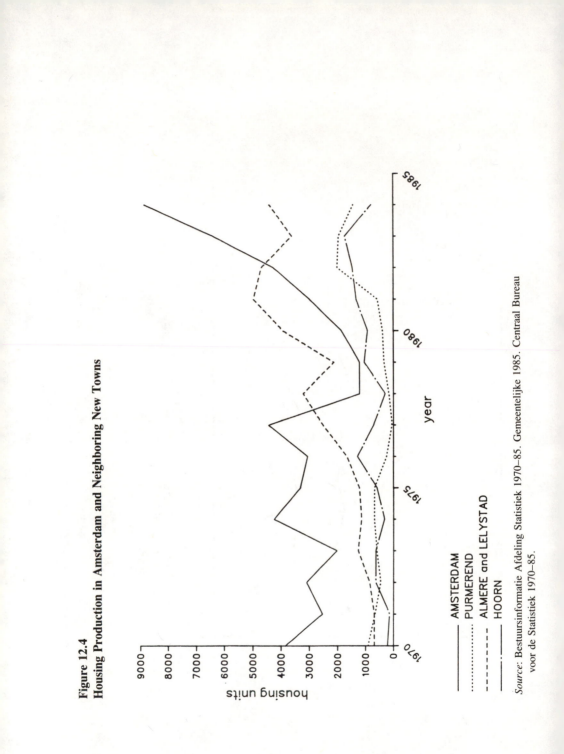

Figure 12.4
Housing Production in Amsterdam and Neighboring New Towns

AMSTERDAM
PURMEREND
ALMERE and LELYSTAD
HOORN

housing units

year

Source: Bestuursinformatie Afdeling Statistiek 1970–85. Gemeentelijke 1985. Centraal Bureau voor de Statistiek 1970–85.

Table 12.1
Source of Income of the New and Prior Tenants of Several High-Rise Buildings in Bijlmermeer, January 1982–April 1983

| | Gliphoeve II | | Buildings | | Develstein | | Gooioord |
| | New | Prior | New | Prior | New | Prior | New |
	%	%	%	%	%	%	%
Labor	39	53	68	93	56	92	70
Study	5	24	6	–	2	1	2
Welfare	41	19	14	–	32	5	15
Unemployment benefits	15	4	12	7	11	3	14
N (=100%)	59	128	176	27	57	104	66

Source: Tenant administration housing associations.

Table 12.2
Composition of the Households of New Tenants of Several High-Rise Buildings in Bijlmermeer and Low-Rise Buildings in Banne Buiksloot, January 1982–April 1983

	Bijlmermeer %	Banne Buiksloot %
Single	34	10
Married	12	19
Married + Children	11	40
Couples living together	25	15
Single-parent families	17	16
N (100%)	429	68

Source: Tenant administration housing associations.

mainly emerged in ethnic origin, household composition (Table 12.2), length of residence, and in the fact that nearly 60 percent of the newcomers (in Bijlmermeer, 30 percent) were "urgent cases" in terms of housing distribution criteria.

In contrast with the ordinary working class population of Banne Buiksloot, Bijlmermeer revealed a concentration of people with a marginal position in society. This concentration could be viewed as a result of a rapid process of downgrading. Compared with the first households in Bijlmermeer, present households have a very low income (Table 12.3). Only half of the tenants who moved to Develstein in the last two years have regular income from a job, and their professions fall into the "lower" occupational types. Also the share of single people and single-parent families increased (47 and 11 percent in Develstein, respectively), as did the proportion of Surinamese and other foreigners (Figure 12.5).

Since 1982, vacancy rates have increased at a high rate. However, despite their adjacent locations (Figure 12.6), not every building has been affected in the same way. The fact that they are run by different housing associations with different allocation and management policies, shows that management and microenvironment were also important factors at this stage of the downgrading process. Nevertheless, the overall pattern gave cause for concern. In the beginning of 1982, 12 percent of the Bijlmermeer population about the age of 20 was on welfare or received unemployment or other social benefits, compared to 8 percent for Amsterdam as a whole. By the end of 1984, these figures were 22 and 13 percent, respectively (Bestuursinformatie Afdeling Statistiek 1982, 1985). In the last elections, the Bijlmermeer percentage of nonvoting eligible voters was the highest in all of Amsterdam, illustrating a widespread indifference toward social issues. The extent of the rent arrears and fly-by-night tenants (Melger 1984a) could also be viewed not only as a sign of growing poverty, but also as a sign of the loss of social ties and values.

THE ANTECEDENTS OF THE DOWNGRADING PROCESS

Bijlmermeer high-rise housing does not conform to the three-stage history of occupancy. One noticeable difference is the rapid pace of the downgrading process, also observed in other high-rise estates, although less pronounced (Herber 1984; Buys and Holt 1984). In fact, Bijlmermeer never reached a stable and viable occupancy, which could largely be explained by its marginal position on the housing market from the outset. The prolonged and massive housing production also influenced the unstable character of even the oldest buildings because it created many new opportunities for subsequent migration streams within Bijlmermeer itself.

Despite the importance of the above-mentioned factors, the downgrading process of high-rise estates does not occur in isolation. Because of its unstable

Table 12.3
Social Composition of the First and Last/Present Tenants of Two High-Rise Buildings in Bijlmermeer, March 1985

	Gliphoeve II		Develstein		
	first	last	first	present	moved in in past 2 years
	%	%	%	%	%
Income level					
low	13	58	–	53	67
	47	36	56	31	20
	38	7	42	16	13
high	3	–	1	–	–
Ethnic Origin					
Dutch	82	31	85	61	52
Surinamese	15	55	11	24	32
European	4	5	4	4	10
else	–	9	1	10	6
Family Status					
Single	21	28	33	47	47
Married	19	6	19	14	18
Married + children	18	25	22	18	12
Couples living together	36	20	24	11	12
Single-parent families	6	21	2	11	13
N (=100%)	263	262	253	204	103

Source: Tenant administration housing associations.

Figure 12.5
The Surinamese Population in Amsterdam on January 1, 1985 (Percentage of Total Population)

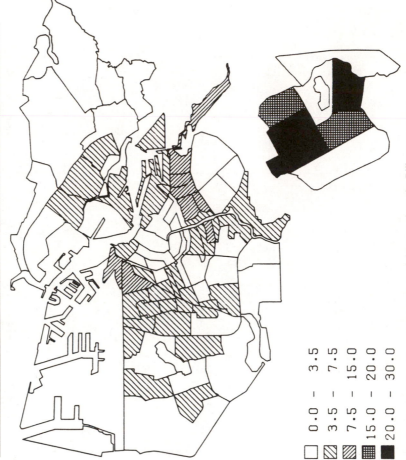

0.0 – 3.5
3.5 – 7.5
7.5 – 15.0
15.0 – 20.0
20.0 – 30.0

The darkly shaded sections at the bottom of the map show the Bijlmermeer area.
Source: Bestuursinformatie Afdeling Statistiek 1970–85.

Figure 12.6
Vacancies in Bijlmermeer

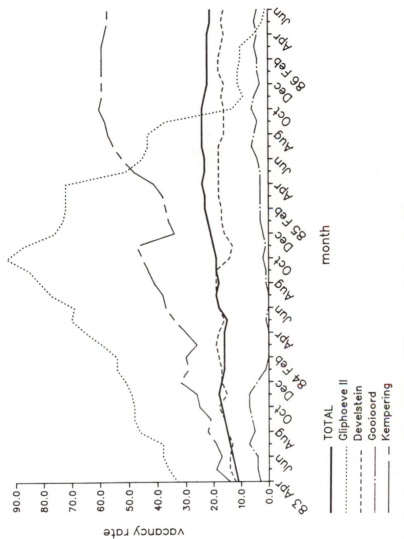

Legend:
- TOTAL
- Gliphoeve II
- Develstein
- Gooioord
- Kempering

Note: From December 1983 and February 1985 onwards, Gliphoeve II and Kempering, respectively, were partly vacated because of a drastic renovation program.
Source: Housing Association "Nieuw Amsterdam."

occupancy, Bijlmermeer experienced from the beginning external pressures and local changes. The following factors are important:

Fluctuations in the housing production in the Amsterdam region: The role of fluctuations in housing production in the occupancy history of Bijlmermeer has been discussed already. The stagnation in housing production in the Amsterdam area at the end of the 1970s, followed by an overall growth of production in the 1980s (Figure 12.4), was accompanied by a sudden increase in migration (Figure 12.3).

The changing population structure of Amsterdam: As is the case in most big cities in Western countries, the population of Amsterdam is decreasing. In the last 15 years, from 1970 to 1985, Amsterdam lost 150,000 (18 percent) of its inhabitants. The structure of its population has also changed. Families suburbanized, single people went to the city—in itself not a totally new or unique development. In Amsterdam, however, the suburbanization process was induced by the spillover policy of the local government. An agreement was reached with the new towns of Hoorn, Purmerend, Almere, and Lelystad to build housing (mostly one-family houses) for households from Amsterdam (about 60 percent of the housing production of the new towns in the mid- and late 1970s was intended for people from Amsterdam). Initially, Amsterdam also had control over the allocation of this housing in the new towns, making it easy for the middle class to migrate. The lower class, however, stayed behind. In 1977 the share of households under or at minimum-income level was estimated to be 30 percent (Gemeentelijke 1978). In 1985, half of the population was composed of singles; people between 20 and 35 years old made up 30 percent of the population, compared with 23 percent in 1970. Amsterdam is impoverishing and rejuvenating. The housing demand is changing accordingly. With its peripheral location, its monofunctional design, its high rent level, and its excess of three-bedroom apartments, Bijlmermeer does not meet this demand.

Immigration of the Surinamese: The immigration surge of the Surinamese people just before the independence of Surinam in 1975 coincided with a growing vacancy rate in Bijlmermeer, leading to a concentration of the Surinamese in some buildings. Overcrowding, ghettoization, and an ongoing stigmatization resulted.

Government interventions such as the introduction of a rent subsidy program attuned to individual circumstances and changes in the housing distribution requirements: The rent subsidy program, introduced in 1975, turned out to be counterproductive for management of the housing stock. On the one hand, housing associations relaxed their income ceiling restrictions; on the other hand, the much-desired single-family housing now came within reach of people who could not afford it before, promoting suburbanization. Apparently the introduction of the rent subsidies accelerated the downgrading of high-rise housing estates such as Bijlmermeer. In 1985, 67 percent of the Bijlmermeer tenants were receiving rent subsidies. The direct effect of alterations in the rent subsidy allocations was a fall in the net income of the tenants (Woningcorporatie 1986). If the current government's plans to abolish the rent subsidy program are implemented, Bijlmermeer would risk getting even more vacancies and becoming even more impoverished.

Economic stagnation, particularly social consequences of the present economic stagnation such as declining purchasing power, increasing unemployment, and a growing number of households living on minimum incomes or government allowances: Because of the marginal position of high-rise units on the housing market, these households became concentrated in high-rise estates, despite their high rent levels. This exacerbated poverty, dependence, and lack of social involvement.

FACTORS INHERENT IN HIGH-RISE HOUSING: SCALE AND CONNECTIVITY

External influences and a low appreciation of high-rise living, however, were not the only factors causing deterioration of the high-rise housing estates. Certain features, inherent in high-rise design, worsened living conditions once the downgrading process had set in. These features pertained to the collective nature of the design. They allowed individual actions to cause collective and often detrimental effects. We can call these features "scale" and "connectivity." Scale refers to the massive nature of high-rise estates and the multitude of dwellings, people, cars, dogs, and so on. Connectivity refers to the fact that people living in high-rise housing have to share numerous spaces and amenities: outdoor and indoor hallways, elevators, garbage chutes, hot water supply, heating, parking lots, lawns, and parks. In environments like the Bijlmermeer with buildings of 500 apartments or more and a design emphasizing collectivity, these features became important and concrete facts of everyday life. They gave rise to the following problems:

Proximity: Where so many people live close together, "deviant" behavior can disturb the whole pattern of living conditions. The man at the end of the gallery who worked the night shift and went to work wearing wooden shoes is a vivid illustration of this problem (Herber 1984). In anonymous surroundings, problems of this kind are often difficult to solve.

Congestion: Insignificant everyday activities or habits can become a problem by their scale and connectivity (Hirsch 1977; Schelling 1974). The problems with the hot water supply in the Gliphoeve buildings are an example. Overcrowding, combined with the habit, imported from Surinam, of taking frequent showers, made it nearly impossible to take a bath during peak hours.

Anonymity and lack of social control: In housing estates with a large and transient population, contact with neighbors is generally either rare or totally nonexistent (Michelson 1970, 188). People do not even know many of the other tenants by face, and particularly in the lower social classes, the tenants often feel socially isolated (Frankenberg 1970; Rainwater 1966). Insofar as research results are available, Bijlmermeer is no exception to this rule. The Bijlmermeer tenants had even less of a tendency than residents of other new urban neighborhoods to identify with their fellow tenants, and they felt more alone (Ferf-van den Brueke and Melger 1974, 46; Dijkhuis 1975). In a recent study of the tenants' problems in coping with their environment, 9 percent mentioned their fellow tenants as its most unpleasant aspect. The lack of safety, however, was cited most frequently, by 18 percent (Melger 1984b). The high-rise design with its many semipublic spaces reinforces feelings of anonymity and vulnerability (Coleman 1985; Newman 1972; Michelson 1977, 51). Hallways, lobbies, elevators, stairwells, and lawns or parks are openly accessible to everyone and, moreover, frequently out of sight from windows or for passers-by (see Figure 12.7). Vandals are rarely known. Anybody is a potential offender.

Figure 12.7

Hallway in Bijlmermeer. Reprinted by permission of Projectbureau Hoogbouw Bijlmermeer.

The incidence of mugging in Bijlmermeer shows the relative lack of safety of semipublic spaces like indoor hallways, elevators, and lobbies. In 1977, 23 percent, 14 percent, and 11 percent of the mugging occurred in those places, respectively.[3]

Lack of feedback: In a massive environment, individual action to solve even concrete problems makes little sense. What is the use of putting garbage in the garbage can in the basement if all the other tenants leave it in the hallway? Why should one try to lower energy costs by closing the windows and switching off the heating? If not all other tenants do the same, this kind of action does not produce any personal advantage. This mechanism partly explains why energy costs and gross rents in high-rise housing with its collective heating system and hot water supply are still so difficult to control. In 1985, energy costs accounted for 22 percent of the gross rent of a three-bedroom apartment. Since they were first built in 1974, gross rent has risen by 81 percent and the net rent by only 45 percent.

Collective action, based on consensus, seems to be a necessary condition to counter these problems. It will be difficult to attain this goal in anonymous and inflexible surroundings with a marginal, dependent, and transient population.

CONCLUDING COMMENTS

If high-rise housing estates are to survive, a number of measures are necessary. Technical renovation programs alone will not do the job. If we take into account the factors acting on the deterioration process three options exist.

Tenant participation: The lack of involvement on the part of the tenants in their surroundings seems to be one of the main reasons for the present problems in high-rise housing estates. Decentralization of the management to shorten the contact lines between the housing association and the tenants is a possible strategy to restore tenant confidence. The (re)introduction of a building superintendent can be a means to this end. Another measure, which has proved its worth elsewhere (Rigby 1985), is the transfer of responsibilities to a tenant association. Up to now, there has been very little experience with this in the postwar neighborhoods in the Netherlands. In the Bijlmermeer, tenant management has only been suggested as a possible strategy for countering the process of deterioration (Verhagen 1985). However, the establishment of a stable, motivated, and able core of tenants who carry managerial responsibilities and who receive the trust of their fellow residents is critical.

Design improvements: Certain design features of high-rise housing become detrimental conditions when a marginal population moves in. Changing these features can be an important step in curtailing the development of problems. Some obvious improvements, most of which have already been proposed or employed in at least one Bijlmermeer building, include:

- The individualization of collective services like the heating system, the hot water supply, and parking lots.
- A reduction in semipublic spaces; areas like indoor hallways and corridors, elevators, lobbies, and lawns or parks require attention. Increasing the number of entrances (and

reducing the number of apartments per entrance), subdividing outdoor passageways, removing indoor hallways and placing apartments instead of storage lockers on the ground floor are all measures that should diminish anonymity and restore social control.

• A reduction in the number of residents. The vertical partition and the topping off of buildings are measures that fall under this heading. Not only anonymity, but also operating costs are the target of measures of this kind (Coleman 1985).

In Gliphoeve I and II, the "problem buildings" where these measures were taken for the first time (with exception of the topping off), there are hardly vacancies anymore and the living climate has improved considerably. However, the question remains whether these measures would be equally effective if they were applied on a large scale without such simultaneous nontechnical measures such as rent reduction.

External conditions: Although changes in management, tenant participation, and design features can improve living conditions in high-rise housing, it remains questionable whether high-rise housing estates can survive without intervention in external conditions. It has been noted earlier how external developments and events influenced the downgrading process of the Bijlmermeer area. To cope with the current problems, it will be necessary to control or affect at least some of these developments, however difficult it may be. In considering measures like a restriction on new housing construction, a rent reduction, or a change of the rent subsidy or housing allocation criteria, we are encroaching upon a different domain. A reconsideration of priorities is imperative—and not exclusively in the field of housing and financing. Questions about quality of life and equity are also at issue. In these matters, politics have the last word.

NOTES

1. The selection of buildings was influenced by the availability of data. The "buildings" in Table 12.1 are in fact only small parts of the buildings under discussion. They are the ones managed by the two housing associations that participated in the research.

2. From September 1, 1983, the housing distribution requirements officially no longer applied to the Bijlmermeer area. In practice, however, the rules had already lost much of their effect (*Rapportage* 1981).

3. Percentages based on internal police data: the so-called Meldingsrapporten.

REFERENCES

Bestuursinformatie Afdeling Statistiek
1970–85   *Amsterdam in cijfers, Jaarboek 1970–1985*. Amsterdam: Stadsdrukkerij.
Biervliet, W. E.
1976   *Bewonersonderzoek, Gliphoeve I, Amsterdam, Bijlmermeer, Deel 1*. Amsterdam, unpublished.
Bock, Manfred
1981   "Nawoord." In *Hoogbouw*, edited by J. Duiker, 51–60. Amsterdam: Van Gennep.
Bourne, Larry S.
1981   *The Geography of Housing*. London: Winston.

Bureau van Statistiek van de Gemeente Amsterdam
1971   *Enkele statistische gegevens omtrent de Bijlmermeer*. Amsterdam.
Buys, Andre, and Andre Holt (eds.)
1984   *Hoogbouw in de problemen?* Amsterdam: unpublished.
Centraal Bureau voor de Statistiek
1970–85   *Maandstatistiek Bouwnijverheid*. 's-Gravenhage: Staatsuitgeverij.
Coleman, Alice
1985   *Utopia on Trial*. London: Hillary Shipman.
Cooney, E. W.
1974   "High Flats in Local Authority Housing in England and Wales Since 1945." In
       Multi Storey Living: The British Working Class Experience, edited by Anthony
       Sutcliffe, 151–80. London: Croom Helm.
Dettingmeyer, Rob
1982   "De strijd om een goed gebouwde stad." In *Het Nieuwe Bouwen in Rotterdam
       1920–1960*, 19–76. Delft: University Press.
Diepen, Maria van, and Ankie de Bruyn-Muller
1976   *De kraakacties in Gliphoeve*. Amsterdam: Gemeentelijke Dienst Volkshuisvesting.
Dijkhuis, J. H.
1975   *Bijlmermeer van binnen*. Delft: Centrum voor Architectuur Onderzoek.
Du Laing, Hugo
1973   *Het proces van stadsuitbreiding. Casestudie: De Amsterdamse stadsuitbreiding
       Bijlmer*. Leuven: unpublished.
Dunleavy, Patrick
1981   *The Politics of Mass Housing in Britain 1945–1975*. Oxford: Clarendon Press.
Ferf-van den Brueke, I., and R. Melger
1974   *Verhuizen naar, in en uit de Bijlmermeer*. Amsterdam: Gemeentelijke Dienst
       Volkshuisvesting.
Frankenberg, Ronald
1970   *Communities in Britain*. Harmondsworth: Penguin Books. (Originally published
       in 1977.)
Gemeentelijke Dienst Volkshuisvesting
1970   *Concept Notitie Bijlmermeer*. Amsterdam: unpublished.
1978   *Een stelsel van inkomenshuren*. Amsterdam.
1985   *Amsterdam, Wonen in cijfers 1984*. Amsterdam: Stadsdrukkerij.
Guffens, Th. M. G., N. J. M. Nelissen, and J. B. Scholten
1968   "Migratie en wijzigingen in de samenstelling van buurten." *Stedebouw en Volks-
       huisvesting* 10, 354–62.
Herber, George
1984   *Het sociale vervalproces van hoogbouwwoningen*. Amsterdam: unpublished.
Hirsch, Fred
1977   *Social Limits to Growth*. London: Routledge and Kegan Paul.
McClintock, Hugh, and Michael Fox
1971   "The Bijlmermeer development and the expansion of Amsterdam." *Journal of
       the Town Planning Institute* 7, 313–16.
Melger, Roy
1984a *Mutaties in de Bijlmermeer*. Amsterdam: Gemeentelijke Dienst Volkshuisvesting.
1984b *Renovatie onderzoek hoogbouw Bijlmermeer*. Amsterdam: Gemeentelijke Dienst
       Volkshuisvesting.

Michelson, William
1970   *Man and His Urban Environment: A Sociological Approach*. Reading, MA: Addison-Wesley.
1977   *Environmental Choice, Human Behavior, and Residential Satisfaction*. New York: Oxford University Press.
Murie, A., P. Niner, and C. J. Watson
1976   *Housing Policy and the Housing System*. London: Allen & Unwin.
Newman, Oscar
1972   *Defensible Space: Crime Prevention Through Urban Design*. New York: Collier Books.
Priemus, Hugo
1984   *Verhuistheorieën en de verdeling van de woningvoorraad*. Delft: University Press.
Rainwater, L.
1966   "Fear and the House-as-Haven in the Lower Class." *Journal of the American Institute of Planners* 32, 23–31.
Rapportage van de Werkgroep Onderzoek Volkshuisvesting e/g-buurt.
1981   Amsterdam, unpublished.
Ravetz, Allison
1971   "Tenancy Patterns and Turnover at Quarry Hill Flats, Leeds." *Urban Studies* 3, 181–205.
1985   "Problem Housing Estates in Britain: The Case of Quarry Hill Flats and Hunslet Grange, Leeds." In *Post-war Public Housing in Trouble*, edited by Niels L. Prak and Hugo Priemus, 43–54. Delft: University Press.
Rigby, Robert
1985   "Community Based Approach to Salvaging Troubled Public Housing: Tenant Management." In *Post-war Public Housing in Trouble*, edited by Niels L. Prak and Hugo Priemus, 19–34. Delft: University Press.
Rossum, J. A., J. F. van Hulst, and A. L. J. Goethals
1981   *Voorstudie naar het beheer en exploitatie van hoge woongebouwen*. Amsterdam: SISWO.
Schelling, Thomas
1974   "On the Ecology of Micromotives." In *The Corporate Society*, edited by Robin Marris. London: Macmillan.
Verhagen, Evert
1985   *De overdracht van beheerstaken aan bewoners in de Bijlmermeer. fase 1: inventariserend onderzoek*. Amsterdam: SWOB.
Waardering van de woonvormen, De
1970   's-Gravenhage, Staatsuitgeverij.
Wielemaker-Dijkhuis, J. H., and D. de Jonge
1972   *Interim rapport Bijlmermeer*. Delft: Centrum voor Architectuur Onderzoek.
Woningcorporatie Nieuw Amsterdam
1986   *Effektrapportage*. Amsterdam: unpublished.
Yancey, W. L.
1971   "Architecture, Interaction and Social Control: The Case of a Large Scale Public Housing Project." *Environment and Behavior* 1, 3–18.

PART V

ASPECTS OF MANAGEMENT
AND OWNERSHIP

The tenure form that has received most attention in recent housing research
is private ownership. Analysts have been particularly concerned about implications of attempts to privatize the financing, management, and ownership
of the housing stock. These concerns, while highly relevant, do not reflect
other noteworthy developments regarding tenure, some of which are discussed in the following chapters. (Readers may also find Chapter 10 by
Franck of interest.)

Woodward, in Chapter 13, describes public housing communes in Sweden
as an alternative to rental tenure in conventional public housing. She reports
on the experiences of four such projects, outlining their goals, achievements,
and difficulties. Although it is early to form a judgment regarding the eventual
success of this experiment in public housing, it seems quite clear that it is
an option that has so far attracted a new and different type of tenant, requiring
adjustments in the managerial style of and administration by the public
housing organizations.

Van Weesep focuses on quite different aspects of tenure and management
in the Netherlands in Chapter 14. He draws on an empirical study of housing
in The Hague to examine questions of broader applicability underlying condominium conversion. In various countries, the loss of rental units to the
owner-occupier sector is seen as creating serious problems. Two such problems are the diminished supply of rental housing and the lack of maintenance
by the new owners. Van Weesep examines these and other questions and
concludes that, due to a number of specific conditions, there is little cause
for concern in The Hague at present, although certain government precau-
tions are in order to avoid the occurrence of future problems.

Chapter 15 is also concerned with rental housing. Baar reviews the historical development of municipal rent controls in the United States, which
currently affect about 11 percent of that nation's rental housing stock. He
then discusses systematically a number of controversial issues to be resolved
in the actual formulation of specific rent control laws and briefly reviews
the evidence regarding alleged impacts of rent control on new construction
and maintenance levels. As Harloe's (1985) recent analysis has shown,

private rental housing in the United States is experiencing serious problems. The difficulties are certain to endure in light of political, economic, and demographic projections. In this context, rent controls will continue to be debated. Baar cautions that questions about their effects and considerations of equity and efficiency, raised in the discussions, should not obscure the political motivations of the main participants.

REFERENCE

Harloe, Michael
1985   *Private Rented Housing in the United States and Europe*. New York: St. Martin's Press.

13

Public Housing Communes: A Swedish Response to Postmaterial Demands

ALISON E. WOODWARD

Abstract. Swedish public housing authorities were the first in the world to introduce shared or communal solutions in normal rental tenure. Public housing communes are a response to the demands of women and alternative groups for new housing forms. This chapter discusses the success of four Swedish projects in attracting a new type of tenant and meeting social and fiscal goals. The experiments attract a new postmaterialist tenant, who values social aspects above material aspects of housing. However, there have been problems regarding organization and scale. These remain to be solved if the communal experiment is to spread to a wider tenancy.

INTRODUCTION

Public housing in Sweden, as in most Western countries, faces a number of serious problems. Costs are higher than income, well-to-do tenants move out, and much of the stock is unattractive and hard-to-rent (Lindberg 1985). As 20 percent of the total housing stock is publicly owned and 48 percent of the rented sector is under public housing management,[1] these problems affect a significant proportion of the population. Further, they represent a major fiscal interest for local governments.

In the 1980s, public housing firms have attempted to come to grips with their problems. Firms reorganized, introduced new forms for tenant influence, and dealt with the vacant stock through both offensive and retreatist tactics. Everything from blowing up buildings (Gothenburg) to turning them into offices, nurseries, and hotels (RESABO) has been tried (*BoFast* 1985).

One of the most creative solutions is the introduction of collective or communal housing into the public housing sector. Collective or public communal housing here refers to dwellings open to *all* household types (that is, not institutional or student housing) centered around common facilities like food service and meeting and hobby rooms. Such projects introduce a new housing form in the traditional public sector. Sweden is the first country in Europe to offer such far-reaching communal living in public rented tenure. This chapter reviews the background to this innovation and its potential for reaching new tenant groups and satisfying "postmaterial" demands.

THE COMMUNAL TRADITION

Sweden has a relatively long history of communal multifamily living. Its roots can be found within the utopian tradition (Vestbro 1982, 1985) as well as in the early Soviet experiments with new family forms (Caldenby and Walldén 1979).[2] In the 1920s and 1930s, a number of experiments in collective housing were built under private auspices. Vestbro (1982) catalogs some 20 Swedish projects with some degree of collective service built before 1965. With increasing labor costs, and rising demands for larger dwellings, most of these projects converted to serviceless rental forms by the 1970s.

Yet in the 1970s, a new interest in the idea arose from different sources. Throughout the industrial world, experiments in "communal" living flourished. Big city apartments were shared (Gorman 1975; Kanter 1979; Palm-Lindén 1982; Petersen 1972) or squatted (Turner 1976) and communes bloomed on rural farms (Jonsson 1983; Berger 1981). As those who instigated communal living forms moved into more established positions in society, the forms themselves also became more established. Legal changes in some countries made it easier for nonrelated people to share housing and improved tenure security. Residents designed and constructed buildings specifically adapted to communal living arrangements. In Denmark, *Faelleboskap* were built, in France and Belgium *habitats autogere*, and in Germany and Switzerland a wide variety of *Wohngemeinschaft* arrangements appeared (Gromark 1983). All are based on resident investment either in the form of a membership fee to a cooperative or through co-ownership.

In Sweden, the form most closely related to these developments, the *storfamilj*, is widespread. The storfamilj is a small commune of unrelated people who share either a larger apartment or a house (Palm-Lindén 1982). Again, these groups are formed through private initiative. The word itself emphasizes the social qualities of the arrangement, as it translates into "big family." One of the problems storfamilj have had, however, has been finding physical settings suited to communal living. Both they and a number of other groups began political pressure for publicly supported alternative housing forms in the 1970s.

An important element in the pressure groups for communal housing besides the storfamilj supporters is the woman's movement. Since the 1920s, Swedish feminists have demanded housing forms that would ease the burden of homemaking and provide more time for working mothers (Åkerman et al. 1975; Cronberg et al. 1979; BIG gruppen 1982). Women were joined in the 1970s by environmental activists and others interested in alternative living. Some areas spawned formal organizations founded for the single purpose of demanding "Communal Houses Now!"

Political action on these demands lagged. Male politicians opposed the idea as a demand from a bohemian minority or as unrealistic, given experience with earlier experiments. It was when the drive for communal housing meshed serendipitously with other issues that local governments seriously considered the alternative. In every community that adapted communal public housing schemes, the demands of activists linked conveniently with other policy motivations. Some cities use the projects as a plank in their social welfare program, providing new forms of integrating social services for the aged and children (Pedersen 1981). Others use communal projects in remodeling unattractive suburban housing (Caldenby and Walldén 1984). In Stockholm, the city hoped to provide sufficient clients for a full-scale restaurant by combining housing for the elderly with a communal solution (Woodward et al. 1984). Communal housing has also been a method of introducing smaller-than-standard apartments into production, bypassing the stringent Swedish norms and cutting costs. Finally, responding to the demand for communal housing can be seen as a method for the public housing authority to gain prestige and a progressive image.

Another change in the policy arena that eased the introduction of communal schemes was the agreement between the Swedish tenants' union and the organization of public housing authorities to introduce wide-ranging tenant influence in management (*bo-inflytande*) (Cronberg 1986). Many argued that the communal dwelling form provided an ideal social base for introducing tenant management (Kärnekull 1982; Hjärne 1982; Sollbe 1982; Madigan 1984).

Today there are some 40 housing projects with communal components either on the drawing boards or completed (Grossman and Vestbro 1982). These projects vary widely in size (from 10 to 200 apartments) and form. They promise a cornucopia of social and fiscal goods.

Politicians hope that many of the social goals ultimately will have fiscal effects. For example, promoting social integration of different generations may help promote mutual aid across age barriers and thereby cut social welfare costs. Attracting a new more educated and steadily employed tenant may improve prompt payment of rent and lower vandalism.

Among the many goals for communal housing are the following:

Social and Political Goals

• Provide housing better suited to new family types and women's changing roles.

• Provide a good form for tenant influence in management.

• Ease social integration and promote aid between households through socially shared situations such as communal eating arrangements and shared work assignments.

• Appeal to new and desirable tenant groups.

Housing Management and Fiscal Goals

• Reduce housing production costs through smaller apartments (reduced kitchens and living rooms).

• Attract tenants to vacant or unrentable properties.

• Reduce housing management costs by lowering vandalism and resident turnover.

• Lower maintenance costs by tenant take-over of maintenance tasks.

THE POSTMATERIALIST TENANT

The first of the new generation of public housing communes opened its doors in 1981. It is still a little early to evaluate the projects and their ability to live up to their goals. However, it is already clear that these projects attract a special sort of tenant.

This housing most directly appeals to a group that has been variously termed the "new class" (Gouldner 1979; Djilas 1966), the "postmaterialists" (Inglehart 1977, 1982), or the elites of the postindustrial society (Uusitalo 1980). The group is small but influential. It is said to value quality of life over material quantity and to prioritize the satisfaction of nonmaterial needs through continuing education, increased leisure, and alternative life-styles. Many are interested in participation and self-actualization (Watts and Wandesforde-Smith 1982). They tend to be well-educated and work in jobs with a high degree of autonomy, frequently in the public sector. A majority were born after 1940 (Inglehart 1982).

In Sweden, these holders of postmaterial values were active in the antinuclear movement. Across Europe, these people form the heart of the environmental movement (Watts 1979). Generally, they subscribe to a Schumacherian "small is beautiful" doctrine (1973) and might be expected to shy away from the standardized mass-produced world of public housing. Much criticism directed at Swedish multifamily suburbia originated with people representing postmaterial world views (see reviews in Franzén 1982; Franzén and Sandstedt 1981). As these people often hold positions of opinion leadership in society, it is in the interest of public housing to win them back.

The feminist and political organizations agitating for communal solutions in public housing share many features with the postmaterial ideal-type sketched here. By providing communal projects, public housing firms may be able to co-opt some of their most virulent critics. In the material that follows, we will show that communal projects have indeed captured the postmaterialist tenant, but that this may have a number of unintended consequences for public housing firms. While the communal housing scheme is very compatible with the postmaterial value complex, it may not be compatible with the organizational structure of a public housing firm.

BIG CITY RESPONSE TO COMMUNAL DEMANDS: UPPSALA AND STOCKHOLM

The city of Stockholm responded to political pressure to provide public communal housing by establishing a committee to investigate potential sites and models (Stockholms Kommuns Kollektivhus Kommitté 1983) as well as directing its public housing firms to include such projects in new production. A number of models evolved. In 1983 we began a study of two of these models to compare outcomes for social integration, tenant involvement, and costs (Woodward et al. 1984). We chose four buildings with two different models.[3] One is small scale and focuses on self-management through tenant participation. Tenants run a food service and provide most daily building maintenance. The other model is large scale and based on employees. A restaurant, a library, and other services are provided under separate management. These projects are combined with housing for the elderly managed by the social welfare office to help underwrite the costs of these services.

The Large-Scale Projects

The two big projects, Rio and Fristad, are located in Stockholm and managed by the same firm. They were among the first communal housing solutions in Stockholm and built with a combination of motivations including the hope that housing for the elderly would be humanized through integration with the communal project. The communal sections are connected to large service apartment complexes for the elderly. The communards share common rooms, library, hobby facilities, and a restaurant with the elderly. Additionally, the communal buildings have a number of their own facilities such as separate meeting rooms, cafe, sauna, and day care.

Project Fristad includes 133 communal apartments and 175 apartments for the elderly (see Figure 13.1). Rio, located in one of the most attractive neighborhoods in Stockholm, has 111 communal apartments and 143 apartments for the elderly. Each has several apartments adapted for people with mobility handicaps. The elderly dominate both projects.

The floor plan in Figure 13.2 indicates the layout of the communal shared facilities in Fristad. Figure 13.3 indicates the physical separation of the elderly from the communards. Project Rio is also separated from the elderly by an extremely long corridor, but employs a similar solution grouping common facilities on the ground floor. Both provide meal service at lunch and dinner. Tenants purchase a fixed number of meal tickets monthly as part of the rental agreement, but they have no influence over food service.

The Small-Scale Projects

The two smaller projects are located in a Stockholm suburb (Prästgårdshagen, 31 apartments) and in the university city of Uppsala (Blenda, 24 apartments). They include extensive common facilities such as a professional-scale kitchen, TV rooms, dining room, sauna, hobby and day-care facilities. The floor plan in Figure 13.4 illustrates the layout in Prästgårdshagen on the ground floor. In both Prästgårdshagen and Blenda, apartments are below the Swedish size norm to provide for greater common space.

Tenants manage these projects and receive rent rebates for their work in building

Figure 13.1

Fristad is set in a wooded area in a Stockholm suburb. The immediate environment is enriched by play space for children and small garden allotments for tenants.

Source: AB Svenska Arkitektkontoret, Stockholm. Reprinted by permission.

Figure 13.2

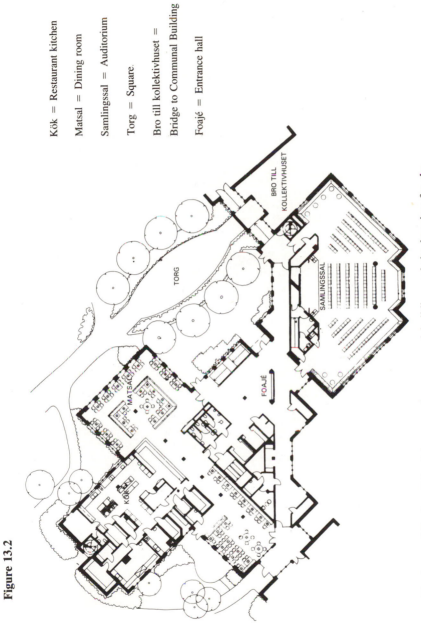

Kök = Restaurant kitchen

Matsal = Dining room

Samlingssal = Auditorium

Torg = Square.

Bro till kollektivhuset =
Bridge to Communal Building

Foajé = Entrance hall

The heart of Project Fristad between the communal building and the housing for the elderly.

Source: AB Svenska Bostäder Arkitektkontoret, Stockholm. Reprinted by permission.

Figure 13.3

Exterior perspective of Project Fristad. On the right apartments for communal housing. On the left service apartments for the elderly.

Source: AB Svenska Bostäder Arkitektkontoret, Stockholm. Reprinted by permission.

maintenance. They prepare weekday meals in teams of two or three. About 30–60 people eat on any given evening for a very moderate price.

Apartments in all projects are officially allocated to households indicating their interest in communal living through application to special housing. All projects are rental. They are all managed under agreements permitting substantial tenant influence. Greatest tenant influence is to be found in Prästgårdshagen, which has the strongest tenant influence agreement in Sweden. Here tenants do cleaning and gardening chores and carry out minor repairs as well as being responsible for interior repainting and renovation.

Neither of the larger projects has taken on any more substantial management or maintenance tasks, although the formal terms of their agreement would allow this. In Fristad, tenants clean halls and stairs. All projects will receive rent rebates if tenants succeed in cutting energy usage.

TENANTS IN FOUR SWEDISH PUBLIC HOUSING COMMUNES

The special character and high motivation of the new residents in communal projects make them a particularly thankful group for sociological study (Lindberg 1978). In the spring of 1985, all adult residents as well as children between 12 and 18 received a long questionnaire. It included items on previous housing, motivation for moving to a communal project, expectations, knowledge about tenant management, and housing satisfaction. The response rate was exceptionally high, due in part to survey assistance from resident committees in each building. Over 90 percent of all households participated, although in some only one of two adults responded. In total, 362 adult residents completed questionnaires.

Results indicate that these tenants represent a virtual carbon copy of the postmaterial ideal type, both demographically and in their expressed housing expectations. Although the projects were open to the general public, they attracted chiefly highly educated and materially established households. The projects are dominated by women and include larger proportions of single-parent households than in public housing in general.

Over 78 percent of the residents had at least high school education and 48 percent had completed a university or postgraduate degree. In the two smaller projects, the figures for university education were even higher. The majority of respondents were in their thirties, although each project also had a number of residents between 18 and 25. Rio, the project in the most attractive location, proved exceptional to this demographic pattern—more than one-third of the tenants there were over 50.

This points to one of the first contradictions between the goals of the different organizations involved in housing and the goals of the communal projects. While the communal projects are founded upon tenant desire to experiment with greater participation and community in multifamily housing, the municipal housing organization may have other goals. In Stockholm, there is an extreme shortage

Figure 13.4
Prästgårdshagen: Floor plans for one typical living floor and ground floor. The ground floor of project Prästgårdshagen includes a number of common facilities, while each floor above focuses around a common living room.

1:200

1. Entrance hall; 2. Dining room; 3. Kitchen; 4. Washing/drying; 5. Workshop; 6. Photography lab; 7. Sauna; 8. Relaxation Room; 9. Other common rooms (weaving, pottery, play room); 10. Day Care center; 11. Bicycle storage; 12. Garbage; 13. Common living room and normal apartments.

Figure 13.4 cont'd.

1:200

Source: Coordinator Arkitekter AB and AB Familjebostäder, Stockholm. Reprinted by permission.

Table 13.1
Social Class in Differing Housing Tenures in Swedish Housing

Social Class	Public Sector Rental	Private Sector Rental	Cooperative	Ownership	Total
Working Class	67	54	55	43	51
Middle Class	29	39	40	49	42
Upper Class	4	7	5	8	7
Sum %	100	100	100	100	100

Source: Lindberg 1985, 68. Based on figures from the Swedish Census (FoB) 1980. Only men from 20–64, nationwide. Total N = 1,777,018.

of centrally located apartments. Therefore, they use new production as a lever to garner attractive exchange objects. New tenants are required to turn over their former apartment to the housing authority when allocated a new one.

Many older tenants were attracted to the Rio project primarily because of its central location and access to services for the elderly rather than its status as a communal project. They often lived in large older apartments with a high market value, which the housing authority coveted. Theoretically they should not have been eligible for an apartment in the communal project, but the need to obtain attractive apartments seems to have overridden the mandate to fill the projects with motivated tenants.

Postmaterialist tenancy is reflected in the project demographics. The tenants are hardly a cross-section of the Swedish population, to say nothing of the population housed in public housing. Generally, Swedish public housing has become more and more segregated socioeconomically since the 1960s (Danemark 1984; Lindberg 1985; Thelander 1984, 1985). Using the standard statistical breakdown of the Swedish class structure into working class, middle class (*tjänstemän*), and upper class (owners and professionals), Lindberg provides an analysis of Swedish housing and class structure based on data from 1980 in Table 13.1.

In analyzing our data we have used a less crude scheme to isolate categories that may be expected to reflect postmaterial orientations (Table 13.2). Using Wright's (1978, 1980) model for the analysis of Western class structure, we see

Table 13.2
Class Composition of Residents in Four Urban Communal Projects as Compared
to the Swedish Class Composition and the Stockholm Class Composition in 1980
(in percent)

Social Class	Tenants	Swedish Population	Stockholm Population
Managers	2	11	19
Advisory Managers	11	3	3.5
Supervisors	13	7	9
Semi-autonomous categories	41	17	18
Workers	28	51	43
Owner-employers	5	11	7.5
N=	249	1180	250

Swedish and Stockholm/Stockholm County figures from the Swedish Class Study, 1980. Category
    Owner-employers includes both self-employed and employers with one or more employees.
Source: G. Ahrne, ''Report on the Swedish Class Structure 1.'' Working Paper Number 4,
    Department of Sociology, University of Wisconsin, Madison, Wisconsin, 1982, pp. 25–26.

the following patterns in the Swedish population at large and in the communal
projects studied here.

A majority of the communal project residents can easily be placed in a ''postmaterialist'' profile. Manual workers, who make up some 51 percent of the
Swedish population and some 67 percent of public housing, are only 28 percent
of the residents in communal projects.

Notable is the high percentage of workers with relatively autonomous jobs or
relatively self-directed employment such as teachers and journalists—the category coded as ''semiautonomous'' workers. This group constitutes 17 percent
in Sweden generally (Ahrne 1982), but makes up over 40 percent of those
responding to the question in our houses. In this study, the smaller the project,
the larger the representation of such tenants. A parallel result was found in one
of the very first Swedish communal projects in Gothenburg, where 90 percent
worked in semiautonomous jobs (Caldenby and Walldén 1984, 100).

Equally striking is the finding that only one-fourth of the respondents work in the private sector. All others are employed by public authorities or in publicly owned enterprises.

MOTIVATIONS

Postmaterialists value social qualities above material comforts. In Stockholm, the Communal House Committee (Stockholms Kommuns 1983) carried out a survey with potential residents to identify motives for seeking communal living. They found both "material" and "social" motivations. For example, those who believed that collective living provided economy of both time and money exemplify material motives for collective living. They feel that buying durable goods such as TVs and videos are cheaper when done in a group. Preparing meals together allows the purchase of food at quantity prices and saves time for the individual homemaker. People with "social" motives for applying for communal housing believed that collective living offered a chance to expand their social network and improve the quality of their everyday life through mutual support and new friendships.

In our study, we replicated a number of items first used in the Stockholm survey. A majority of the respondents in all projects moved in because they were interested in living communally. However, there was great variation between the projects. In the smallest project, 84 percent moved primarily to try out communal living, while in Rio only 55 percent had communal motivations. The smaller the project, it seems, the higher the motivation of the resident to live up to communal ideals.

In answers to open-ended questions about reasons for moving in, a striking majority of the respondents emphasized the social aspects of the living experience. Few mentioned material motivations such as saving time and money. A key word that cropped up again and again was "community." Residents anticipated the security of knowing neighbors, a better environment for their children, and a less socially isolated life-style than is common in Swedish apartment living. They stressed social idealism rather than material advantages.

This idealism is mirrored by the fact that 92 percent of the new communards gave up cheaper housing to move to the new form. Generally, new rental housing is the most expensive housing form available for middle-income families (Sandelin & Södersten 1978; Frykman 1985). In interviews, many couples stressed that they made economic sacrifices to live in the new projects, putting other values before their own private economy. However, they also noted that they may be able to lower rents in the long run by participation in management schemes.

Table 13.3 illustrates the domination of social over material values among new communards in evaluating their housing. Respondents rated the importance of various aspects of the dwelling experience. Some can be considered purely social, such as "community," while others can be considered to be more material, such as "potential to lower food costs." Some reveal both social and

Table 13.3
Social and Material Aspects of Housing Rated as Important or Very Important (percent)

	Blenda N=32	Prästgårds- hagen N=41	Fristad N=154	Rio N=134
Social Aspects *				
Community	86%(2)	83%	85%(2)	77%(4)
Community for children	80 (4)	93 (1)	83 (3)	80 (1)
Security	80 (4)	76	86 (1)	79 (2)
Meals	81 (3)	90 (2)	48	53
Social Rooms	93 (1)	85 (5)	74 (5)	65
Material Aspects				
Potential to lower rent	15	88 (3)	80 (4)	78 (3)

Potential to
  influence bldg.
  maintenance
	56	85 (4)	67	61

Potential to lower food costs	28	61	66	68 (5)
Hobby rooms	78	80	70	63
Sauna	40	56	52	47

*Numbers in parentheses indicate ranking of first five items

material aspects. For instance, hobby rooms offered a material improvement by adding an extra dimension to the rental apartment, with space for a loom or carpentry material. Yet these rooms also provide important centers for social contacts. Likewise, expanded tenant management provides both social and material benefits.

Tenants in Prästgårdshagen, who have the most elaborate tenant involvement scheme, found the potential to affect building management extremely important, in part because recurrent management chores such as spring cleaning also provide a common social ritual. They rated this aspect as much more important than did residents in buildings with more restricted schemes.

Generally, the aspects most frequently rated as "very important" or "important" were social aspects. "Community for children," for instance, was in the top five in all four projects. That children live an entirely different life in a communal project than in a standard rental apartment building is obvious even to the most casual observer. Children aged two and up take over the semipublic space of corridors and commons as their own. They involve adults socially through their active use of normally dull and lifeless environments. Parents and nonparents alike are positive about this aspect of communal living.

One especially interesting finding presented in Table 13.3 is the evaluation of common meals. Eating centrally is the clearest difference between a communal project and other apartment living. Yet in the larger projects, where an outside food service handles meals, only half of the respondents rate the meal service as an important aspect of communal living. In the smaller projects, meals are among the five most important aspects of the project. Tenants prepare meals themselves and can control quality, portion, and type of food. Eating together in these buildings is the heart of the communal experience.

It is difficult to say if this significant difference is a consequence of scale or of social organization. Within the larger projects, spontaneous rotating potlucks have sprung up among residents to avoid the institutional restaurant food and yet still enjoy the advantages of sharing cooking chores.

PROBLEMS IN PARADISE: HOUSING MANAGEMENT GOALS AND CONSTRAINTS

These projects have attracted a new type of tenant. The postmaterialist communard seems generally to value social aspects of housing above material aspects, and to have the economic and cultural wherewithal to demand it. With this new tenant, however, public housing firms have also encountered a new group of problems, in part related to their goals. Public housing firms, especially the largest ones, have not been equipped to deal with postmaterialist demands. While extensive reorganization has been undertaken to revamp public firms to deal with new requirements for tenant participation and more decentralized forms of management (Cronberg 1986), there are still significant areas of tension. The experiment with communal living helps reveal these weaknesses. A general problem of not having the organization or the personnel to deal with tenant influence found in all public housing in Sweden (Hjärne et al. 1979; Bengtsson 1981, 1985) becomes acute when dealing with highly organized tenants.

The postmaterialist in the public job sector can get time off from work to negotiate with the landlord. The highly educated communard knows lawyers and can confront managers during office hours. In all these projects, tenants are tenacious in demanding repairs of faulty construction, renegotiating rents, and getting proper information on upkeep. Managers have had to attend evening meetings with complaining, highly verbal tenants. While in many "normal" rental projects, where tenant influence agreements are in effect, active tenants make up less than 10 percent of the population, in these communal projects attendance at management meetings is always about 35 percent of all residents. In the smaller projects, attendance is usually around 75 percent. While this sounds like an ideal situation for tenant participation, it has created extra demands on managers. As one maintenance supervisor commented, "It wasn't really the idea to manage the communal projects as an exception. They should be part of the normal stock." However, given the exceptional tenant, exceptional management has been called for.

One of the largest housing firms in Sweden manages the two big Stockholm projects. It has lacked the flexibility and decentralized organization necessary to handle "an exception." Further complicating its task is the fact that the projects are caught in an inflexible network of other connections to the Social Welfare Office, the Housing Authority, the Bureau for the Elderly, and the restaurateur. These connections hamper freedom in negotiation with tenants. For example, tenants want more influence over the restaurant. The situation has resulted in tenant boycotts in both projects. Some of the conflict is based on tenant post-material values. About half the tenants in the larger project moved in with hope of changing the large-scale format to a more intimate self-help situation. The community they seek is not compatible with the institutional restaurant structure. The tenants and the housing firm have developed an adversary relationship. Given the cultural resources of the tenants and the power of the firm, the standoff has led to protracted legal negotiations that drag on and on.

Thus, although one of the goals of the communal effort has been tenant influence, public housing firms have found that fulfilling this goal involves restructuring and unanticipated resource mobilization. On the positive side of tenant involvement, there is a low incidence of internal vandalism. Tenant pride seems to be high. They decorated halls and commons themselves so that all the projects have a personal touch. In the long run, tenant control of the environment and involvement in management may help these projects end up on the plus side of the management ledger.

Another fiscal goal of the projects has been cutting production costs. Here, too, the projects have had mixed results. Generally, tenants with minimized apartments express satisfaction. The most common cutback is in kitchen size. In the smaller projects where food service is most successful, some families report they are even willing to forgo more kitchen equipment. They claim they need less storage space when they eat regularly in the building. All families have accepted the trade-off of generally smaller rooms for larger common facilities. This could indicate a possible place to cut production costs in the future, but only if producing the common rooms is less expensive than building larger apartments.

However, a real problem more generally is the high cost of all new housing. The biggest complaint in all projects is cost. Despite rent rebates for maintenance chores, rents are high. The availability of cheaper housing, including single-family homes, is threatening tenant stability. Among tenants who thought they might move in the next five years (varying from 10 to 30 percent in the four projects), the primary motivation was economic. High costs also work against realizing any goal of socioeconomic integration, as families with low incomes cannot afford the rent.

In the long run, a communal project with high tenant involvement may slightly cut costs for maintenance. Yet, other factors remaining constant, the effect of a communal project on fiscal strain as measured in money is probably nil. The real importance of the project is as a symbol that the public housing firm is open to change and responsive to social pressure.

CAN THE POSTMATERIALIST COMMUNE CHANGE PUBLIC HOUSING? GOALS AND REALITIES

The Swedish public housing communes came about through political pressure. They had a number of social goals appealing to feminists and political activists. However, the projects became reality only when it could be shown that social goals were compatible with the needs of the public housing firms themselves. For the public sector to take on the risks of such an experiment required a pragmatic coupling to potential economic benefits. This coupling of social idealism with economic pragmatism has characterized most modern Swedish housing policy (Woodward 1987). In spirit, the communal experiment is hardly a deviation, even if internationally it may seem radical.

Social Goals

We have seen that the projects examined here have been successful in living up to a number of social goals. The studied communal projects offer alternatives for many different family types. For example, multigeneration living where a parent lives in housing for the elderly while the son or daughter lives in the communal project is feasible and convenient. Some of the projects demonstrate new living arrangements for divorced parents. Parents sharing child care had separate apartments in the same communal project. Of course such experiments depend on the willingness of the housing authority to find new models for allocation that better fit the needs of various family types.

All of the projects here offered good forms for tenant involvement, but the forms found content only in the smaller projects. This suggests that scale will be important in planning future communal buildings. The issue of scale is relevant not only for the project, but also for the managing firm. The smaller housing firms seemed better able to deal with the communal experiments' growing pains than did the larger Stockholm firm. Each of the smaller firms had a staff member who took personal responsibility for the project. For the larger projects, much work remains to institute real tenant participation. At times progress seems to have been hindered by the very size and complexity of the management firm itself.

While it is still too early to judge the success in promoting social integration, the percentage of respondents who know their neighbors was striking. In the smaller houses here, as well as in Gothenburg (Caldenby & Walldén 1984), tenants were on a first-name basis and knew most of the children in their houses. This is a far cry from the usual anonymity of Swedish multifamily housing, and comes about through the sharing of common tasks. It can be hypothesized that this development also lays the base for mutual aid, but testing this will require further research.

Finally, the social goal of appealing to new and desirable tenant groups seems to have been attained. The communards are highly educated. Their value profile can be termed postmaterialist. They seem to share a number of the ideals found in other European alternative social movements (Offe 1984, 1985; and Frankel 1986). They belong to the social class most likely to purchase a single-family home rather than staying in rental housing. Attracting these tenants can help public firms break a trend of becoming a retreat for the poorest, oldest, and youngest. However, thus far these projects are still experimental and appeal to a postmaterial sort of elite. The form could be attractive to a wider public, but first the firms must dare to believe that it is viable.

Management Goals

Turning to management and fiscal goals, we see more problems. All of the projects involved many municipal offices in their planning and management. In most public administrations, a number of conflicting goals exist simultaneously within the same organization. These conflicting goals (Pressman and Wildavsky 1979), as well as organizational inertia and defensive game playing (Bardach 1977), are cited in the implementation literature as factors slowing innovation in the public sector. An organization may be commanded to carry out a political task but not have the means, or alternatively have the means but not the will. Both situations lead to implementation failures. When several organizations are involved in implementing a program, the potential for failure increases. The larger Stockholm communal projects provide an illustration of such intraorganizational implementation barriers. The municipal housing authority has an overarching goal of solving acute housing problems. To achieve this end it may fill communal projects with tenants uninterested in communal living but with attractive exchange apartments. It puts priority on its overarching goal over the lesser goal of insuring the success of communal experiments. Likewise, a goal of the integrated elderly-communal projects was to promote social integration of the aged. The Social Welfare Office, whose primary obligation is to meet the most crying needs, allocated elderly housing to the most needy rather than those with a potential for taking part in common activities with their younger neighbors. The result is that the median age of the elderly in the projects is 88. This dampens any realistic hope of social integration.

Interviews in 1986 with tenant groups about their most pressing problems revolved around this dilemma. Problems in obtaining cooperation from all concerned administrations to make the projects a success drain tenant enthusiasm. That this does not have to be the case is illustrated in the first Swedish communal project in Linköping (Stolplyckan treated in Pedersen 1981). The various municipal offices formed a cooperative management group to overcome such territorial and goal conflicts. This suggests that a major task facing tenant enthusiasts and management is building the bridges between concerned public offices and removing the burdens of suspicion and/or complacency that have hindered innovation.

The four projects here have succeeded in introducing smaller apartments and attracting solvent tenants who pay their rent on time. However, their potential to lower management costs in the long run depends on the solution of a number of related organizational dilemmas. In the larger projects, some of the most committed tenants have moved or plan to move because of frustration. Committed tenants in Rio, for example, feel that if apartments continue to go to those uninterested in communal living, the experiment will eventually die.

The public housing commune touches only a few households in Sweden. After five years of experimentation, however, the results provide grounds for optimism. The form can potentially house new family forms and provide a source of renewal for public housing.

While the details may seem to have come from the special situation of a powerful Swedish public housing sector, the broad idea can suggest solutions for other countries experiencing postmaterial demands. Future research should focus on identification of the most successful management forms and physical layouts to underwrite the fiscal and social goals of public housing communes.

NOTES

This chapter presents results from the project "Management and Social Integration in Collective Housing," financed by the Swedish Council on Building Research and the Royal Institute of Technology, Department of Building Function Analysis. Thanks to colleagues Maj Britt Grossman and Dick Urban Vestbro, as well as to an anonymous reviewer.

1. In larger cities, public housing makes up a greater proportion of all housing. In 1980, 28 percent of all housing in Stockholm was public (Lindberg 1985).

2. G. Wright (1981) and Hayden (1981, 1984) document American attempts with communal housing, including the apartment hotel. The goal of many of these solutions

was to ease the housekeeping burden in families without personal servants. However, they were also the forerunners of the multifamily communal housing solutions.

3. Three of the four projects are presented and illustrated in the Swedish architectural magazine *Arkitektur* (1985). An English summary and floor plans are included there.

REFERENCES

Ahrne, Göran
1982   "Report on the Swedish Class Structure." Working paper from Class and Class Consciousness Project, Department of Sociology, University of Uppsala, Sweden.
Åkerman, Britta et al.
1975   *Service och gemenskap där vi bor i Stockholm.* Stockholm: Tiden.
Arkitektur
1985   Theme issue on collective/communal housing. 85, 3–30.
Bardach, E.
1977   *The Implementation Game: What Happens After a Bill Becomes a Law.* Cambridge, MA: MIT Press.
Bengtsson, Bo
1981   *Boendedemokrati och boendeinflytande.* Gävle: Statens Institut för byggnadsforskning.
1985   *Lokalt hyresgästinflytande i allmännyttiga och privata fastigheter: en jämförelse.* Gävle: Statens institut för byggnadsforskning (publication M85:4).
Berger, Bennet
1981   *Survival of a Counter-Culture: Ideological Work and Everyday Life Among Rural Communards.* Berkeley: University of California Press.
BIG-gruppen
1982   *Det lilla kollektivhuset: En modell for praktisk tillämpning* (T14:1982). Stockholm: Statens råd för byggnadsforskning.
BoFast
1985   Theme issue on response to apartment vacancies. 3, 5.
Caldenby, Claes, and Walldén, Åsa
1979   *Kollektivhus: Soviet och Sverige omkring 1930.* Stockholm: Statens råd för byggnadsforskning.
1984   *Kollektivhus Stacken.* Gothenburg: Bokförlaget Korpen.
Cronberg, Tarja
1986   "Tenants' Involvement in the Management of Social Housing in the Nordic Countries." *Scandinavian Housing and Planning Research* 3, 65–87.
Cronberg, Tarja, et al. (eds.)
1979   *Bygge och bo pa kvinners vilkar. Rapport fra en konferense i Kungälv 4–6 mai 1979.* Copenhagen: Nordiske kvinners bygg og planforum.
Danemark, Berth
1984   *Boendesegregationens utveckling i Sverige under Efterkrigstiden* (DS Bo 1985, 4). Stockholm: Bostadsdepartement.
Djilas, Milovan
1966   *The New Class.* London: Unwin.
Frankel, Boris
1986   *The Post-Industrial Utopians.* Cambridge: Polity Press.

Franzén, Mats
1982   "Vänstern och den romantiska pessimismen." *Zenit* 75, 5–17.
Franzén, Mats, and Eva Sandstedt
1981   *Grannskap och stadsplanering: Om stat och byggandet i efterkrigstidens Sverige.* Academic dissertation. Department of Sociology, Uppsala University. Stockholm: Almqvist & Wiksell.
Frykman, Tofte
1985   "Bostadssubventioner och jämlikhet i boendet." In Byggforskningsrådet, *Forskare om bostadspolitik och bostadsmarknad* (T6: 1985), 63–85. Stockholm: Statens råd för byggnadsforskning.
Gorman, Clem
1975   *People Together: A Guide to Communal Living.* St. Albans, Herts.: Paladin.
Gouldner, Alvin
1979   *The Future of the Intellectuals and the Rise of the New Class.* New York: Seabury.
Gromark, Sten
1983   *Boendegemenskap: En kritisk granskning av boendegemenskap som samhällsangelägenhet, av dess värden, villkor och förutsättningar.* Gothenburg: CTH Arkitektur, Institution för byggnadsplanering.
Grossman, Maj Britt, and Dick Urban Vestbro
1982   *Aktuella kollektiva bostadsprojekt.* Stockholm: Kungliga Tekniska Högskolan, byggnadsfunktionslära.
Hayden, Dolores
1981   *The Grand Domestic Revolution: A History of Feminist Designs for American Homes, Neighborhoods and Cities.* Cambridge, MA: MIT Press.
1984   *Redesigning the American Dream: The Future of Housing, Work and Family Life.* New York: Norton.
Hjärne, Lars
1982   "Inte bara for sociala atleter—om dynamiken i kollektivboende." *Bo kolektivt,* edited by B. Sollbe, 133–40. Gävle: Statens råd för byggnadsforskning.
Hjärne, Lars, Hilda Lennartson, and Tiiu Soidre-Brink
1979   *Hyresgästinflytande-På vems villkor?* (R115:1979). Stockholm: Statens råd för byggnadsforskning.
Inglehart, Ronald
1977   *The Silent Revolution: Changing Values and Political Styles among Western Publics.* Princeton, NJ: Princeton University Press.
1982   "Changing Values and the Rise of Environmentalism in Western Societies" (preprint 1982–14). Berlin: International Institute for Environment and Society, Wissenschaftszentrum.
Jonsson, Britta
1983   *Alternative rörelse och samhällsutveckling i Sverige.* Academic Dissertation, Department of Sociology, Uppsala University, Sweden.
Kanter, Rosabeth Moss
1979   "Communes in Cities." In *Co-ops, Communes and Collectives: Experiments in Social Change in the 1960's and 1970's,* edited by John Case and Rosemary Taylor. New York: Pantheon Books.
Kärnekull, Kerstin
1982   "Upplåtelseformer for kollektivboende: Problem kan lösas om viljan finns." In

Bo Kollektivt (M82:20), edited by B. Sollbe, 67–72. Gävle: Statens Institut för byggnadsforskning.

Lindberg, Göran
1978   "Arguments for Studying Collective Houses." Paper presented at International Sociological Association Uppsala Congress, Session 2, "Housing and the Physical Environment," August 16.
1985   "Ekonomi, organisaton och kooperation i kooperative bostadsförvaltning." In Byggforskningsrådet, *Forskare om förvaltning och förnyelse* (T7:1985), 63–84. Stockholm: Statens råd för byggnadsforskning.

Madigan, Michael
1984   *Kollektivhus-hyresrättsliga aspekter på ägande och boende.* Stockholm: SABO.

Offe, Claus
1984   *Contradictions in the Welfare State.* London: Hutchinson.
1985   "New Social Movements: Challenging the Boundaries of Institutional Politics." *Social Research* 42, 817–67.

Palm-Lindén, Karin
1982   *Att Bo i Storfamilj* (Rapport R2:1982). Lund: Lunds Universitet, Arkitektursektionen, Byggnadsfunktionslära.

Pedersen, Britt
1981   *Stolplyckan: Kommunalt kollektivhus i Linköping.* Lund: Lunds Universitet, Arkitektursektionen, Byggnadsfunktionslära (Unpublished working paper).

Petersen, Paul
1972   *Wohngemeinschaft oder Grossfamilie-Versuch einer Neuen Lebensform.* Wuppertal: Jugendienst-Verlag.

Pressman, Jeffrey, and Aaron Wildavsky
1979   *Implementation.* Berkeley: University of California Press.

Sandelin, B. and B. Södersten
1978   *Betalt för att bo.* Stockholm: Raben & Sjögren.

Schumacher, E. F.
1973   *Small Is Beautiful.* London: Blond and Briggs.

Sollbe, B. (ed.)
1982   *Bo Kollektiv-erfarenheter och visioner* (M82:20). Gävle: Statens Institut för byggnadsforskning.

Stockholms Kommuns Kollektivhus Kommitté
1983   *Kollektivboende i Stockholm. Slutrapport från Kollektivhuskommittén.* Stockholm: Stockholms stad.

Thelander, Anna Lisa
1984   *Bostad efter behov. Jämlikhet och integration i boendet på 80-talets bostadsmarknad* (Rapport R 26:1984). Stockholm: Statens råd för byggnadsforskning.
1985   "Den svenska bostadssituationen. Förändringar och utvecklingsmönster." In Byggforskningsrådet, *Forskare om förvaltning och förnyelse*, 15–36. Stockholm: Statens råd för byggnadsforskning.

Turner, J. F. C.
1976   *Housing by People: Towards Autonomy in Living Environments.* London: Marion Boyars.

Uusitalo, Liisa
1980   "Post-Industrial Society and Environmentalism." (reprint IIUG 1980–19) Berlin: International Institute for Environment and Society, Wissenschaftszentrum.

Vestbro, Dick Urban
1982   *Kollektivhus fran enkökshus till bogemenskap*. Stockholm: Statens råd for byggnadsforskning.
1985   "Socialistiska och borgerliga bostadsutopier." *Zenit* 87, 17–35.
Watts, Nicholas
1979   "Post-Material Values and Political Change: Hypotheses for Comparative Research." Paper presented at Meeting of the International Society of Political Psychology, Washington, DC.
Watts, Nicholas, and Geoffrey Wandesforde-Smith
1982   "Post-material Values and Environmental Policy Change." In *Environmental Policy Formation*, edited by Dean E. Mann, 29–42. Lexington, MA: Lexington Books.
Woodward, Alison
1987   "Social Ambitions: Planning for Community in the United States and Sweden." In *Research Reports from the Department of Sociology*, no. 2. Uppsala: Uppsala University.
Woodward, Alison, Maj Britt Grossman, and Dick Urban Vestbro
1984   "Projektbeskrivning: Förvaltning och integration i kollektivhus." Research proposal submitted to Swedish Council for Building Research, April 1984. Stockholm: Kungliga Tekniska Högskolan, Arkitektursektionen, Byggnadsfunktionslära.
Wright, Erik O.
1978   *Class, Crisis and the State*. London: New Left Books.
1980   "Class and Occupation." *Theory and Society* 9, 177–214.

14

Coping with Condominiums in the Netherlands

JAN VAN WEESEP

Abstract. Condominium conversion has become a volatile issue in large cities in the Netherlands. The turning of rental units into owner-occupier tenure is widely considered to be a threat to the government's allocation and management of rental housing. In addition, the owner occupiers of the units are thought to be overburdened with management problems. This research reports on such management problems of housing authorities as well as owner occupiers in The Hague. Effects of conversion differed in the various market sectors. The decline of the rental sector tended to be less severe than housing authorities feared. Most owner occupiers were able to maintain their property, but results of the analysis suggest that government should intervene in the condominium associations to ensure proper maintenance in the future.

INTRODUCTION

Part of the private rental sector in the Netherlands housing market has undergone a change of tenure to home ownership. Condominium conversion has become a controversial part of this process. Its focal position reflects the anxiety of housing authorities, who feel that conversion impedes their efforts to effectuate an equitable distribution of housing. Throughout the postwar period, they allocated the vacant rental housing, but the rationale of this practice is undermined when the number of rental units plummets as a result of tenure conversion.

Unlike in the United States, the conversion of rental dwellings to owner-occupier status in the Netherlands needs only the vehicle of condominium conversion where it involves multiunit property, as Dutch law allows vertical subdivision of the typical row house complexes. Condominium conversion is concentrated in the large cities (Amsterdam, Rotterdam, and The Hague) because of their large proportion of multiunit structures and their large share of rental housing (Maas 1981). Owing to the preponderance of population groups that depend on (low-cost) rental housing and the persistent lack of vacancies, the process of condominium conversion is eyed with great suspicion (Burgemeester en Wethouders 's-Gravenhage 1983). Conversion was blamed for the tightening of the market, and, therefore, the large cities sought legislative action to stop it. However, the 1975 national legislation requiring official permission to convert older buildings was ineffective, as the permit could rarely be denied (Aussems 1981). Subsequently, local ordinances were enacted by the cities to bar the owner of a converted property from using it. But when these provisions were challenged, the courts considered them to be discriminatory (Van Weesep and Maas 1984). The authorities remain apprehensive, although much of their suspicion proves to be unfounded.

The demise of the private rental sector is a process common to a large number of countries (Harloe 1984). Likewise, aided by special statutes, the sale of units in multiunit property has mushroomed everywhere. The cause of condominium conversion is found in the declining profitability of rental property. Landlords can no longer operate at a profit when they face the high costs of necessary maintenance and renovation of the older rental stock. In areas dominated by older rental complexes, wholesale conversion may therefore occur as owners seek capital gains rather than long-term investment yields. Condominium conversion accounts for the increase of owner occupiers in inner-city areas (Cribbet 1963). It has been linked to the conversion of commercial structures (''lofts'') to residences (Zukin 1982; Van Weesep et al. 1985) and to gentrification (Hamnett and Randolph 1986). Yet whereas the process is internationally similar, in the national and local contexts different issues are identified as problematic (Hamnett and Van Weesep 1986).

The American condominium experience offers a case in point. As property taxes are an important source of income for local jurisdictions, the conversion process has been welcomed in some cities as it boosts values. But negative effects have also been stressed, leading to a heated debate over the merits of condominium conversion. The debate focused on the issue of displacement (Lauber 1980). In 1980 the U.S. Congress asked the Department of Housing and Urban Development (HUD) to report on the scope, the causes, and the impact of conversion. While the study played down the total amount of displacement, its occurrence among lower income groups and the elderly was acknowledged (U.S. Department of HUD 1981a). The HUD study identified the resulting steep increase of housing costs for displaced renters and for sitting tenants who bought their unit as a second major problem (U.S. Department of HUD 1981b). Consequently, the thrust of the battle over conversion in the United States is to protect tenants from the hardships of displacement.

The present study of the effects of conversion in The Hague provides evidence that condominium conversion does not cease to be an issue when tenants are protected. As a result of conversion, home seekers find it hard to obtain suitable housing. The demand for condominiums is related to the persistent housing shortage (Van Weesep 1984b). The housing authorities are hard put to find housing for households on their waiting list. Unlike in many other Dutch cities, the housing authorities in The Hague do not allocate the houses owned by private landlords, who control 56 percent of the stock. Above all, the allocation of dwellings stagnates because so many rental dwellings that become vacant are no longer for rent but for sale. Between 1975 and 1982, 3,750 conversion permits were issued citywide, which created at least 15,000 condominium units in the pre-1940 housing stock alone! The Dutch experience shows that even when displacement is not an issue, another kind of problem emerges as the most serious drawback of the conversion process: management. At a general level, housing authorities have to cope with the problems of managing a diminishing rental stock. At the same time, owner occupiers have to cope with the management of their own property; their high housing costs may impede adequate maintenance.

Placing the issue in a comparative perspective does not give conclusive guidelines for policy. Each housing system harbors specific characteristics that can turn a similar process into a very different issue. The protection of tenants from eviction is the major reason that the issue of condominium conversion in the Netherlands is different from that in the United States (Hamnett and Van Weesep 1986). In the Netherlands, conversion and unit sales have become separate processes. The substantial value difference between rented dwellings and vacant ones (Hamnett and Randolph 1984) and the inability of owners to remove sitting tenants slow the sales; sitting tenants can not be threatened into buying, and prospective owner occupiers will buy only vacant dwellings. The decline of the rental stock is thus less severe than the number of conversions suggests. In addition, the U.S. experience shows that other developments may cushion the effect of conversion on the functioning of the rental market (Eilbott 1985; O'Connell forthcoming). Consequently, the impact of conversion on the management problems of the Dutch housing authorities may have been exaggerated. Likewise, the management problems of owner occupiers may be less severe than expected. Conversion has made inroads in widely disparate market segments and has thus encountered large variations in management styles (Van Weesep 1984a).

Our investigation of condominium conversion in the city of The Hague was designed to shed light on these management problems of the authorities and of the owner occupiers. The variations among market segments are highlighted in the first section of this chapter by comparing the record of the conversions in different neighborhoods. In the next section, the four selected neighborhoods and the characteristics of their condominiums are reviewed. Condominiums accounted for 52 percent of their housing stock. Substantial variation, however, exists among the four areas; together they showed the entire range of condominium types and management styles. Subsequently, evidence is presented to argue that the decline of the rental sector as a consequence of conversion is less serious than is commonly assumed. Finally, the focus turns to the activities of owner occupiers with respect to maintenance and improvement of their property.

THE CONTEXT OF THE STUDY

Housing characteristics (age, type, quality) tend to vary by neighborhood. In order to trace the range of effects of condominium conversion, four neighborhoods were selected to represent the variations of the condominium sector in the city of The Hague (see Table 14.1). First, an inventory of the condominiums was made to document the process of accretion and the rate of sales to owner occupiers.[1] This part of the research utilized data from the Land Register and from city registers; all properties were included. Second, a survey of owner occupiers was conducted. In the four neighborhoods 3,589 owner occupiers were identified. Random samples were selected with a 95 percent confidence interval, and 384 interviews were completed, generating an average response rate of 67 percent. The survey provided information on the owner occupiers, including their previous housing market position and their motives to buy. At the same time, the survey was used to collect data on the owner's ways of managing the property and on the functioning of the condominium associations.

Laakkwartier-Oost dates from the 1930s and was built for the lower middle class. It is a relatively attractive neighborhood with parkways and other green areas. The dominant type of housing is the characteristic three-story townhouse ("brownstones"), whereby each unit has its own street access. Most are still privately owned rental units, but wholesale condominium conversion is boosting the number of owner occupiers. The conversion process has been very strong: By 1985, condominiums made up 83 percent of the neighborhood housing stock.

Most homes in *Valkenboskwartier* date from the first quarter of this century. The area was destined for the working class and lower middle class, with a sprinkling of housing for higher income groups. All buildings are multifamily, and most units are relatively large. Fewer than 10 percent have only one or two rooms, and about 30 percent consist of five rooms or more. The population of the area is changing rapidly as younger people move in and as ethnic minorities increase. This area was selected because of its large condominium sector and because it had not been canvassed as intensively as other neighborhoods of this type. Although the exact size remained undermined, almost 3,400 condominium units (approximately 60 percent of the stock) were counted in the land register.

Statenkwartier also dates back to the early decades of this century, but some small apartment blocks were built after World War II. The area was destined for an elite population and has retained its status; it is sought after by those who can afford to live here. In general, the housing stock deviates from the city's average. The condominium sector has expanded rapidly, mostly in the smaller multiunit townhouse and in the postwar blocks. The area had 1,863 condominium units (47 percent of the stock).

The fourth area, *Mariahoeve*, was developed in the 1960s. Though built at low densities, it appears monotonous, because of the predominance of apartment blocks. In spite of this, the area's status is substantial. Amenities and services are above average, and the apartments are relatively spacious (mostly two- and three-bedroom units). The rental sector is evenly divided between nonprofit and private owners; many of the private rental dwellings are owned by pension funds and other institutions. As institutional owners are purely "rational" managers, condominium conversion is likely to occur among their properties; as soon as

Table 14.1
The Housing Stock by Type on January 1, 1985 (percentages)

Housing Type	Laak-kwartier	Maria-hoeve	Staten-kwartier	Valkenbos-kwartier	The Hague
Single-family dwellings	6.7	9.5	37.8	6.6	14.2
Apartment blocks	0.1	78.5	15.4	2.4	26.6
Multi-unit townhouses	86.9	3.5	12.4	53.6	42.8
Other	6.3	8.5	34.4	37.5	16.4
N (=100%)	4817	7708	4043	5623	196612

Source: City of The Hague, Real Estate Register.

operating subsidies run out and maintenance costs rise, the units are sold. The number of owner occupiers in the area is increasing and 60 percent of them own apartments. Over 3,100 (residential) condominiums were counted here. Leasehold has not deterred conversion: 75 percent of the condominiums are sited on land leased from the city.

The selected neighborhoods present the entire range of housing market sectors in the city; likewise, the condominiums demonstrate a wide variety. The selection of neighborhoods allows for comparisons within the condominium sector to estimate the effect of the conversion on the decline of the rental stock and to show the entire range of management styles. Valkenboskwartier is representative of a number of neighborhoods characterized by conversion of low-quality, cheap rental housing. Part of the area is undergoing urban renewal and deferred maintenance is a ubiquitous problem. Statenkwartier is representative of the older high-income areas. Its numerous condominium complexes are small, well-cared-for, and attract a different group of buyers than do the condominiums in the other older areas. Laakkwartier represents the vast middle range of condominiums in The Hague. The inclusion of Mariahoeve brings in the conversions of relatively modern apartment complexes, which supposedly demand fewer renovations. But there were additional reasons to include a new area. Most of the condominiums formed part of large homogeneous complexes, and it was assumed that these were professionally managed. Moreover, many of the converted buildings had been built as cooperative complexes, and the long-term occupants, now the unit owners, were accustomed to communal management decisions. Their experience could provide some useful lessons for the condominium owners elsewhere, and might help to identify useful policy avenues.

THE DECLINE OF THE RENTAL SECTOR

Condominium conversion itself does not necessarily remove any rental units from the market, as the units are often not sold. The sitting tenant is protected from eviction, and as long as the unit cannot be sold vacant for occupancy, the value remains depressed. If the dwelling is sold, it is often sold to another investor, who pays a speculative investment value, hoping that the sitting tenant will die, move, or buy. Nor can the condominium units in use by owner occupiers at the time of the survey simply be looked upon as assaults on the rental sector. The occupant may have been the sitting tenant, may have vacated a rental unit by moving, or may have been a prospective renter. In all these instances, the rental stock diminishes, but the demand for rental units is proportionally reduced. The total effect of the conversion on the rental market is difficult to quantify, but may be estimated by comparing the size of the condominium sector, the volume of sales, the previous housing market position of the owner occupiers, and the motives for buying.

The size of the condominium sector in the four neighborhoods was surprisingly large. In Laakkwartier, 83 percent of all dwellings proved to be condominiums;

in Statenkwartier and Valkenboskwartier, 50 to 60 percent of the stock had been converted. In Mariahoeve the condominium sector accounted for 40 percent of all dwellings, which implies that 75 percent of its private rental stock had been converted. Owners of rental property indicate that they routinely convert their entire property to increase its value and to evade possible future obstacles.[2] Many conversions in the older neighborhoods took place before 1975, when the conversion permit was introduced. In the older neighborhoods, conversion still continues, but at a much slower pace. This may have been caused by the fall in price of residential property after 1978, but it may also be related to the depletion of the unconverted stock.

By 1983, some 50 percent of all condominium units in the three older neighborhoods had not been sold at all. In Mariahoeve 86 percent had been retained by the owner who converted, clearly a reflection of the many former cooperatives that had been converted to condominiums. In addition, it became clear that many sales did not involve owner occupiers. In Valkenboskwartier less than 40 percent of all buyers intended to occupy the unit; a slight majority of the transactions in Laakkwartier were also among traders. But in Mariahoeve as well as in Statenkwartier owner occupiers made up 75 percent of all buyers. The former landlords are more inclined to sell entire complexes to speculators than to retail the units themselves. Some of the new owners push hard for sales to sitting tenants, other bide their time until the unit is vacated before they sell to an owner occupier. It is obvious from the sales volume and from the pattern of sales among categories of owners that the rental stock erodes slowly. To the housing authorities, the slow pace of the decline of the number of rental units brings little solace. They have to deal with the problem that the dwellings will not be rerented when the present occupants leave.

The share of owner occupiers varied from 48 percent in Statenkwartier to 22 percent in Mariahoeve. Some of the condominium units were sold to sitting tenants. In Mariahoeve, this number was very high because some 50 percent of all owner occupiers had been shareholder-residents of the cooperatives that had been converted; in the other complexes, less than 10 percent were former tenants (see Table 14.2). The largest share was registered in Valkenboskwartier, where 20 percent of all owner occupiers were sitting tenants. Most former tenants preferred owning to renting, possibly because they were offered discount prices. Other owner occupiers, from 25 percent in Laakkwartier to 50 percent in the other areas, had moved from a different dwelling to the present condominium (Table 14.2). Some of them had moved to The Hague from elsewhere; others had owned their previous dwelling. The net effect of the adaptation moves within The Hague varied substantially. As few as 3 percent of the new owner occupiers in Mariahoeve vacated a rental dwelling in the city. In Statenkwartier and Valkenboskwartier the group accounted for 25 percent, in Laakkwartier for 15 percent. Thus while condominium conversion does promote adaptation moves— a high priority in the city's housing policies—the rate at which rental units become available obviously falls short of the number lost through conversion.

Table 14.2
The Housing Status of the Owner Occupiers upon the Acquisition of the Present Condominium Unit (percentages)

Housing Status	Laak-kwartier	Maria-hoeve *	Staten-kwartier	Valkenbos-kwartier
Starter	58.9	25.7	29.6	27.8
Sitting tenant	13.4	8.6	13.3	25.8
Occupant of other home	27.7	51.4	57.1	46.4
Unknown	-	14.3	-	-
n (=100%)	112	35	98	97

* In Mariahoeve the previous members of the cooperatives have been omitted.

Finally, the effect of the sale of units on the rental market may be cushioned by the diversion of potential renters to the condominiums, decreasing the demand for rental units. In Laakkwartier 46 percent of the sample would have preferred to rent; elsewhere, the group varied in size, from 13 percent in Mariahoeve to 35 percent in Valkenboskwartier. The most important reason (42 percent to 69 percent) for these owners to buy was the anticipated long wait for a suitable rental dwelling. In Mariahoeve, and to a somewhat lesser extent in Statenkwartier, the other high-cost area, a substantial number bought because they could not find what they desired in the rental sector.

Thus, as units are being sold to owner occupiers, the rental sector declines. Some buyers make rental units available, others had been interested in a rental dwelling; and by buying a home, they helped decrease the demand for rental units. In Statenkwartier, where 48 percent of the units were sold to owner occupiers, the loss was compensated in half the cases. In Laakkwartier and Valkenboskwartier, one-third of the very large condominium sector had been sold to owner occupiers, and in one-quarter of these cases the loss of the rental unit was not compensated. In Mariahoeve, three out of every four units sold to an owner occupier caused a decline of the rental stock. The two higher-cost neighborhoods thus registered the largest net losses, but fortunately most of these had been more expensive rental units, of which there is no real shortage.

MAINTENANCE AND RENOVATIONS IN THE CONDOMINIUM STOCK

Activities of the Unit Owners

The objections to condominium conversion are not based solely on the anticipated consequences of loss of rental housing. They also express the housing authorities' fear of rapid dilapidation of condominiums, which would eventually necessitate urban renewal. At a time when the city is attempting to make ends meet by enforcing deep budget cuts, this would constitute a very strong argument against condominium conversion and provide the justification for severe restrictions.

The research, however, demonstrated that the situation was not serious. In the older stock, this is in part a result of the compulsory building inspection that follows the application for a conversion permit. The building inspectors carry out their task assiduously, leading to the correction of serious defects. There is a more important reason for the better-than-anticipated situation: In contrast to expectations, the great majority of the owners can well afford to maintain their dwellings and, indeed, much work is being done.

Some owner occupiers have not undertaken any work at all on their units; in Mariahoeve and Statenkwartier this group comprised one-third of the owners. A frequently given reason was that the—often relatively new—unit did not need any maintenance or improvement. In the other two areas, more than 30 percent of the owners undertook five or more separate activities. In the areas with modest dwellings, it was common to improve the floor plan by knocking down partition walls. In all three older neighborhoods wiring, water, and gas pipes were frequently replaced. Everywhere, even in Mariahoeve, kitchens, baths, and other facilities were upgraded. Other activities, clearly concentrated in the more expensive neighborhoods, include such niceties as installation of fireplaces (compare Chapter 5).

Within each neighborhood the survey recorded significant variation in repair and maintenance activities among unit owners. A number of regularities were observed. In general, the number of activities increased with the age of the owners. Also the cost of maintenance and improvements is directly related to age, but this may be an effect of who did the job: the owner or a contracted professional. The elderly hired more outside help. This may explain why low-income owners (including many elderly) spend more on repairs and maintenance than do middle-income owners. In Mariahoeve, differences showed up among complexes: in former cooperatives, with their many elderly owners of long tenure, different types of activities were undertaken than in the converted rental complexes with young high-income owners. Neither occupational status nor family status were related to number of activities or to the cost. It may be significant that those who had professed a preference for a rental dwelling did as much maintenance as those who registered their preference for home ownership. Apparently, the two groups do not have a different opinion on how to manage their units. In general, length of tenure was positively related to number of activities, suggesting a cumulative improvement strategy.

In all four neighborhoods much work was done by the owners themselves, with or without the help of friends. In relatively few cases everything was left to professionals. Owners in Laakkwartier and Valkenboskwartier were most actively involved; in 50 percent of the cases the work was done without professional help. At the other end of the range was the elitist Statenkwartier, where only 17 percent of the owners performed all the work by themselves with or without the help of friends. The use of subsidies tended to decrease the extra financial burden resulting from the involvement of professionals.

A disappointingly small number of owners had applied for subsidy payments. In Valkenboskwartier one in every three owners who had undertaken maintenance or improvements had applied for support. Possibly the owners here were more familiar with the programs, because urban renewal was taking place in the area. Elsewhere, no more than 20 percent of the owners applied for a subsidy. The respondents in Mariahoeve gave several reasons why they refrained from applying for subsidies. One-third were unfamiliar with the programs. One-half knew about the programs but had not applied: they thought that the type of work they undertook fell outside the program; they did the job themselves; or they hired a moonlighter for unreported (black market) wages (compare Chapter 6). However, where subsidies were granted, they did have a positive effect: More money was spent on the work and professionals were more often involved.

Clearly, subsidies are important, both for improved maintenance standards and for creating jobs.

The Performance of the Condominium Associations

The physical integrity of the condominium is not only dependent on the way the owners care for their units; each condominium complex has common elements that need to be maintained. Although the precise delineation varies, the common elements always include the structural parts of the building, such as foundations, outside walls, utility mains, and so on. The law has vested the responsibility for these common elements in the condominium association, the meeting of unit owners. The association is founded when the condominium is registered as such. Condominiums established under the old 1951 act may not have an association. In fact, the clarification of the mutual relationships and the responsibilities of the unit owners were central to the 1971 amendments. The description of the association provided unambiguous rules concerning the management of the property. The association is responsible for day-to-day management and for maintenance and repairs of the common elements. The law prescribes that the members must meet at least once a year, appoint officers, and decide on the unit owners' contributions for common expenses, including necessary maintenance and repairs of the common elements. The associations decide what is to be done, and they are the key to understanding the differences in care for the buildings. It is therefore important to describe how the associations in the four neighborhoods function, before studying the variations of activities.

The results of the survey are alarming.[3] Both in Statenkwartier and in Valkenboskwartier a vast majority of the owners (66 and 90 percent, respectively) did not know about their association. In Laakkwartier nearly 35 percent of the unit owners had no information on their association. In contrast, in the larger, more recently converted complexes in Mariahoeve, the existence of the associations was acknowledged by every respondent. Likewise, the postwar complexes in Statenkwartier put the formal structure into practice more than the other complexes in the same neighborhood do. Obviously, larger complexes require more formal interaction structures, and apparently, when the need is demonstrated and the associations are properly set up, the owners support them.

The best situation was reported from postwar Mariahoeve. All owners were familiar with their association. The prescribed meetings take place, and attendance figures are high. All associations seem to have adequate financial reserves. Few conflicts reportedly existed within the associations. This may result from two causes: owner occupiers are a majority in all complexes, and while informal consultations do occur, all important decisions are arrived at in scheduled meetings of all owners. Most owners reported to be very satisfied with the way the condominium complex was being run. On the basis of this evidence one would conclude that running the association by the book leads to harmonious condominium complexes. Following the rules, however, can be dispensed with, as the evidence from Statenkwartier shows. A large majority of the unit owners here stated that the association did not meet its obligations—in fact, most denied its existence—but they did not find this to be a problem. The reason for this is that these condominium complexes tended to be very small (fewer than five units), socially homogeneous, and with majorities of owner occupiers. With so few people involved, and few potential problems, informal decision making takes the place of formal meetings. Few of the existing associations had financial reserves beyond what was needed for operating expenses. Larger expenses are covered from special assessments.

When the association does not function well, the owners have no recourse to standard and legally enforceable procedures to deal with conflicts over their joint responsibilities. This can lead to bitter strife among the unit owners, to dissatisfaction, and to deferred maintenance. Evidence of such situations was gathered in Laakkwartier and Valkenboskwartier. In Laakkwartier some associations functioned well, and in some that did not meet the requirements of the law the management was arranged informally. But no fewer than 10 percent of the owners complained about conflicts between owner occupiers and absentee landlords. Quality differences within the complexes were frequently the cause of other problems. Many owners were adamant about their refusal to pay for repairs on houses of a different quality, sometimes as far as a half block away. Likewise, the associations in Valkenboskwartier were often reduced to inactivity (or worse) by internal conflict. These conflicts cast a shadow on the condominium, as they diminish the social benefits of home ownership and can easily stave off the needed and desired maintenance.

Maintenance of the Complexes

Regular maintenance of common elements is at least as important as work on the individual units for the future of the housing stock. As buildings age, more effort is required to keep them in good condition. Therefore, the condominiums in the older neighborhoods demand more maintenance than those in the postwar areas. In reality, the buildings in the older areas are not given more care than the newer ones. On the contrary, the number of activities per complex is larger in Mariahoeve than elsewhere. The larger number of activities here reflects in part the long tenure of many owners in Mariahoeve, who can consequently recount a long history of sporadic maintenance activities. But the owners of units in recently converted rental complexes also reported significant activity. In the other three neighborhoods, some 30 to 40 percent of the owners reported no activity on the common elements. Some owners declared that no work was necessary, but many reported that conflicts of opinion among the owners and/or lack of money was the reason that necessary work did not take place.

The type of activities also varied among the neighborhoods (Table 14.3) Work on the roof is common, possibly because a good roof is essential to the integrity of the building and the comfort of its occupants; necessary roof repairs are always

Table 14.3
Type of Maintenance and Improvement Activities of Common Elements (percentages)

	Laak-kwartier	Maria-hoeve	Staten-kwartier	Valkenbos-kwartier
Roof	44	56	74	67
Outside walls	22	24	21	33
Sewers, drains	24	-	18	40
Water & gas mains	6	8	16	12
Thermopane	•	12	19	5
Painting	43	77	79	59
Repair of balconies	8	-	18	5
n (=100%)	63	67	68	58

• no data

urgent and are always carried out. There are also differences in activities that are more preventive in nature (painting) or that are intended to increase the comfort of the occupants (installation of thermopane); these are significantly more common in the higher income areas of Statenkwartier and Mariahoeve. In the two other neighborhoods urgent repairs take place, but other work is apparently put off.

Expenditures for work on common elements (per owner) are much lower than the average cost of work on the individual units. In Laakkwartier and Statenwartier, 60 percent of the owners had spent more than 10,000 guilders on their individual units. (One guilder equaled $0.48, April 1987.) In contrast, in Laakkwartier, the owners in only 11 out of 61 complexes where work was done had each spent over 2,500 guilders on the common elements; in Statenkwartier, only 17 percent of the owners had spent more than 5,000 guilders on the common elements. A similar imbalance existed in Valkenboswartier. Here, 73 percent of all unit owners had spent more than 10,000 guilders on their own units, and only 30 percent contributed more than 5,000 guilders to maintenance and repairs of common elements. (In Mariahoeve the condominium associations paid the bills from the reserves, and many owners did not know their exact share.) In the three older neighborhoods, special assessments are common practice, and this hampers rational decision making in cases where social relations are not good. In several instances, owners reported having paid for urgent repairs of "their" common elements, without being able to collect from the others.

This analysis demonstrates that the larger homogeneous complexes with formally run associations promote good maintenance. The same is true of the very informally run smaller associations where the social relations among the owner occupiers are good. But when the unit owners in the same complex differ in opinion about the necessity of work on the common elements, the most urgent problems get dealt with but, in general, less work gets done. In fact, the way management decisions are arrived at can aggravate the tensions among the unit owners. Differences of opinion on work on the common elements were recorded not only between owner occupiers and absentee landlords, but also among resident owners. A well-functioning condominium association could help resolve such problems, but to have a fair chance of success, the establishment of the association would have to be treated with more care.

CONCLUSIONS AND POLICY RECOMMENDATIONS

Conclusions

The research revealed that thousands of condominium units have been created by the conversion of rental buildings in The Hague. By implication, the potential loss to the rental sector is great, but a significant proportion of the units continue to be rented. Large investors customarily convert, without the intention to sell individual units in the short run. When they do sell, they prefer to sell all units at once. They are not in the business of selling individual units, and they do not want to have to deal with other owners in the transition period. Thus, dealers take the middleman position and thousands of units are already in their hands. Eventually, a substantial loss of rental units should be expected. As owner occupiers move into the condominiums, the demand for rental dwellings will decrease, but not proportionally. Consequently, the housing authorities will have to cope with a tight rental market in the future.

The most significant finding from the research is that the effects of conversion are different in the various neighborhoods. The owner occupiers themselves exhibit a diversity of personal and household characteristics. No evidence was found of an overall financial crisis, and there is no reason to believe that the average owner would not be able to afford the cost of normal maintenance. Indeed, the maintenance efforts of owner occupiers are much better than anticipated by housing officials; almost all owners undertake activities, and in numerous cases have spent significant amounts of money on their units. Work on the common elements of the complexes, however, is less than optimal. The most urgent problems are taken care of, in one way or another. But especially at the lower end of the market, tensions seem to rise over this issue; elsewhere, the situation is much better. The major reason for the observed differences lies in the functioning of the condominium associations. Only in Mariahoeve do they abide by the letter of the law. In Statenkwartier good informal relations within small homogeneous complexes prevent the emergence of grave problems. Well-run associations do not necessarily guarantee good maintenance practices, but, conversely, poorly functioning associations almost always lead to strife. Large associations seem to work well when they are physically homogeneous; small associations have used informal decision making successfully when the owner occupiers predominate and maintain good social relationships. Few owner occupiers were aware of their rights and obligations, and even fewer had attempted to use the legal instrument of the association by-laws to take care of necessary maintenance and repair work.

Toward a Policy

As the consequences of condominium conversion vary significantly, a differentiated policy is recommended. A general conversion moratorium is not necessary, as the problem of the declining rental stock is less pronounced in the more expensive neighborhoods. Neither these units nor their buyers are part of the housing market segments on which the housing authorities concentrate their efforts. The decrease of rental units in other neighborhoods is a greater cause for concern, as housing authorities can hardly afford to lose this part of the rental market. This would support the current proposal to withhold conversion permits for housing of which there is an acute shortage. But the research showed that these types of housing have already been converted; the eventual sale can hardly be stopped. It seems unlikely that any commercial investor would be able to buy the complexes and continue to rent them at a profit; nonprofit organizations would need substantial subsidies to operate them. The units will almost certainly be lost to the rental sector, and the housing authorities would be wise to try to stimulate positive effects of the increase of home ownership.

Three separate fields of action can be identified. First, the functioning of the condominium associations should be improved. The members should be better informed about their rights and obligations. Procedures within the associations should be clarified. The founding of an Institute of Condominium Associations must be stimulated, to disseminate information, to develop management instruments, and above all to provide individual owners with an easily accessible arbiter in case of conflicts.

Second, conversion procedures should be improved, especially as far as the delineation of individual complexes is concerned. Large complexes can operate well if they are perceived as meaningful entities by the unit owners. If the converter simply pools diverse properties in one condominium complex, problems are imminent. Unit owners are reluctant to share the cost of upkeep of buildings that they do not consider their own, especially if quality differences clearly violate the principles of mutuality. Subdivision of a property into horizontal segments—that is, condominium units—should be preceded by an appropriate vertical subdivision, the delineation of the complexes. This would help to avoid the large heterogeneous complexes with their poorly functioning condominium associations that remain sources of conflict.

Finally, the city should explore the possibility of joining forces with well-intending owners whose efforts at proper maintenance are being frustrated by others. By buying individual units, the housing authorities could become members of condominium associations and help sway the balance in the condominium association when maintenance issues are being voted on. The city customarily acquires housing within the context of its urban renewal program; it could apply the same method to promote private renewal without having to initiate new programs.

Unlike in other countries, the conversion of rental property in the Netherlands does not lead to displacement of tenants. Existing housing legislation prevents rapid increases as a consequence of the increasing shortage of rental units. In spite of many housing market controls, however, there are many ways in which an increase in the number of condominiums—and especially in the subsequent sale of units—can frustrate municipal housing policies. At the same time, the increase in home ownership may harbor benefits in a period characterized by fiscal austerity, a retreat of the public sector, and an increasing appeal to private initiative. A foresighted housing authority should reassess the potential of the condominium when it has so clearly established its presence, and not be sidetracked by outdated ideological positions.

NOTES

1. The research on which this chapter reports is part of the Urban Problems research program (STEPRO) of Utrecht University. The data were gathered by J. Dijkman, M.

Garretsen, T. Hoogland, and J. Kolpa, graduate students of the Free University in Amsterdam. M. W. A. Maas helped supervise the project. The research was carried out at the request of the Department of Urban Development of the city of The Hague. Permission by the Land Register (Rijkskadaster) to copy data from its files is gratefully acknowledged.

2. Information on landlords and their strategies are preliminary outcomes of research by graduate students of the Department of Geography of Utrecht University.

3. Information on the associations was gathered among the owners. In the case of small associations the information may have been taken from a single source. This may have built a bias into the analysis, where the respondent was asked to report on the functioning and activities during his or her tenure. The outcomes thus reflect the individual's involvement or length of tenure, as well as the profile of the association.

REFERENCES

Aussems, T.
1981   "De verkoop van partikuliere huurwoningen en de stadsvernieuwing." *Wonen TA/BK* 18, 21–27.
Burgemeester en Wethouders 's-Gravenhage
1983   *Nota Woningsplitsing*. 's-Gravenhage: Gemeentebestuur.
Cribbet, John E.
1963   "Condominium—Homeownership for Megalopolis." *Michigan Law Review* 61 (May), 1207–44.
Eilbott, P.
1985   "Condominium Rentals and the Supply of Rental Housing." *Urban Affairs Quarterly* 20, no. 3, 389–99.
Hamnett, C., and W. Randolph
1984   "The Role of Landlord Disinvestment in Housing Market Transformation: An Analysis of the Flat Break-up Market in Central London." *Transactions, Institute of British Geographers*, N.S. 9, 259–79.
1986   "Teneurial Transformation and the Flat Break-up Market in London: The British Condo Experience." In *Gentrification of the City*, edited by N. Smith and P. Williams. London: Allen and Unwin.
Hamnett, C., and J. Van Weesep
1986   "The Social and Political Impact of Condominium Conversion: A Comparative Analysis." Paper presented at the Annual Meeting of the Association of American Geographers, Minneapolis.
Harloe, M.
1984   *Private Rented Housing in the United States and Europe*. London: Croom Helm.
Lauber, D.
1980   "Condominium Conversions: The Number Prompts Controls to Protect the Poor and the Elderly." *Journal of Housing* 36, 201–9.
Maas, M. A. W.
1981   "De splitsing van appartementen geinventariseerd in de grote steden." *Bouw* 36, no. 11, 27–30.
O'Connell, B. J.
n.d.   "Cooperative and Condominium Conversion." In *Handbook of Housing and the Built Environment in the U.S.*, edited by E. Huttman and W. Van Vliet—. Westport, CT: Greenwood (forthcoming).

U.S. Department of Housing and Urban Development
1980   *The Conversion of Rental Housing to Condominiums and Cooperatives. A National Study of Scope, Causes, and Impacts.* Washington, DC: U.S. Department of HUD.
1981a   *The Conversion of Rental Housing to Condominiums and Cooperatives. Impacts on Elderly and Lower Income Households.* Washington, DC: U.S. Department of HUD.
1981b   *The Conversion of Rental Housing to Condominiums and Cooperatives. Impacts on Housing Costs.* Washington, DC: U.S. Department of HUD.
Van Weesep, J.
1984a   "Condominium Conversion in Amsterdam: Boon or Burden?" *Urban Geography* 5, no. 2, 165–77.
1984b   "Intervention in The Netherlands: Urban Housing Policy and Market Response." *Urban Affairs Quarterly* 19, no. 3, 329–53.
Van Weesep, J., and M. W. A. Maas
1984   "Housing Policy and Conversion to Condominiums in The Netherlands." *Environment and Planning A* 16, 1149–61.
Van Weesep, J., T. J. Hulsebosch, and M. W. A. Maas
1985   "Revitalisering in Amsterdam: de aanbodzijde belicht." *Geografisch Tijdschrift*, Nieuwe Reeks (New Series), 19, no. 2, 133–45.
Zukin, S.
1982   *Loft Living: Culture and Capital in Urban Change.* Baltimore: Johns Hopkins University Press.

15

Peacetime Municipal Rent Control Laws in the United States: Local Design Issues and Ideological Policy Debates

KENNETH K. BAAR

Abstract. Prior to the 1970s, U.S. rent controls were limited to war-generated emergencies, except in New York City, which has been under rent controls since 1942. Since 1970, municipal rent control laws have been adopted by approximately 100 New Jersey municipalities, 13 California cities, Boston and neighboring suburbs, and Washington, D.C. In addition, about 40 California cities have adopted ordinances which regulate the rents of spaces occupied by "mobile" homes. At present, approximately 3 million of the 28 million rental units in the United States are subject to local rent regulations.

U.S. rent controls typically permit annual across-the-board increases and, in addition, permit individual landlords to petition for rent adjustments based on "fair return" or capital improvements. Rent regulations have been the subject of intense political debate. Analyses and discussions of their impacts are largely ideological, although framed in scientific technical terms. Rent control supporters push for municipal legislation, while rent control opponents advocate state and federal limits on the powers of localities to control rents and evictions.

INTRODUCTION

Peacetime rent controls are a relatively new entrant into U.S. housing policy. Until 1970, rent regulations were enacted only as temporary measures aimed at war-generated emergencies. The one exception has been New York City, which has been under rent controls continuously since 1942.

In the early 1970s, municipal rent controls became widespread on the East Coast. They were adopted in 100 municipalities in New Jersey, Boston and several neighboring cities, and Washington, D.C. In the late 1970s, rent controls became widespread in California. As of 1986, approximately 3 million of the 28 million rental units in the United States were subject to some form of rent regulation (Baar 1983).[1]

In response to these developments and fears that rent controls will become more widespread, there have been federal and state efforts to curb local rent regulations. The President's Commission on Housing (1982) proposed that cities with rent controls lose eligibility for federal mortgage insurance and certain types of federal aid. Eleven states have banned local controls. In jurisdictions where rent controls are in effect, there have been continuous battles over their form and future.

The debate over rent controls takes place on the municipal, state, and federal levels, because each of these levels of government has power over local housing policies. In many states, municipalities have the power to adopt rent controls. States have the power to institute rent controls and they have the power to grant or remove municipal authority to regulate rents. The federal government can condition federal benefits on particular local policies. The debate also takes place in the courts because they have the power to invalidate rent control laws, or particular provisions within them, on constitutional grounds.

The discussion over whether rent controls should be adopted takes place in a political and social arena that contains an underlying premise that the "free" market leads to the best results. While the discussion is clothed in terms of technical analysis, in reality, it consists largely of a combination of sweeping factual conclusions that are not supported by any empirical data, and of ideological comments about the social inequities caused by the presence or absence of such regulations.

Opponents of rent control liken the policy to a disease that will rot a city and hurt, rather than help, its intended beneficiaries. Their principal arguments are that it causes landlords to reduce maintenance, halts construction of new rental units, and unfairly benefits tenants who are not in need. Supporters of rent control claim that tenants, who have little real bargaining power in tight markets, need to be protected from unconscionable rent gouging and claim that regardless of whether or not rents are regulated, the volume of new rental construction will be insufficient to stabilize rents.

The past few years have been marked by significant developments in the rent control debate. Tenant pressures for the expansion of rent controls seem to be increasing as rent increases have exceeded increases in the cost of living in some regions.[2] At the same time, apartment owners have been frustrated in their efforts to obtain judicial relief from tenant-oriented legislation. As a result, political struggles and public policy debates over rent regulations have intensified. Conservatives, who traditionally have been advocates of local control, have focused their efforts on obtaining preemption of local rent control policies at the state and national levels, where tenants are in the minority and are politically ineffective. The most critical change in the next few years may be a shift in judicial attitudes toward rent and eviction restrictions, as members of the judiciary are replaced by more conservative justices.[3]

The purpose of this chapter is to recount the evolution and lessons of a decade and a half of peacetime rent controls in the United States. First, it reviews the predecessors to the current generation of "moderate" controls; then it describes the design of current regulations. It concludes with a discussion of the debates over the impacts of contemporary rent controls.

THE EVOLUTION OF U.S. RENT CONTROLS

The principal purpose of U.S. rent controls has been to provide tenants with security of tenure by stabilizing rents and requiring just cause for eviction. In the absence of rent and eviction regulations, tenants may be evicted without "just cause" or their rents may be increased without limit, after only 30 days' notice.[4]

The underlying "stabilization" goals of U.S. rent controls may be distinguished from "fair rent" schemes of other nations, which set rents without consideration of their relationship to current rent levels. An example of the fair rent approach is Italy's Equo Canone, which has established fair rent levels according to 13 objective criteria.[5] Such a fair rent approach would be politically unacceptable in the United States, to the extent that it led to significant rent increases for some units, and the courts may rule that it would be unconstitutional if it reduced the profit levels of some properties below preregulation levels.

Contemporary U.S. rent controls laws usually:

1. establish "base" rents at levels in effect just prior to the adoption of controls;
2. permit automatic annual across-the-board increases;
3. authorize rent increases or decreases for individual buildings or units for a variety of purposes, including "fair return," capital improvements, and/or reductions in maintenance and services;[6]
4. exempt new construction from regulation;[7] and
5. require "just cause" for eviction.

A substantial portion of U.S. rent control laws include vacancy decontrol provisions. Under such provisions, the initial rent for a new tenant is not subject to regulation. Subsequent rent increases are regulated as long as the same tenant remains in the unit. However, the initial rent for the new tenant, which is established independent of any controls, becomes the "base" rent for the purpose of calculating future allowable increases.

Post-World War I Regulations

Some understanding of the history of U.S. rent controls is a prerequisite to an understanding of the design of contemporary regulations and of the debates over their impacts.

Rent controls were first adopted in the United States just after World War I (Drellich and Emery 1939). The laws of that period usually did not specify how much rents could increase. Instead, they authorized tenants to raise the defense in eviction cases that the increase in their rent was excessive or unreasonable, but did not define these concepts.

At that time, "freedom of contract" was considered a central constitutional right by the Supreme Court, and economic regulations such as minimum wage and maximum hours laws were subject to judicial invalidation (for example, *Adkins v. Children's Hospital* 1923). In 1921, consistent with that view, the Supreme Court ruled that rent control laws were valid during an "emergency," but would not be valid as permanent peacetime measures (*Block v. Hirsh* 1921; *Marcus Brown Holding Co. v. Feldman* 1921). While courts did not hold, at that time, that rent controls per se were unconstitutional, they did hold that they must permit apartment owners a fair return on the "value" of their property (*Hirsch v. Weiner* 1921; *Karrick v. Cantrill* 1922). This development was particularly significant because it marked the entry of the judiciary into the role of defining rent increase standards.

In 1924 the Supreme Court directed the lower courts to closely question whether there still could be an "emergency" based on war-generated temporary shortage conditions (*Chastleton v. Sinclair* 1924). By the end of that year, all rent controls had been terminated, except for New York City regulations, which remained in effect until 1929. During the next decade, when national economic regulation became pervasive in response to the Depression, the Supreme Court substantially narrowed the scope of its review of economic regulations and held that price regulations did not have to be justified by an "emergency" (*Nebbia v. New York* 1934).

World War II Era Rent Controls

U.S. entry into World War II was accompanied by the passage of a federal rent control statute, which established "base rents" at prewar levels and authorized the Office of Price Administration (OPA) to promulgate guidelines for rent increases. Pursuant to its power, the OPA authorized across-the-board increases that reflected regional increases in apartment operating costs. It also authorized adjustments in individual cases involving capital improvements, rents not established in arms-length transactions, or fair return issues (operating cost increases in excess of cost increases or operating costs in excess of a designated percentage of gross income).

From 1942 through 1953, millions of individual adjustments were authorized. However, during this era, the courts rejected the 1920s judicial view that landlords had a constitutional right to a fair return on the value of their property. In 1943 the U.S. Court of Appeals concluded that such an approach was circular, since the rental income of a building determines its value (*Wilson v. Brown* 1943).

Since the World War II era, the concept of permitting individual, as well as across-the-board, increases has been incorporated in virtually all rent control ordinances, although the individual adjustment standards have varied enormously among laws. The view that rent control regulations must consider the special circumstances of individual properties has played a central role in U.S. rent controls and has distinguished them from types of price regulations that treat all regulated businesses uniformly.

Rent Control in New York City

In 1953, federal rent controls were terminated; but local regulations continued in effect in some areas. In the following years, state courts invalidated the local laws on the basis that there was no longer an emergency, notwithstanding the Depression-era judicial abandonment of the emergency test in price regulation cases. An exception was the high court of New York State, which also applied the emergency test, but continually found that an emergency still existed (Baar and Keating 1975).

Under the New York law in effect from 1953 through 1969, no across-the-board rent increases were authorized. Instead, the principal rent increase mechanism was a limited vacancy decontrol provision under which rents could be increased by 15 percent each time a unit became vacant. In addition, individual adjustments were authorized to cover the cost of capital improvements and increases in services or to provide a fair return, which was defined as 6 to 8 percent of assessed value.

New York City's experiences from 1953 through 1969 left an indelible mark on public perceptions of rent controls. As a result of the limited vacancy decontrol, there were enormous differences in rents between comparable units within the same building, which were attributable to variations in turnover rates. The vacancy increase mechanism provided incentives for landlords to engage in tactics that would increase tenant turnover such as harassment and reductions in maintenance (Sternlieb 1972; Housing and Rent Study Group 1973). At the same time, it acted as a disincentive to tenant mobility. The image of the little old widow who remained in her enormous apartment, at an extremely low rent, long after the departure of her husband and children, became the stereotype of New York City rent control.

By the 1960s, central-city decay was becoming widespread in older Eastern cities as middle-class households moved to the suburbs, leaving the poor and elderly behind. During that era, there was widespread abandonment of slum buildings by landlords (U.S. Comptroller General 1978; Sternlieb et al. 1974). In New York, the largest city in the United States, the problem was most severe in absolute terms and the public was convinced that New York's severe abandonment problems were attributable to its rent controls, despite the fact that abandonment rates were higher in other cities without rent controls.

In 1969 and 1970, the New York rent regulations were amended to allow for substantial across-the-board rent increases,[8] and to extend coverage of the law to units constructed between 1947 and 1963, which had previously been exempted from regulation. However, by then rent control had gained a reputation as a cancer that destroyed cities and kept the rents of middle- and upper-income tenants at unreasonably low levels. Its legitimacy was considered questionable.

"Moderate" Peacetime Rent Controls

The Northeast. In the early 1970s, political pressure for rent controls emerged in New Jersey suburbs of New York City, Boston and neighboring suburbs, and the Washington, D.C., metropolitan area, as the rental market in those regions tightened and rents escalated. Rent control organizing efforts were particularly successful in suburban communities that had substantial middle class tenant populations concentrated in larger apartment projects (Baar 1977). The rent controls that were adopted in response to this movement differed substantially from the regulations of previous eras. Generally, the regulations permitted annual across-the-board increases that were adequate to cover operating cost increases. (New Jersey tenants called their measures "rent leveling" ordinances instead of rent controls, in order to disassociate them from the New York laws.)

Where rent controls were adopted, they were attacked in court as unconstitutional on every conceivable ground. In 1975 and 1976, the high courts of New Jersey, Maryland, and California ruled that the emergency standard was a throwback to the 1920s, which was no longer applicable, and that rent controls were constitutional as long as they were reasonable and permitted a fair return to property owners. In contrast, the Florida Supreme Court continued to apply the emergency standard (Baar 1983, 755).

After courts ruled that rent controls were constitutional in peacetime, landlords shifted their legal attacks to issues relating to the constitutionality of particular facets of local ordinances. The subsequent round of legal debate was primarily over whether or not the laws permitted a "fair return." No one disputed the principle that landlords were entitled to an adequate return, but there was no judicial or administrative consensus as to what methodology should determine what constituted a fair return.

In 1975, the New Jersey Supreme Court concluded that a return on market value approach would be circular in the context of price regulation. But, based on its understanding of British fair return standards, it then concluded that a fair return on "hypothetical" value should be permitted. For fair return purposes, it defined value as

the value of the property in a rental housing market free of the aberrant forces which led to the imposition of controls. . . . the worth of the property in the context of a hypothetical market in which the supply of rental housing is just adequate to meet the needs of the various categories of persons actively desiring to rent apartments in municipalities (*Troy Hills Village v. Township of Parsippany-Troy Hills* 1975).

However, only three years later, the same court reversed itself and concluded that the standard of fair return on "hypothetical" value, which it had mandated three years earlier, was "practically unworkable" (*Helmsley v. Borough of Fort Lee* 1978). Also, during this period, the Massachusetts courts concluded that a return on value theory was circular and unworkable in the context of price regulation (*Niles v. Boston Rent Control Administrator* 1978).

New Jersey landlords, after failing to obtain relief in the courts, found highly successful avenues for reform on the political level. Starting in the second half of the 1970s, they succeeded in convincing the public that homeowners' municipal property taxes were increasing as a result of rent controls, because such regulations reduced the value of apartments and, therefore, reduced apartments' share of the property tax base.

While homeowners had not been particularly concerned about the impact of rent controls on landlords, they were extremely concerned about their property taxes, which typically ranged from 1 to 4 percent of market values. These concerns about the impact of rent controls on the property tax base played a critical role even in cities where apartments constituted only a small portion of the tax base. In response to such concerns, many cities loosened their rent regulations by adding vacancy decontrol provisions and others repealed them altogether. The property tax issue became the Achilles' heel of rent control in New Jersey.

In fact, the relationship between rent controls and homeowners' property taxes was extremely uncertain and the debate was highly emotional. Studies by academics and appraisers attributed the diminution in apartments' share of the property tax base to the imposition of rent controls, without noting the role of changes in property valuation methods, new construction, and overall shifts in the values of different types of properties. They also failed to note that the relationships between assessed values and actual values were so tenuous as to make it impossible to determine whether changes in assessed values were attributable to changes in values or in assessment practices or to updating and improving assessments (Baar 1984).

California Rent Controls. While the property tax issue substantially weakened New Jersey rent regulations, it spurred the rent control movement in California. In the second half of the 1970s, there was an enormous surge in California property values and a resulting surge in property taxes. In 1978, in response to these developments, California voters passed an initiative, Proposition 13, which cut property taxes by two-thirds.[9]

Tenants, who were accustomed to hearing that rent increases were necessitated by property tax increases, now expected rent decreases. Instead, they were met by continued increases in rents, which reflected a tightening rental market. For example, in the 12-month period following the passage of the tax initiative, Los Angeles area rents increased by 10 percent, despite the fact that the reduction in property taxes was equal to about 7 percent of the gross rental income of properties.[10]

Furious tenant reactions led to the passage of rent control ordinances in San Francisco, Los Angeles, San Jose, Oakland, and eight other cities. In addition, in the following years, approximately 40 cities passed rent control ordinances that were applicable only to mobile home park spaces.[11] The tax initiative, besides stimulating the tenant movement for rent control, cut off potential home owner fear of a property tax shift due to rent controls. Supporters of rent control could not have been more brilliant than the conservative authors of Proposition 13 in devising a strategy that would stimulate the passage of rent controls and then insulate them from potential home owner opposition. Most of the California apartment rent control ordinances have permitted substantial annual rent increases and contain vacancy decontrol provisions.

As on the East Coast, landlords have sought relief from the rent controls in the courts, especially from the ordinances that have not included vacancy decontrol provisions. At first, some California trial courts ruled that owners were constitutionally entitled to either a fair return on the value of their property or to rents that were adequate to cover mortgage payments. Provisions allowing the recovery of mortgage payments led to particularly high rent increases for recent purchasers of property, who paid high prices for buildings in anticipation of free market appreciation in property values. However, in 1983 and 1984, state appellate courts rejected the fair return theories of the trial courts.

DEBATES OVER RENT CONTROLS

Design Issues

There has been an abundance of debate over the impacts of rent control. However, very little has been written about the alternative types of provisions in rent control laws, despite the significance of the differences in the standards that have been included in such laws. (For discussions of drafting issues, see Baar 1983; Lett 1976; Selesnick 1976.)

This section of the chapter discusses vacancy decontrols, alternate types of across-the-board increase standards, standards for individual adjustments for fair return and for capital improvements, rent administration registration and financing mechanisms, exemptions, grounds for evictions, and demolition and conversion controls.

Vacancy Decontrols. The principal distinction between rent control laws has been whether or not they have included vacancy decontrol provisions. (Some ordinances have followed an intermediate approach of permitting limited increases upon vacancies, typically in the range of 10 to 15 percent.) Vacancy decontrols are particularly significant in the U.S. context because tenant turnover rates are high, averaging from 25 to 50 percent per year.

From a political perspective, rent regulations with vacancy decontrol have been an attractive alternative for local legislators, because they enable landlords to pursue their common practice of reserving substantial rent increases for vacancies, while insuring that tenants are not forced to move by excessive rent increases.

Opposition to vacancy decontrol has been based on the view that it provides incentives for reductions in maintenance and harassment of tenants. From a broader policy perspective, opponents of vacancy decontrol argue that permitting rents to increase to market levels reduces the overall affordability of the rental housing stock. Proponents of vacancy decontrol have argued that such mechanisms are necessary to insure that landlords can obtain enough income to maintain and upgrade their units. From an equity point of view, it is claimed that it is unreasonable to regulate the rents of vacant units, since prospective tenants are free to accept or reject a unit based on its rents. Where rent control laws have authorized a combination of substantial annual across-the-board rent increases and vacancy decontrol, the laws' impact on the overall rate of increases in rent may be minimal.

Annual Across-the Board Increases. Under most rent control laws, all owners are entitled to automatic annual rent increases. The types of mechanisms that have been used to determine the amounts of these increases include:

1. *Fixed percentage*: Under this type of standard, the same percentage rent increase is permitted each year. This approach offers the advantage of simplicity, but suffers from the obvious weakness that the designated percentage does not bear any particular relationship to operating cost increases or the rate of inflation. As a result, provisions of this type are frequently either amended or replaced with Consumer Price Index (CPI) standards as the designated percentage becomes inadequate or excessive in light of fluctuations in inflation rates.

2. *Increases tied to the Consumer Price Index*: Ordinances that use this type of standard often permit annual increases equal to two-thirds or three-quarters of the percent increases in the CPI. However, a significant portion permit full CPI increases. Since operating expenses usually consume 40 to 60 percent of gross income, full CPI increases are not necessary to cover operating cost increases and to permit some growth in income. Some ordinances place a maximum or a minimum on the increases authorized pursuant to such a formula, with ceilings of 7 or 8 percent and floors of 3 or 4 percent being most common.

The Consumer Price Index is considered to be a credible guide for determining allowable annual increases, since it reflects overall trends in the cost of living. However, the incorporation of such standard in rent laws has often run into stiff political opposition from either landlords or tenants, depending on the rate of inflation at the time the standard is proposed. In fact, the rate of increase in the CPI does not necessarily bear a substantial relationship to the rate of increase in apartment operating costs, since the marketbasket of household expenses that is used to measure the CPI differs substantially from the types of expenses associated with the ownership of apartment buildings.

3. *Increases determined by a rent administration based on an annual study of apartment operating cost increases*: Under the operating cost methodology, a weighted price index of local apartment operating costs is developed each year

in order to determine what size across-the-board rent increases will cover apartment operating cost increases. It is common for jurisdictions that use this approach also to provide for an adjustment in apartment owners' net operating income. (Table 15.1 illustrates this methodology.)

While from a theoretical point of view this approach has the strength of tying rent increases to apartment operating cost increases, from a practical point of view, its use presents a number of problems. Ratios of some types of operation costs to gross income and their rates of increase are not easily determinable, since apartment owners' expense records are generally not available to a rent board. While precise estimates may be made of increases in expenses that are publicly regulated (for example, water and refuse collection), precise estimates of increases in maintenance expenses cannot be made without expense records. Therefore, when operating cost studies are performed for rent boards, it is commonly assumed that maintenance costs have increased at the same rate as the CPI.

Generally, ordinances that authorize the use of operating cost studies to determine allowable rent increases do not indicate what factors should be taken into account, how they should be weighted, nor how increases in the particular types of costs should be estimated. As a result, designs and applications of this approach may be manipulated toward producing desired results. Furthermore, even if a formula is objectively derived, the issues surrounding its development are so complex that its application is seen as political.

Under all three types of annual across-the-board rent increase methodologies, it has been common to authorize additional increases for landlords who pay for gas and electricity expenses. Some ordinances permit dollar-for-dollar passthroughs of increases in property taxes or other types of expenses. Commonly, such passthroughs are authorized for substantial increases in expenses that both vary significantly in size among properties and are beyond the control of landlords.

Individual Adjustments for Fair Return. Virtually all rent control ordinances allow landlords to petition for rent increases for individual properties based on fair return standards. However, there are major differences in the concepts underlying alternate fair return standards depending on whether they consider mortgage payments, "value," or only operating costs. These differences determine the numbers and classes of property owners they benefit (for example, recent purchasers, owners of apartments in poor neighborhoods, highly mortgaged properties). In some jurisdictions, fair return adjustments play a major role as a rent increase mechanism, while in others they are insignificant. Typically, the rents of only 1 or 2 percent of all rent controlled units are adjusted through fair return mechanisms.

The debate over what types of fair return standards are appropriate and reasonable has been waged for 60 years within the judicial forum. The critical distinction between U.S. fair return standards and those of other nations has been that U.S. standards have tied fair return to operating expenses and property

Table 15.1
Calculation of Across-the-Board Rent Increases: Weighted Index (Hypothetical Case)

Expense	Ratio to Gross Income		Pct. Increase over prior yr.		Pct. Rent Increase Required
Property Taxes	.15	x	5	=	.75
Water	.02	x	15	=	.30
Sewer	.02	x	3	=	.06
Refuse Collection	.03	x	10	=	.30
City licenses & fees	.01	x	25	=	.25
Maintenance	.14	x	6	=	.84
Insurance	.02	x	10	=	.20
Management	.06	x	6	=	.36
Gas (hot water only)	.02	x	18	=	.36
Elec. (common areas)	.02	x	5	=	.10
Net operating income (adjusted by 50% of pct. increase in CPI)	.51	x	3	=	1.53
					————
Across-the-Board Increase					5.05

Source: Baar (1985).

yields, while the fair return standards of other nations have been based on factors such as rents for comparable units, equilibrium market, or value as defined by some physical measure.

The fair return formulas that have been used in the United States may be divided into five general categories.

1. *Cash flow*: Under this type of formula, landlords are entitled to rents that are adequate to cover operating expenses and mortgage payments.[12] This standard favors owners who have invested less of their own cash and have obtained larger mortgages. To the extent that the market permits, it allows landlords to regulate their rents through regulation of their financing arrangements. In markets where property values have been increasing, the standard operates most favorably for recent purchasers.

2. *Return on investment*: Under this type of standard, a landlord is entitled to rents adequate to yield a designated rate of return on investment, as well as covering operating expenses and mortgage payments. Where property values have been increasing over time, the purchase date becomes the chief determinant of what rent will be permitted, under this formula. Since investment is a business decision that is governed by expectations as to future income, the use of this standard in a price regulation context is somewhat circular. In the market, the burden is on the investor to determine what investment is reasonable in light of existing regulations. Under this formula, the investment governs what result shall be permitted under the regulations.

3. *Return on value*: Under a return on value standard, an owner is entitled to rents that are adequate to cover operating expenses and yield a specified rate of return on value. Mortgage interest is not considered as an expense, since the return is calculated on the full value of the property, rather than on the owner's investment. When this formula has been used, value has been defined as either fair market value, as determined in a rent hearing, or assessed value. As indicated, the courts have repeatedly concluded that this type of formula is circular, because value is determined by the rents that are permitted.

4. *Percentage net operating income*: This standard insures that net operating income shall equal a designated percentage of gross income (or, conversely stated, expenses do not exceed a designated percentage of gross income). Typically net operating income ratios of 40 to 50 percent are guaranteed.

5. *Maintenance of net operating income*: Under this formula, fair return is defined as the net operating income that a property yielded in a base period. Typically, the base period net operating income is adjusted for inflation in defining current fair net operating income. In effect, landlords are entitled to rent increases that cover operating cost increases and provide some growth in net operating income. The use of this formula has become widespread. It insures stability in the yield of rental properties and provides an incentive to maintenance because it allows for a passthrough of increases in maintenance expenses, regardless of prior profit levels. At the same time, the formula cannot be manipulated through mortgage or investment arrangements. The chief criticism of the

formula is that it perpetuates preregulation net operating income levels, without consideration of whether they were high or low. However, this policy is consistent with the underlying purposes of U.S. rent regulations, which have been to stabilize rents. Some jurisdictions have attempted to address the criticisms of the maintenance of net operating income formula, by using a percentage net operating income formula in conjunction with it.

Individual Adjustments for Capital Improvements. Virtually all rent control ordinances authorize individual adjustments for capital improvements. However, standards for capital improvement increases and mechanisms for processing applications vary substantially among ordinances. Some ordinances broadly define capital improvements to include such matters as painting and replacements of carpets and roofs. Others limit the definition of capital improvements to new facilities or physical additions, while excluding replacements. Some laws do not permit increases for improvements that are not necessary to maintain the structure, unless a specified percentage of the tenants approve of them. Under some laws applications are processed administratively, while under others applications are reviewed at a hearing at which tenants may raise other issues.

There is no empirical research on whether capital improvement increase mechanisms have had a significant effect on housing maintenance or have merely been used to obtain rent increases for work that would have been performed anyway. The volume of capital improvement applications has been substantial in some jurisdictions, while in others it has been minimal. The nature of the application process may be the most critical determinant of differences in the volume of applications.

Individual Adjustments for Reductions in Maintenance or Services. Under most rent control laws, tenants may petition for rent reductions based on reductions in maintenance or building services (such as the loss of heat, elevator, or swimming pool). Usually, the standards for determining how much rents shall be reduced for particular reductions are vague, since it is not possible to establish an objective formula that would operate in a reasonable manner, in light of the wide variety of possible circumstances relating to a particular type of loss of services. In practice, tenants are usually hesitant to petition for rent decreases, because they fear retaliation and prefer to avoid unpleasant confrontations with their landlords.

Registration. Some ordinances require that landlords complete registration forms that provide basic information on their units, such as base period rents and amenities. Registration requirements aid tracking of base period rent levels, which determine current legal rent levels under laws that do not contain vacancy decontrol provisions.

Rent Administration Financing. The concept that public funds should be used to administer rent control programs has suffered from a lack of legitimacy relative to other local public expenditures. Commonly, funding for rent control programs has been provided through landlord registration fees, which may be passed through to tenants on a prorated monthly basis.

Exemptions and Evictions for Owner Occupancy. Typically, evictions are permitted for owner occupancy, and smaller owner-occupied buildings (four units or less) are exempted from rent controls. Decisions to exempt such units are typically based on the view that landlords who live in their buildings are less likely to set their rents on the basis of profit-maximization considerations. Another principal motive for exempting smaller owner-occupied dwellings may be the desire to reduce opposition to rent controls by resident owners who may be numerous, while owning relatively few units.

There has been widespread criticism that this exemption and ground for eviction permits landlords to move temporarily into their units in order to evict tenants who are paying low rents and to obtain an exemption from regulations. In recent years, a number of jurisdictions have placed restrictions on owner-occupancy evictions such as presumptions that the eviction was not in good faith if the owner occupant does not move in for a specified amount of time, limits on the frequency of such evictions, extended notice periods, relocation benefits requirements, and bans on allowing owner-occupancy evictions in larger buildings.

Other exemptions that are nearly universal in rent control laws include new construction, government-owned or -subsidized units, care facilities, boarding houses, fraternities and sororities, and transient facilities. Exemptions that are common, but not universal, include single-family dwellings, ''luxury'' units, and substantially renovated units. Some ordinances exclude all buildings that contain less than a specified number of units, regardless of whether they are owner occupied. Under some laws the exemptions are automatic, while under others an exemption certificate must be obtained from the rent administration.

Condominium Conversion and Demolition Controls. Condominium and co-operative controls are standardly adopted in rent controlled jurisdictions (and non-rent controlled jurisdictions) for the purposes of preventing displacement and diminution of the rental housing stock. However, the forms of controls have differed radically among states. One form of regulation, which is standard in California cities, prohibits the conversion of the units in an apartment building into individually marketable parcels.

Another form of regulation, which is in effect in New Jersey and New York, permits division of the units in a building into separately marketable apartments, but delays or prohibits the eviction of some classes of tenants from those units. Regulation of evictions from units converted to condominiums, rather than of the conversion process itself, has significant practical effects. Since the owner-occupancy value of a converted unit far exceeds its rental value, the tenant often becomes the object of strong pressures or financial incentives to move.

Demolition controls have been instituted in some areas where land values associated with alternate uses exceed rental values. However, their legal and political status is in a state of uncertainty. After the California Supreme Court ruled that demolition controls were constitutional (*Nash v. City of Santa Monica*

1984), the California legislature responded by passing a law that guarantees to apartment owners the right to evict their tenants for the purpose of going out of business. While the U.S. Supreme Court has dismissed constitutional challenges to apartment demolition controls, the newly appointed Chief Justice Rehnquist has argued that they are unconstitutional (*Fresh Pond v. Rent Control Board of Cambridge* 1983).

Rent Control as a Housing Policy

Rent control may or may not be a wise housing policy. However, analysis over its impacts has been far removed from reality. Economists and representatives of the real estate industry commonly justify their opposition to rent control with their conclusion that it is bad for tenants, although tenants have supported such measures.

Reports on rent control by "impartial expert" commissions summarily make sweeping conclusions that rent controls have terrible effects, without even bothering to describe what rent increases have been permitted under such laws and without even obtaining the benefit of meaningful empirical research (for example, President's Commission on Housing 1982). Alternatively, economists have used econometric equations to demonstrate the impacts of rent regulations. Often these sweeping unsupported conclusions and econometric equations become the sole basis for the conclusions of other experts. In the face of the complexities of analyzing the impacts of one particular policy within a sea of variables that govern housing trends, experts seem to have substituted intuition for serious analysis.

Frequently, the experiences of a particular city have been used to make broad generalizations about the impacts of rent control. Discussions of the impact of rent controls often draw broad conclusions based on New York City's experiences, despite the fact that its rent controls of the 1950s and 1960s were markedly different from contemporary regulations. Some reports even draw conclusions from experiences under European rent regulations that froze rents for decades, without noting the critical differences between these laws and U.S. regulations (for example, Block and Olson 1981).

Impact on New Construction. When research on the impacts of rent controls on new construction has been performed, variations in construction levels have been used to draw broad conclusions in situations where the impact of other intervening variables, such as fluctuations in interest rates and changes in zoning policies, have far outweighed the impact of rent regulations. Also, arguments are made about the need for a free market solution without much consideration of whether such a paradigm is appropriate in light of local zoning and land use policies that severely restrict apartment construction (Baar 1986).

During the past decade, prominent housing experts have claimed that lags in rent increases, relative to the rate of increase in the cost of living, deter new rental construction (Downs 1983, 92–116; Lowry et al. 1983, 103–35). However, they have not bothered to test this hypothesis. In fact, contemporary construction data from the areas of the nation with the highest and lowest rates of increase in rents raise doubts about its validity.[13] Studies that actually go to the effort of collecting available data do not support the conclusion that rent controls have had a negative impact on new construction (Gilderbloom 1981; Los Angeles Rent Stabilization Division 1985; Baar 1986).

Impact on Maintenance. A number of studies have attempted to measure the impacts of rent control on maintenance (Sternlieb 1972, 1974; Rydell et al. 1981). However, quantification of actual maintenance patterns poses severe practical problems. In the alternative, some economists have used econometric equations in order to estimate actual impacts. Another methodology has been to interview tenants about changes in maintenance patterns since they moved into their units. However, such responses may be biased by tenant income levels and perceptions about the reasonability of their rents.

"Equity and Efficiency." In recent years, as the arguments about the impacts of rent control on maintenance and new construction have become less convincing, discussion and analysis of rent controls has shifted in emphasis toward consideration of whether lower-income or middle- and upper-income groups are the principal beneficiaries of the benefits of rent controls (Clark and Heskin 1982; Devine 1986). Often the premise for such discussion has been that protection of middle- and upper-income households constitutes an unreasonable "subsidy." Rent control ordinances contain statements of purpose that focus on the need to protect low-income households from excessive rent increases. However, such laws protect all tenants of rent controlled units without regard to their income level. If a rent control law applied only to units rented to low-income households, landlords would have incentives to avoid renting to such households, thus eliminating the political support of middle-income households, which is necessary to obtain the adoption of rent regulations. While a means or need test is commonly used in evaluating the legitimacy of rent controls, it carries no real weight in the evaluation of the legitimacy of housing policies that benefit home owners, such as deductions of mortgage interest or zoning restrictions that exclude multifamily dwellings.

Rent controls have also been criticized for producing particular results that otherwise have been supported as the desirable goals of other housing policies. For example, critics of rent control chastise it for causing a loss of rental units through their conversion to the owner-occupied sector. However, historically, the central goal of U.S. housing policy has been to increase home ownership and reduce tenancy. Rent controls are standardly criticized for reducing rental housing construction, although a central goal of zoning policies has been to reduce or severely curb multifamily rental construction. Another criticism of rent control has been that it reduces tenant mobility, although traditionally tenants have been considered as less desirable citizens than home owners because they are more transient.

CONCLUSION

The lessons of a decade of U.S. rent controls may more clearly illuminate how policies are formulated and how policy debates are conducted than indicate the real impacts of rent controls. They illustrate how analysis of a policy of national importance may rely on seemingly intuitive analysis, even by those regarded as experts. The analysis of the President's Commission on Housing, which includes the following conclusions, illustrates the highly ideological nature of the debates.

Moreover, rent control yields an income redistribution from landlords to tenants by implicitly taxing landlords for the benefit of tenants. In general such a tax is inefficient and inequitable. Rental property owners are often small-scale investors who do not have large-scale resources. More importantly such a tax ignores the fact that individuals can move to another area to avoid or take advantage of local redistribution programs (President's Commission on Housing 1982, 92).

While the introduction of security of tenure and predictable rent increase patterns may not have a place in the cost-benefit analyses and the equations of economists, they may be invaluable to tenants. In their absence, tenants in tight housing markets do not know, at any time, if their rents will not be increased at all or will be increased drastically.

While the debate over the impacts of rent controls may be largely ideological and may have little to do with their actual design, the forms of U.S. rent controls are particularly worth noting. They include the concepts of annual across-the-board rent increases, individual adjustment standards that guarantee the right to a growing net operating income (under maintenance of net operating income formulas), increases for capital improvements, and exemptions for new construction, as well as limits on rent increases and evictions.

NOTES

The author gratefully acknowledges the editorial assistance of Karen Westmont.

1. This estimate does not include units that have controlled rents by virtue of the fact that they are publicly owned or subsidized. Several million units are in these classes.

2. From 1960 to 1980, the U.S. rent index increased at approximately 60 percent of the rate of increase in the Consumer Price Index—all items. From January 1980 to January 1986, the rent index increased at 119 percent of the rate of increase in the all items index. The all items index increased by 40.8 percent, while the rent index increased by 48.5 percent. In some regions the rent index increased by a much greater percentage during this period (for example, Los Angeles 65 percent, San Francisco 70 percent).

3. At the federal level, new judges have been appointed by a conservative president since January 1981. (Nominations have to be confirmed by the Senate, but rejections of presidential nominations are rare.) In California, in November 1986, three liberal justices of the state supreme court lost judicial confirmation initiatives, thereby giving a conservative governor the opportunity to appoint three new justices.

In February 1987, the U.S. Supreme Court agreed to hear an appeal from a California supreme court decision upholding a provision in a San Jose rent control ordinance which includes "hardship to a tenant" as a factor in individual rent adjustment hearings. *Pennell v. City of San Jose*, Cal. 3d. (1986), U.S. (1987). No other ordinances include a provision of this type. The significance of the case will depend on whether the Court's analysis extends to other rent control issues.

4. Evictions are governed by state laws and are usually permitted for any reason, except for reasons specifically prohibited, such as discrimination based on race, sex, or age or retaliation for housing code complaints.

5. Factors that are considered include unit size; amenities; type, condition, and age of building; neighborhood desirability; region; and city population (Legislazione Italiana 392 [July 27, 1978]).

6. Differences in administrative mechanisms play a major role in determining the impacts of individual adjustment standards. Under some laws, rent board staff members may approve applications for increases, unless the tenants object, and tenants may only raise issues that are raised by the rent increase petition. Under other laws, hearings are required in all cases.

7. Typically laws exempt units that were constructed after the adoption of the rent regulation. Some laws exempt only the initial rent of newly constructed units or only new units for a designated number of years.

8. Under rent control, which was applicable to units covered under the old law, rent increases of 7 percent per year were permitted. Under rent stabilization, which is applicable to units constructed after 1947 and rent controlled units, which subsequently became vacant, annual rent increases are set by a rent guidelines board.

9. Property tax rates were reduced from an effective rate of approximately 3 percent of current market value to 1 percent of 1975 assessed value. Assessment increases are limited to 2 percent per year, except that properties are reassessed at market value when sold.

10. See annual reports of the Institute of Real Estate Management, Apartments, Income/Expense Analysis, Chicago, for a comparison of property tax expenses for California apartments before and after the initiative.

11. "Mobile homes" are hardly mobile. They are prefabricated houses, which are commonly located in mobile home parks with up to several hundred spaces. It costs from $5,000 to $10,000 to move the mobile homes and often there are no vacant spaces to which they can be moved. California has approximately 380,000 mobile homes.

12. A variation of the cash flow formula is a return on gross rent formula under which an owner is entitled to rents that provide a net rental income equal to a percentage of the rent in addition to covering operating expenses and mortgage payments.

13. In the San Francisco area, which has experienced the greatest rent increases of any area in the United States (70 percent increase in rents, versus a national average of 48 percent in rents and 40 percent increase in the cost of living, since January 1980), the rate of new construction has been low (Baar 1986, 49). At the same time, apartment construction has boomed in Texas and Arizona, where there have been regional oversupplies and rent increases have been far below national averages. The differences may be explained by variations in construction costs and the fact that it is easy to obtain permission to build apartments in Texas and Arizona, while the process ranges from tortuous to impossible in the San Francisco area. An alternate explanation is that Texas and Arizona do not permit rent controls, while California does. However, the increases

in rents obtainable under California rent control ordinances have far exceeded the increases obtainable in the "free" markets of Arizona and Texas.

REFERENCES

Baar, K.
1986   "Facts and Fallacies in the Rental Housing Market." *Western City* 62, no. 9, 47.
1985   "California Rent Controls: Rent Increase Standards and Fair Return." *Real Property Law Reporter* (California Continuing Education of the Bar) 8, no. 5, 97.
1984   "The Impact of Rent Controls on the Property Tax Base: The Political Economic Relationship." *Property Tax Journal* 3, no. 1, 1–20.
1983   "Guidelines for Drafting Rent Control Laws: Lessons of a Decade." *Rutgers Law Review* 35, no. 2, 723–885.
1977   "Rent Control in the 1970's: The Case of the New Jersey Tenants Movement." *Hastings Law Journal* 28, no. 3, 631–83.
Baar, K., and W. D. Keating
1975   "The Last Stand of Economic Substantive Due Process—The Housing Emergency Requirement for Rent Control." *Urban Lawyer* 7, 446–509.
Block, Walter, and Edgar Olson (eds.)
1981   *Rent Control Myths and Realities*. Vancouver: Fraser Institute.
Clark, W. A. V., and A. Heskin
1982   "The Impact of Rent Control on Tenure Discounts and Residential Mobility." *Land Economics* 58, no. 1, 109–17.
Devine, R.
1986   *Who Benefits from Rent Control?* Oakland, Calif: Center for Community Change.
Downs, Anthony
1983   *Rental Housing in the 1980's*. Washington, D.C.: Brookings Institution.
Drellich, Edith, and André Emery
1939   *Rent Control in War and Peace*. New York: National Municipal League.
Gilderbloom, J.
1981   "Moderate Rent Control." *Urban Affairs Quarterly* 17:125–29.
Housing and Rent Study Group, Temporary State Commission on Living Costs and the Economy
1973   New York City
Lett, Monica
1976   *Rent Control Concepts, Realities and Mechanisms*. New Brunswick, NJ: Rutgers University, Center for Urban Policy Research.
Los Angeles Rent Stabilization Division
1985   *Rental Housing Study: Housing Production and Performance Under Rent Stabilization*.
Lowry, Ira, Carol Hillestad, Syam Sarma
1983   *California's Housing Adequacy, Availability, and Affordability*. Santa Monica, CA: Rand Corporation.
Niebanck, Paul (ed.)
1985   *The Rent Control Debate*. Chapel Hill: University of North Carolina Press.
President's Commission on Housing
1982   *Report of the President's Commission on Housing*. Washington, DC: U.S. Government Printing office.

Rydell, P., et al.
1981   *The Impact of Rent Control on the Los Angeles Housing Market*. Santa Monica, CA: Rand Corporation.
Selesnick, H.
1976   *Rent Control: A Case For*. Lexington, MA: Lexington Books.
Sternlieb, George
1974   *The Realities of Rent Control in the Greater Boston Area*. New Brunswick, NJ: Rutgers University Press.
1972   *The Urban Housing Dilemma*. New York: Office of Rent Control, New York City Housing and Development Administration.
Sternlieb, G., R. Burchell, J. Highes, and F. James
1974   "Housing Abandonment in the Urban Core." *APA Journal* 40, no. 3, 321–332.
U.S. Comptroller General
1978   *Housing Abandonment: A National Problem Needing New Approaches*. Washington, D.C.

COURT CASES

Adkins v. Children's Hospital, 261 U.S. 525 (1923)
Block v. Hirsh, 256 U.S. 135 (1921)
Marcus Brown Holding Co. v. Feldman, 256 U.S. 170 (1921)
Chastleton Corp. v. Sinclair, 264 U.S. 543 (1924)
Fresh Pond Shopping Center, Inc. v. Rent Control Bd. of Cambridge, 464 U.S. 875 (1983)
Helmsley v. Borough of Fort Lee, 394 A.2d. 65 (1978)
Hirsch v. Weiner, 190 N.Y.S. 111 (1921)
Karrick v. Cantrill, 277 F. 578 (1922)
Nash v. City of Santa Monica, 207 Cal. Rptr. 285 (1984)
Nebbia v. New York, 291 U.S. 502 (1934)
Niles v. Boston Rent Control Adm'r, 374 N.E.2d 296 (1978)
Pennell v. City of San Jose, Cal. 3d.
Troy Hills v. Township of Parsippany-Troy Hills, 350 A.2d. 34 (1974)
Wilson v. Brown, 137 F.2d. 348 (1943)

PART VI

SPECIAL POPULATION GROUPS

In the final part of this book an issue is taken up that has been gaining much attention in recent years: the relation of housing and neighborhoods to special population groups. With the growing differentiation of life-styles in advanced societies, groups that have special housing needs are rapidly coming into the forefront of research and public policy considerations. Two such groups are female-headed households and households headed by the elderly.

In the United States, where there is so little public input into housing and a rather weak rental sector, it is common for these new population groups to have relatively unequal access to quality housing and decent neighborhoods. Such is clearly the case with female-headed households in metropolitan areas, as is pointed out in Chapter 16 by Smith and Thomson. One of the fastest growing population groups, these women have difficulty participating in the housing market because of their relatively low incomes, because of exclusionary zoning policies and discrimination in mortgage lending practices, and also in many cases due to their race.

The housing situation of special groups is often more satisfactory in other advanced nations. In Israel, as Chapter 17 by Ginsberg describes, the elderly living in central Tel Aviv are by and large very satisfied with both their housing and their residential environments. She discusses the reasons for this satisfaction, one of the most important being the availability of friends.

Both chapters suggest that it is socially wise housing policy to build communities with diverse housing types and tenure forms so that population groups with special needs do not become geographically isolated.

16

Restricted Housing Markets for Female-Headed Households in U.S. Metropolitan Areas

REBECCA L. SMITH AND C. LEE THOMSON

Abstract. The study in this chapter employs U.S. census data to examine the distribution of female-headed households in metropolitan areas. Housing costs, tenure status, and spatial distributions of single female-headed, single male-headed, and couple-headed households are compared. Four factors that influence women's access to housing are discussed: income, race, exclusionary zoning, and discrimination in mortgage lending practices. Women, like blacks, experience unequal access to housing due to income constraints and discrimination directed at them because they are nontraditional households. Housing and planning policy must make provisions for these nontraditional households to prevent such inequalities.

INTRODUCTION

Over the last two decades, Americans continually have had to revise attitudes and policies that deal with a variety of social issues as women have become a more pervasive and recognized social force. During these two decades, women have entered the labor force as wage earners in great numbers, and have arisen as a potent political force. Also changes in family structure have meant that increasing numbers of women have become heads of households. Owing to changes in the age of marriage and to increases in divorce rates, the number of families and nonfamily households headed by women has grown rapidly since 1970, so that today 27 percent of all American households are headed by women.

Since each household must be housed, it follows that women, as household heads, are now the primary housing consumers of 27 percent of housing units in the United States. Constraints placed on the ability of these households to obtain housing have put them at a disadvantage in the competitive housing market. The housing status of female-headed households in many ways bears strong resemblance to the housing status of black households, suggesting that women face barriers similar to those faced by black households in obtaining equality in housing.

Much has been written on the social and economic status of women in the

United States, but this literature has curiously omitted a consideration of their housing status (U.S. Commission on Civil Rights 1983; U.S. Department of Labor 1979). Outside the United States, women have been more fully recognized as a distinct housing class (Klodawsky, Spector, and Hendrix 1983; Brion and Tinker 1980), with concerns such as day care and personal safety, and restricted incomes. Failure to recognize the needs of women as a class of housing consumers will likely prolong their disadvantaged status. This chapter is intended to shed light on the housing status of female-headed households in U.S. metropolitan areas. Statistics describing the housing status of female-headed households are first reviewed. This is followed by an examination of the types of discrimination that have affected these households.

HOUSING CHARACTERISTICS

Several measures of housing status are reviewed here, including tenure, cost, quality, and location of housing. An attempt has been made to provide national statistics where they are available. Springfield, Massachusetts, was chosen to provide, in a single metropolitan area, a level of detail not available at the national level. Female-headed households comprise 30 percent of all households in the Springfield area, close to the national average. It is also a fairly typical city in terms of size, ethnic diversity, and average income, and as such is a good microcosm of the nation, for reference where national statistics are not available.

Household Types

As of 1983, 27 percent of American households were headed by a single female (U.S. Department of Commerce 1984). These households are categorized into two major groups: family and nonfamily households. Family households are composed of two or more persons related by blood, marriage, or adoption, as defined by the U.S. Census Bureau. Owing to a rise in divorce rates in recent years, the number of single women heading family households has increased faster than any other type of family households (see Table 16.1). More than 90 percent of single-parent families are headed by women; 60 percent of single female-headed families include children under the age of 18, compared to 36 percent of single male-headed families.

Nonfamily households are composed of single individuals, or two or more people who are not related. An increase in the number of nonfamily households since 1970 is associated with changing attitudes about marriage. Table 16.1 indicates rapid growth in both male-headed and female-headed households between 1960 and 1983, although it is clear that the growth of female-headed households has outpaced the growth of either male-headed or couple-headed households—58 percent of nonfamily households have a female householder.

Table 16.1
Growth of Families and Households

	1960	
	Families	Households
Couple-Headed	87%	74%
Single male-headed	3%	8%
Single female-headed	10%	17%

	1970	
	Families	Households
Couple-Headed	86%	69%
Single male-headed	3%	10%
Single female-headed	11%	21%

	1980	
	Families	Households
Couple-Headed	83%	61%
Single male-headed	3%	14%
Single female-headed	10%	17%

	1983	
	Families	Households
Couple-Headed	81%	59%
Single male-headed	3%	14%
Single female-headed	15%	27%

Source: U.S. Census of Population, U.S. Summary, 1960, 1970, 1980; Current Population Reports, Series P–20, No. 388, 1984.

Housing Tenure

Home ownership is a valued housing status in the United States. The federal government encourages private ownership of single-family housing through government-sponsored mortgage guarantees and tax breaks for interest paid on mortgage loans. Nationally, 65 percent of all households own their housing unit. This figure camouflages sizable differences in home ownership rates of couple-headed households compared to other types of households. Almost 80 percent of couple-headed households are home owners, as compared to close to 50 percent of single male-headed and single female-headed households. Family households are 5 percent more likely to own their housing than nonfamily households.

In Springfield, the home ownership market is clearly dominated by couple-headed households, who comprise 76 percent of home owners in the metropolitan area. Single male householders are 6 percent of the owners, and single female heads of households are 17 percent of owners. Female heads of household make up 46 percent of the rental housing market there, and are the single largest class of rental housing consumers.

Housing Costs

Income constraints have an effect on any household's ability to obtain housing. Women, whether married or single, generally have lower incomes than do men. However, the data presented in Table 16.2 suggest that the generally low-income status of female heads of households is not directly linked to the housing costs paid by these households. Households headed by women consume lower cost housing than either married couple or single male households, but not low enough to reflect their level of income. Of the households that rent in the Springfield metropolitan area, female householders have a median income that is roughly one-third (39 percent) the median income of married-couple households, and only one-half (53 percent) that of male-headed households. Yet the median rent paid by female householders is 84 percent of what married couples pay, and 96 percent the median rent level of single male heads of household.

A similar relationship exists between income and housing costs for home owners. Single women who own their housing have a median income of 45 percent and 67 percent the income of married couple and single male householders, respectively. Yet the corresponding housing costs for single female householders are not that much lower in comparison to the other households. Monthly housing costs for female owners is 88 percent of the costs paid by married couples, and 95 percent of the payments made by single males. Median house values for the three household types show the same relative balance as monthly housing costs.

These data suggest that female householders pay relatively more, as a percent of their income, for housing than do other households. This relationship is spelled out even more explicitly if we look at rent as a percent of income (Table 16.2).

Table 16.2
Comparison of Household Characteristics: Springfield SMSA

	Married-couple households	Single male households	Single female households
Tenure			
All households	85%	12%	30%
Owners	76%	6%	17%
Renters	34%	20%	46%
Costs			
Median income: Owners	$23,610	$15,690	$10,540
Median house value	$39,100	$32,300	$32,100
Monthly housing costs	$ 365	$ 341	$ 323
Median income: Renters	$15,336	$11,155	$ 5,961
Median rent	$ 246	$ 215	$ 207
Rent as a % of Income			
under 25	66%	57%	36%
25 - 34	17%	17%	19%
35 - 50	9%	10%	15%
over 50	8%	15%	29%

Source: U.S. Bureau of the Census, Metropolitan Housing Characteristics, Springfield-Chicopee-Holyoke, Mass., 1980.

U.S. federal housing policy has long maintained that households should pay no more than 25 percent of their income for housing, although this figure has more recently been increased to 30 percent. Table 16.2 indicates that among renters in the Springfield area, most married couple households and two-thirds of the single male householders rent housing for less than 35 percent of their income. Among single-female householders, by contrast, almost half pay more than 35 percent of their income for rent. In fact, a striking 29 percent spend over half of their income on rent.

The foregoing discussion suggests that female householders do not obtain substantially lower cost housing than do other types of householders, even though the incomes of female householders are on average substantially lower. Possible explanations for these findings include a shortage of lower cost housing, or an unwillingness on the part of female householders to inhabit cheaper, and hence lower quality, housing.

Housing Quality

From the meager data presented in the Metropolitan Housing Characteristics for Springfield, it is possible to draw the tentative conclusion that female-headed households do not reside in lower quality housing any more than do other types of households. Using crowding and lack of plumbing as indicators, the percent of female-headed households living in substandard housing conditions is roughly equivalent to the percentage of other households living in such conditions. Furthermore, female householders are not congregated in the older units of the housing stock. In fact, women who rent tend toward slightly newer housing, an effect perhaps of the newer age of many apartment buildings.

HOUSING CONSTRAINTS

These statistics clearly suggest that women who head households and are therefore primary consumers of housing do not enjoy equal participation in the housing market. They pay a higher percent of their income for housing, they are less likely to own their housing, and they are overrepresented in the central cities. What are the constraints that limit the housing choice of female householders and concentrate them in the central city? Here, four sources of constraint are discussed: income, race, discrimination in mortgage lending practices, and exclusionary zoning.

Income and Poverty

The economic status of women is declining as women are the fastest growing segment of the poverty population. Two-thirds of all adults below the poverty level in the United States are women, and one-half of all families below the poverty level are female-headed families. The President's National Advisory

Council on Economic Opportunity predicted in 1981 that if the proportion of the poor in female-headed families continued to increase at the same rate that it increased between 1968 and 1978, by the year 2000 the poverty population in the United States would be composed solely of women and their dependent children (National Advisory Council on Economic Opportunity 1980).

Detailed data from the Springfield, Massachusetts, SMSA show that there is no clear relationship between the income and housing or rental costs of female householders. Women tend to overpay for their housing, paying a higher proportion of their income for housing than do other types of households.

Income affects housing choice in ways other than the cost paid for housing. One reason, for instance, that fewer women own rather than rent their housing is the lack of funds available for the down payment required for a home purchase. Lower incomes also make it difficult for female householders to qualify for home mortgages. The home ownership market in Springfield is clearly dominated by married couple households, as is no doubt true in other metropolitan areas as well. With prices inflated to meet the demand of these higher-income households—whose incomes are often augmented by the wages earned by two workers—it is difficult for other households to compete for housing.

Because women by and large rent rather than own their housing units, they also do not benefit from the tax reductions and equity buildup accruing to home owners. Therefore, the housing costs paid are real costs that cannot be recouped with the filing of a tax return or the sale of a house.

Lower incomes can indirectly influence housing choice when housing costs are balanced with other household costs. Households commonly trade off higher housing costs with lower transportation costs. In the United States, women tend to be more dependent on public transportation and less likely to have a private automobile. The presence of public transportation in central city areas (and its relative absence in suburbs) may exert an important influence on the housing choice of female householders. This income effect would therefore show up in locational choice, but not necessarily in the price paid for housing.

Race

The influence of race on the housing status of single women is difficult to unravel. Black women are overrepresented among female householders: nationwide, while only 11 percent of all households are black, 29 percent of single female-headed households are black. Black women who are householders are twice as likely as white women to live in central cities: in 1983, 64 percent of single black mothers lived in central cities.

Several recent studies have shown strong correlations between high proportions of black households, female-headed households, and low-income households (Cook and Rudd 1984; Roncek, Bell, and Choldin 1980). These studies leave unanswered the question of whether female-headed households, regardless of race, live in areas with high concentrations of black households, or whether the aggregated data employed in these studies have simply overemphasized the concentration of a substantial number of black female-headed households in predominantly black neighborhoods.

In Springfield, where a large proportion of all households are female-headed (30 percent) but only a small percent of these black (8 percent), analysis of census tract data suggests that female householders of either race reside in the same districts as do black householders. Using percent of families that were headed by a single female as the dependent variable, multiple regression analysis showed that only 3 of the 14 independent variables included in the analysis explained significant levels of variation in the concentration of these households. Both the percent of households below the poverty level and the percent of households that are black were positively related to percent of female-headed households. A third variable, measuring the presence of various other racial and ethnic groups, showed a strong negative relationship. The remaining variables, measuring a variety of housing and economic characteristics, failed to enter the regression equation at significant levels.

Black and female-headed households both characteristically have lower incomes than other households. This common link could explain their similar concentrations in central-city tracts, rather than the race of the female householders, who in Springfield are much more commonly white than black.

A third factor that should be considered is discrimination in housing practices that have adversely affected both black and female households. Two forms of institutional constraints on housing choice are discussed: discrimination in mortgage lending and exclusionary zoning.

Discrimination in Mortgage Lending

Only since 1974 has it been against the law to refuse a person a mortgage because she is a woman. The Housing and Community Development Act of 1974 amended Title VIII of the Civil Rights Act of 1968, which had prohibited discrimination against blacks, by extending fair housing practices to women. Now black and female householders must meet only the criteria established by the lender in order to obtain a mortgage. There are two basic criteria: (1) the household must have sufficient income, and (2) the household must have sufficient stability as a credit risk.

Low incomes prevent many female householders from obtaining mortgage credit. Decisions about the stability of the household and its income are often based on rules of thumb that make generalizations about women as a class: that they are higher credit risks than men; that they are less reliable debtors; and that they are only temporarily in the labor force. While actuarial tables on expected income growth and income stability for women show these beliefs to be ill-founded (U.S. Department of Housing and Urban Development 1976), it is difficult to change attitudes through legal prohibition against discrimination, particularly when such discrimination can be justified as sound business practice.

Women's real access to mortgage credit in the United States is an important issue that requires further investigation.

Discrimination in Zoning and Rental Practices

Zoning laws are commonly used in the United States to influence the residential character of communities, particularly suburban communities. The purpose of many such zoning practices is to maintain income homogeneity and the "family" atmosphere of areas, especially areas of single-family housing. Many communities define a "family" for purposes of restricting the type of household that may reside in such districts. Most commonly, family is defined in zoning ordinances as a group of persons related by blood, marriage, or adoption. Many areas limit or prohibit residence by nonfamily households, or the sharing of housing units by unrelated individuals.

While such laws are not directly intended to prevent single female householders from residing in these communities, that is often a side effect. As an example, consider the situation of a woman who has remained in her suburban home following the death or divorce of her spouse. She very likely will not be able to afford housing payments after the loss of her husband's income, and may wish to rent a portion of her home to a nonfamily member. Such action would be against the law in many suburban communities. The "nouveau poor," as these women have been dubbed, are often forced to leave their house and their community (Netter and Price 1983). Doubling up by two unrelated households may also be prohibited in many areas.

Quite commonly, rental housing is excluded from all or part of a suburban community. This restriction places constraints on the locational choice of all rental households, but particularly affects female householders who comprise a large portion of the rental housing market in metropolitan areas. Similarly, the ban on children that is practiced by private landlords constrains the housing options of single mothers. It is estimated that in the United States 26 percent of the rental housing stock is off limits to families with children (Children's Defense Fund 1979).

DISCUSSION

This chapter has highlighted several distinct features that characterize the housing status of female-headed households. First, women do not partake equally in the benefits of home ownership. To a greater extent than is true for other household types, women who head households must rent their housing. In fact, female-headed households comprise the largest segment of the rental housing market in some cities. Second, female householders pay more, as a percent of their available income, than do male- or couple-headed households for comparable housing. A substantial proportion of female householders pay more than one-half of their income for housing. Third, women experience greater constraints in their choice of location and are more likely to reside in central cities rather than suburbs, regardless of whether they are raising children.

Previous studies of women's housing patterns have concluded that the distribution of female-headed households in metropolitan areas is most closely associated with race and income. Since a large proportion of female householders are both poor and black, these findings make intuitive sense. However, this relationship is not as straightforward as it might seem. Census tract data for Springfield show a similar distribution of tracts with a high proportion of black and a high proportion of female-headed households. In Springfield, however, only 8 percent of all female-headed households are black, suggesting that white female householders reside in tracts where there is a concentration of black households.

Low-income status may appear to be the common link between these two groups of housing consumers. A third factor that deserves further exploration, however, is discrimination against women as heads of nontraditional households. Certain attitudes about what are considered "desirable" versus "unsavory" influences in a neighborhood have been introduced into the housing market through the activities of mortgage lenders, local zoning boards, and even the housing construction industry. Large segments of American suburbs were built with a particular type of household in mind: the traditional married couple with a working man and economically dependent woman and children (Saegert 1980; Fava 1980). Female householders are prevented from living in these areas by a combination of high costs, lack of rental housing, lack of other essential services, such as public transportation, and, historically at least, discrimination in mortgage lending. Current access by women to mortgage credit is something that should not be taken for granted, given the pervasive nature of attitudes that have worked to their disadvantage in the past.

Many female householders are in a transitional stage in their lives. Some recently divorced and young single women may be expected to become part of a couple at some point in the future. However, the overall rate of increase in the number of female-headed households suggests that many women may remain in this status for longer periods than has been true in the past. Obviously, different solutions may be required to meet the housing needs of transitional as opposed to permanent or semipermanent female households. Recently, a number of innovative approaches to providing transitional housing for women and their children have been initiated in the United States and elsewhere (Cools 1980; Cook 1984; France 1985). Solving the housing inequities that face women as householders in general, however, will require removing some of the current barriers to housing choice that are posed by income constraints and discrimination. It is no longer either accurate or adequate to plan communities and provide housing with only the "traditional" family in mind, since doing so means that the growing number of nontraditional households face an uphill battle in gaining equal access to housing.

REFERENCES

Brion, M., and A. Tinker
1980   *Women in Housing*. London: Housing Centre Trust.
Children's Defense Fund
1979   National Proceedings from a Round Table on Discrimination Against Children in Housing (unpublished).
Cook, Christine
1984   "Transition Housing in Twin Cities, Minnesota." *Women and Environments* 6, 4–14.
Cook, Christine, and Nancy M. Rudd
1984   "Factors Influencing the Residential Location of Female Householders." *Urban Affairs Quarterly* 20, 78–96.
Cools, Anne
1980   "Emergency Shelter: The Development of an Innovative Women's Environment." In *New Space For Women*, edited by Gerda Wekerle, Rebecca Peterson, and David Morley, 311–18. Boulder, CO: Westview Press.
Fava, Sylvia F.
1980   "Women's Place in the New Suburbia." In *New Space for Women*, edited by Gerda Wekerle, Rebecca Peterson, and David Morley, 129–50. Boulder, CO: Westview.
France, Ivy
1985   "Hubertusvereniging: A Transition Point for Single Parents." *Women and Environments* 7, 20–22.
Klodawsky, Fran, A. N. Spector, and C. Hendrix
1983   *The Housing Needs of Single Parent Families in Canada*. Ottawa, Ont.: Ark Research.
National Advisory Council on Economic Opportunity
1980   *Critical Choices for the Eighties*. Washington, DC: National Advisory Council on Economic Opportunity, 12th Report.
Netter, Edith M., and Ruth G. Price
1983   "Zoning and the Nouveau Poor." *American Publishing Association Journal*, Spring, 171–81,
Roncek, Dennis W., Ralph Bell, and Harvey Choldin
1980   "Female-Headed Families: An Ecological Model of Residential Concentration in a Small City." *Journal of Marriage and the Family* 42, 157–69.
Saegert, Susan
1980   "Masculine Cities, Feminine Suburbs." *Signs* 5, S96–S111.
U.S. Commission on Civil Rights
1983   *A Growing Crisis: Disadvantaged Women and Their Children*. Washington, DC: U.S. Government Clearinghouse Publication No. 78.
U.S. Department of Commerce
1984   *Household and Family Characteristics: March 1983*. Washington, DC: U.S. Government Printing Office.

U.S. Department of Housing and Urban Development
1976   *Women in the Mortgage Market*. Washington, DC: U.S. Department of HUD, Office of Policy Development and Research.
U.S. Department of Labor
1979   *The Socioeconomic Status of Households Headed by Women*. Washington, DC: U.S. Government Printing Office.

17

The Elderly in Central Tel Aviv

YONA GINSBERG

Abstract. This chapter examines how elderly residents (a sample study of 384) cope with their environment in central Tel Aviv. Most were satisfied with their neighborhood and wished to stay there. The central location of the area seemed to be its main advantage. A majority had extensive social networks, although friendships were rather dispersed. In contrast to other studies, fear of crime and safety was not a major problem.

INTRODUCTION

Various studies stress the problems faced by the elderly in coping with their environment (Gubrium 1973; Lawton 1974; Shuval et al. 1982). It seems that the more their physical and sensory capacities decline, and the more their independence diminishes, the less the elderly able are to deal with their environment. According to Lawton's environmental press-competence model (1974), as the level of competence decreases, the effect of the environment increases. Among the environmental forces that have an impact on the elderly's behavior, Lawton (1974) mentions the "suprapersonal environment," that is, the characteristics of other people in the physical proximity of the individual.

It has been suggested that age concentration is a positive factor contributing to the elderly's morale, activity, and social interaction (Lawton et al. 1984). Therefore, planned homogeneous housing projects have been recommended for older people. Despite the fact that various studies demonstrated that morale is higher and social contacts are more frequent among elderly living in age-concentrated housing projects (Lawton et al 1984; Rosov 1967), the evidence is inconclusive. Others found no significant differences in the well-being and social involvement of the elderly in natural communities compared to the elderly in senior citizen housing (Poulin 1984).

Several studies found that age segregation also provides social support for the elderly, and that those social support networks have a positive impact on the feeling of safety and security (Gubrium 1974; Sundeen and Mathieu 1976).

Indeed, for inner-city elderly residents the issues of safety and fear of crime seem to be a major problem. Studies found that the level of neighborhood satisfaction among inner-city elderly is low, and that fear of crime and problems of safety are the main causes for the lack of satisfaction (Jirovec et al. 1984; Lawton 1980). Those studies conclude that inner-city neighborhoods are not desirable locations for elderly people.

The purpose of this chapter is to examine how the elderly cope with their environment in the inner neighborhoods of Tel Aviv. More specifically, it focuses on: (1) housing and neighborhood satisfaction and the variables related to them; (2) social support networks—including relatives, neighbors, and friends; and (3) feelings of fear and safety and the impact of personal, ecological, and social variables on these feelings.

THE AREA

In the 1940s and 1950s the central neighborhoods of the city of Tel Aviv were considered a middle-class area. However, in the last two decades this area has been undergoing changes similar, in some respects, to those of central areas in Western cities. The total population has been decreasing and the proportion of the elderly increasing. Some 37 percent of the current residents are 65 years or older. These are the old-timers who remained in the neighborhoods while the younger population moved to the suburbs.

Once wholly residential, the area now has mixed land uses. Many commercial enterprises moved into the neighborhoods because of its proximity to Tel Aviv's central business district. Offices often occupy vacant apartments, replacing the families who have moved out. According to the sample, 60 percent of the residential buildings have one or two apartments used as offices. The buildings, mostly of three or four stories, are relatively old and some are not properly maintained. Many commercial and public services, such as stores, health clinics, and synagogues, are located in the area. Public transportation is very good and there are many open spaces, such as parks and boulevards.

In contrast to inner-city neighborhoods in some other countries, lower-class people have not moved into the area. Thus, the neighborhood consists mainly of middle-class elderly people and nonresidential land uses. Crime is no worse here than in any other part of the city.

In recent years there have been some signs of a "back to the city" movement, and younger people have been moving into the area. Most newcomers are under the age of 35, singles or couples without children. A majority rent their apartments and it is questionable whether they will remain in the neighborhood for a long period of time. Furthermore, this does not appear to be a large-scale trend.

THE STUDY

The study was based on structured interviews with a systematic random sample of 384 people, aged 60 and over: 63 percent of the respondents were 70 years or more; 54 percent were married, 35 percent widowed, and the rest single or divorced. Some 71 percent of the respondents had children, but as one would expect, almost all their children lived outside the parental homes. Thus, most households were small and consisted of one or two inhabitants.

The population was homogeneous in its socioeconomic characteristics. A majority of the sample was born in Eastern Europe and immigrated to Israel 40 or more years ago. Fully 75 percent were retired; in the past they were employed as professional, business, or clerical workers. Thus the sample consisted mainly of a retired middle-class population. The main sources of their present income were retirement pensions and social security benefits. Only 8 percent of the respondents were welfare recipients. Only a small minority owned a car, but over 90 percent had telephones.

Almost half (47 percent) lived in two-bedroom apartments, and 35 percent in three-bedroom apartments. Since most families were small, there was little crowding. Not quite 40 percent owned their apartments and the rest were renters. Over half of the elderly residents had been living in the same building for 25 years or more.

RESULTS

Residential Satisfaction

Satisfaction with the building: Various studies indicated that elderly people perceive their housing as satisfactory (Delvin 1980; O'Bryant 1983). Also in this study satisfaction with the building was high and 68 percent of the sample were satisfied or very satisfied. Satisfaction with the building was related to the building's age and condition: The newer the building and the better its condition, the higher the degree of satisfaction. Owners were more satisfied than renters. Whether or not part of the apartments in the building were used as offices did not have an impact on satisfaction.

Satisfaction with the neighborhood: In general elderly people demonstrate a high level of neighborhood satisfaction (Carp and Carp 1982), although this does not seem to be the case among elderly people living in the inner city (Lawton 1980). However, the elderly living in the inner city of Tel Aviv did express a high level of neighborhood satisfaction: 26.2 percent said they were very satisfied with their neighborhood and 53.4 percent said they were satisfied with their neighborhood, while only 13.5 percent said they were not quite satisfied, and 6.9 percent said they were not satisfied at all with their neighborhood.

Thus, 80 percent of the elderly were either very satisfied or satisfied with their neighborhood. The main reason for neighborhood satisfaction was its location. A vast majority of the respondents (91 percent) felt there were enough commercial and public services in the area, such as groceries, other stores, health clinics, and synagogues. The elderly also regarded public transportation as satisfactory. Most did not patronize clubs and restaurants, but those who did thought there was no shortage in those services either. Neighborhood satisfaction was positively related to satisfaction with the services (Gamma = .46). On the other hand, the main cause of dissatisfaction was environmental nuisances such as noise. Only 12 percent of the elderly complained about the offices replacing families in the area. No difference in the level of neighborhood satisfaction was found among those living on main streets and those living on quiet side streets.

As in other studies (Jirovec et al 1984; Lawton 1980), neighborhood satisfaction was related to housing satisfaction (Gamma = .62). In addition, owners indicated a higher level of neighborhood satisfaction than renters.

Social Networks

The importance of social ties for elderly people has been pointed out in various studies (Dorfman et al. 1985; Gubrium 1974; Heller and Mansbach 1984; Shuval et al. 1982). The social network of the respondents consisted of relatives, friends, and neighbors.

Relatives: Almost all (91 percent) of the elderly had relatives: 71 percent had children, and about half had siblings. Only 14 percent of the respondents had relatives living in the same area; the remainder of the relatives were dispersed in other parts of the city as well as in other places. This fact, however, did not deter the elderly from meeting with their relatives: Most said they met their children at least once a week. Contacts with siblings was less frequent and it seems that telephone calls were a substitute for seeing more distant relatives face to face.

Friends: One would expect people who had lived for over 20 years in the neighborhood to have localized social ties: 81 percent of the elderly said they had friends; 19 percent had all their friends within their own neighborhood; 40 percent had all their friends outside of their neighborhood, and 22 percent had friends both in their neighborhood and in other areas. Thus, despite the stability in residence, most elderly people had a rather dispersed social network. Moreover, although 41 percent said they had friends in the area, over half had friends in other places as well. Thus, local friendships did not seem to be a substitute for extra-neighborhood contacts.

About one-third of the elderly met their friends at least once a week, while those whose friends lived in the neighborhood did so even more often. The open spaces around the area were often used as meeting places, and over half of the respondents visited one of the seven neighborhood parks at least once a fortnight. In short, most elderly people had quite active friendship ties inside the area or in other places.

Neighbors: Contacts with neighbors were quite frequent: 43 percent visited neighbors and 50 percent exchanged help. Assisting neighbors was usually centered around daily needs, and only a small minority helped their neighbors in case of sickness. Most respondents preferred to turn to relatives in case of an emergency. As ascertained by others (Shuval et al. 1982; Chatters et al. 1985), kinship is the predominant source of support for the elderly. Contacts with neighbors were in addition to relations with friends and did not substitute for them; respondents who did not interact with neighbors had less friendship ties than those who interacted with them.

Lawton et al. (1984) suggested that the more homogeneous the neighborhood, the more the elderly interact with each other. Although no objective data were available on the homogeneity of the "microneighborhood," respondents were asked if their neighbors were similar to themselves regarding their age. About half (53 percent) of the elderly perceived their neighbors as being similar to themselves in age.

No association was found between having friends, neighbor relations, or perceived homogeneity on the one hand, and neighborhood satisfacton on the other. It seems that satisfaction with the area was not dependent on the social networks of the elderly.

Safety and Fear

One of the major problems of the elderly in inner-city neighborhoods is fear of crime and issues of safety (Clemente and Kleiman 1976; Yin 1980). A major objective of this study was to find out how the elderly residents of the central neighborhoods of Tel Aviv cope with safety problems.

Most elderly people were aware that their neighborhood had been changing in recent years. Two-thirds realized that at least some of the residents in their buildings had changed, mainly because people had died or had moved to old-age homes. According to the respondents, half of the empty apartments had been replaced by offices. As for changes in the neighborhood, the main change was, according to the respondents, that young people were missing from the area; 15 percent mentioned positive changes in the area such as renovation of some buildings. Despite perceived population changes, two-thirds of the elderly maintained that they knew at least some of the people they encountered on the street.

Two measures were used to determine feelings of safety and security among the elderly. The first was a behavioral measure ("are you going out after dark?"), and the second attitudinal ("do you think that your neighborhood is a safe place?").

Going out after dark: 38.7 percent of the elderly said they always go out after dark and another 24.6 percent sometimes go out after dark. Only 36.6 percent of the respondents said they never go out after dark. Moreover, when asked for the reasons for not going out, only 39 percent of those who did not go out mentioned that the reason was fear. The rest gave other reasons for not going

Table 17.1
"Do you think your neighborhood is a safe place" by "Do you go out after dark" (percent)

	Thinks neighborhood is a safe place		
Goes out after dark	Yes	Depends When	No
Yes (always)	47.1	45.7	18.5
Sometimes	27.0	27.1	18.5
Never	26.0	27.1	63.0
N	294	70	108

$\chi^2 = 46.66$ d.f. = 4 $p \leq .000$

out, such as poor health, old age, or because there was no place to go. Only 11 out of 384 respondents had been victimized in recent years.

Is the neighborhood a safe place: Over half of the respondents (53.4 percent) felt their neighborhood was always safe; another 18.2 percent considered it a safe place during daytime, and only 28.5 percent felt the neighborhood was not a safe place.

Although both measures were related, the level of association is not very high (Gamma = .41). As indicated in table 17.1, those who felt the neighborhood was safe only during the day time did go out at night as frequently as those who claimed the neighborhood was always safe. Only those who perceived the neighborhood as an unsafe place wanted to go out at night less than the rest: 63 percent (of 108) said they never go out after dark. It seems that the two measures are not necessarily two different expressions of the same variable, but might be measuring different variables. It may well be that behavior and attitude in this respect were not totally congruent.

Jirovec et al. (1984, 265) found that "safety is the environmental characteristic most predictive of neighborhood satisfaction among the elderly." Indeed, neighborhood satisfaction was significantly related to "going out after dark" (Gamma = .18) and "is the neighborhood a safe place" (Gamma = .25), although the level of association in both cases was low. The differences seem to lie in the two extremes: 64 percent of the "very satisfied" thought the neighborhood was always safe, in contrast to 62 percent of the "not satisfied at all" who felt the neighborhood was never safe.

Problems of fear and safety contribute to neighborhood satisfaction (or dissatisfaction), and to the quality of life. Thus, safety can be treated as an independent variable. However, one could also regard safety as a dependent variable and try to explain the variance in the feeling of safety. Three kinds of variables were used in order to explain both measures of safety:

1. *Personal characteristics*: These were respondent's age, sex, marital status, level of education, and owning a car. The hypothesis was that the relatively old, the women, those who are not married, the less educated, and those who do not own cars feel less secure than the rest.

2. *Ecological variables*: Environmental forces, such as beauty, quietness, space seem to have an important impact on the elderly residents' behavior (Jirovec et al. 1985; Lawton and Cohen 1974). Since the central neighborhoods of Tel Aviv now have mixed land uses, it was hypothesized that the less residential the immediate neighborhood, the less the feeling of security. Two ecological variables were used: are there any apartments in the elderly residents' buildings that are used as offices, and what is the type of street on which the respondent resides (streets were divided into four groups from purely residential to main commercial arteries).

3. *Social networks*: Other studies have demonstrated that the social support network is an important element for reducing fear and increasing the feeling of security (Gubrium 1974; Sundeen and Mathieu 1976). Three variables were included: the number of relatives in the area, the number of friends, and knowing people on the street (from all to none).

Multiple regressions were used for the questions "Do you go out after dark?" and "Is your neighborhood a safe place?" (see Table 17.2). We could account for 21.3 percent of the variance of the first question, compared to 10.4 percent of the second. Thus, a higher percentage of the variance in the behavioral variable could be explained. Five out of the ten variables entered the equation at a 5 percent significance level in the first question, and four in the second.

Going out after dark was related to sex, age, and education. Males, the relatively younger people, and the more educated ones tended to go out after dark more than the others. Neither of the two ecological variables entered the equation at a significant level. Going out after dark was not associated with the type of building or street. On the other hand, social networks seemed to contribute to going out after dark; the more friends one had and the more people one knew on the street, the more one would go out. Only 17 percent of those not having any friends did go out after dark, compared to 41 percent who had one or two friends, and 65 percent who had three friends. However, having relatives living in the area did not contribute to going out at night.

As for the notion that the neighborhood was a safe place, the men perceived it to be a safer place than did the women. In contrast to the behavioral measure, all other personal attributes did not seem to be related to attitudes toward the neighborhood's safety. Of the two ecological variables, the type of street in which one lives adds to the explanation, but not as one expects. Contrary to the hypothesis, the elderly living on main commercial arteries regarded the neighborhood as a safer place than those living on purely residential streets (69 and 46 percent, respectively). Perhaps elderly residents felt the busier the street, and

Table 17.2

Regression Analysis for "Goes out after dark" and "Thinks neighborhood is a safe place"

Independent Variable	Goes out after dark			Thinks neighborhood is a safe place		
	Simple R	Beta	F	Simple R	Beta	F
Sex	.088	.137	7.45*	.214	.204	14.64**
Marital Status	.149	.011	.05	.114	.039	.52
Age	-.330	-.318	40.30**	-.026	-.010	.03
Education	.189	.136	7.89*	.032	.035	.46
Car	.125	.024	.24	.080	.023	.25
Street	.072	.043	.84	.120	.122	5.80*
Offices	-.034	-.015	.09	-.023	-.065	1.65
Relatives	.082	.008	.02	.129	.114	4.99*
Friends	.274	.189	14.77**	.158	.130	6.21*
Knows people	.122	.112	5.65*	.054	.042	.69

$R^2 = .213$ $R^2 = .104$

*p < .05
**p < .001

the more "eyes upon the street" (Jacobs 1961, 45), the greater the amount of social control. Again, living in a building in which some apartments were used as offices had no impact on the feeling of safety.

Social networks contributed also to the feeling of safety: the more relatives one had in the neighborhood and the more friends one had in general, the safer the neighborhood appeared. The last point seems to be important: the number of friends the elderly had contributed both to going out after dark and to the perception that the neighborhood was a safe place. Various studies have emphasized the importance of local support networks in enhancing the feeling of security among the elderly (Gubrium 1974; Sundeen and Mathieu 1976). However, in contrast to those studies, no difference was found between elderly persons having friends inside the neighborhood and those having friends in other places. In other words, regardless of the place of residence of the friends, the more friends one had the more often one would go out after dark, and the more one would think the neighborhood was a safe place. Moreover, the more friends one had, the more dispersed the social network. Those elderly persons who had a relatively large number of friends drew them from different places (r = .65), thus having had a more dispersed network. In other words, in contrast to other studies, dispersed rather than localized social support networks contributed to the feeling of safety and security. On the other hand, elderly persons who were isolated and did not have any friends—in the neighborhood or outside—felt the least secure in their neighborhood.

These findings suggest the need to reconsider the role of social support networks for the well-being of elderly people. What seems to be important for them is the fact that they have friends rather than that the social network is localized.

CONCLUSIONS

Most elderly residents of the central area of Tel Aviv were satisfied with their housing and neighborhood, and did not wish to move. The central location of the area and the abundance of services seemed to be its main advantage from the respondents' point of view.

The majority of the sample had extensive social networks consisting of relatives, neighbors, and friends, although friendships were rather dispersed. Fear of crime and problems of safety did not seem to be a major concern. Victimization rates among the respondents were low, and only a minority did not go out after dark and considered the area to be unsafe.

Inner-city neighborhoods are generally not considered a desirable location for elderly people. In contrast to the findings of this study, other studies have pointed out that crime and safety are major problems for those residents, social ties are few, and residential satisfaction is low (Jirovec et al 1984; Lawton 1980; Sundeen and Mathieu 1976). The lack of a localized support network is considered one reason for the feeling of insecurity among inner-city elderly residents (Gubrium 1974). The findings of this study indicate that social support networks indeed contribute to the feeling of safety, but these were not necessarily localized social ties.

Lawton (1974) has suggested that one solution to the problem that elderly residents are facing in coping with their physical and social environment is segregated age-homogeneous housing. Planned housing projects are supposed to contribute to the morale, well-being, and social interaction of elderly residents.

The question of whether or not planned homogeneous housing projects are preferable to natural communities poses a difficult policy problem to those dealing with housing policy in general, and housing of the elderly in particular. If the findings of this study have any broader implications, it seems the answer is not clear-cut. A natural community with mixed land uses might be an advantage for elderly residents. Localized social networks are no doubt important for the elderly, and age peers facilitate social interaction. However, one could ask what proportion of the elderly constitute the "critical mass." In this case, over one-third of the population seemed to be sufficient. Moreover, one of the disadvantages of Tel Aviv's inner neighborhood was the absence of young people, and the incoming young residents were regarded as a positive change. In this respect it would appear that the respondents prefer a somewhat heterogeneous neighborhood.

Another question is the advantage or disadvantage of a purely residential area compared to one with mixed land uses. Mixed land uses not only add services to neighborhoods, but might also contribute vitality and life to an area, and perhaps even enhance the feeling of security of the residents.

Neighborhoods are not alike, and inner-city areas differ from one place to another. The inner city of Tel Aviv is not a crime-ridden area, nor did it encounter social or ethnic transitions. It is a sparsely populated neighborhood, predominantly with elderly middle-class residents, and a mixture of nonresidential land uses. In a case like this a natural unplanned mixed community would seem preferable to a planned homogeneous housing project for the elderly. However, the question, both for research and policy, is not whether a given type of neighborhood is more desirable for the elderly. The important issue is which specific elements of a community contribute to the well-being and quality of life of elderly residents.

REFERENCES

Carp, F. M., and A. Carp
1982   "Perceived Environmental Quality of Neighborhoods: Development of Assessment Scales and Their Relationships to Age and Gender." *Journal of Environmental Psychology* 2, no. 4, 295–312.
Chatters, L. M., R. J. Tayler, and J. S. Jackson
1985   "Size and Composition of the Informal Helper Network of Elderly Blacks." *Journal of Gerontology* 40, no. 5, 605–14.
Clemente, F., and M. B. Kleiman
1976   "Fear of Crime among the Aged." *The Gerontologist* 16, no. 3, 207–10.

Delvin, A. S.
1980   "Housing the Elderly, Cognitive Considerations." *Environment and Behavior* 12, no. 4, 451–66.

Dorfman, L. T., F. J. Kohout, and D. A. Heckert
1985   "Retirement Satisfaction in the Rural Elderly." *Research on Aging* 7, no. 4, 577–600.

Gubrium, J. F.
1973   "Apprehension of Coping, Incompetence, and Response to Fear in Old Age." *International Journal of Aging and Human Development* 4, no. 2, 111–25.
1974   "Victimization in Old Age." *Crime and Delinquency* 20, no. 3, 245–50.

Heller, K., and W. E. Mansbach
1984   "The Multifacet Nature of Social Support in a Community Sample of Elderly Women. *Journal of Social Issues* 40, no. 4, 99–112.

Jacobs, Jane
1961   *The Life and Death of Great American Cities*. New York: Random House.

Jirovec, R. L., M. M. Jirovec, and A. Bosse
1984   "Environmental Determinants of Neighborhood Satisfaction among Urban Men." *The Gerontologist* 24, no. 3, 261–65.
1985   "Residential Satisfaction as a Function of Micro and Macro Conditions among Urban Elderly Men." *Research on Aging* 7, no. 4, 601–16.

Lawton, M. P.
1974   "Competence, Environmental Press and the Adaptation of Older People." In *Theory Development in Environment and Aging*, edited by P. G. Windley, T.O. Bryent, and F. G. Ernest, 18–83. Washington, DC: Gerontological Society.
1980   "Housing the Elderly: Residential Quality and Residential Satisfaction." *Research on Aging* 2, no. 3, 309–28.

Lawton, M. P., and J. Cohen
1974   "Environment and the Well-being of Elderly Inner-city Residents." *Environment and Behavior* 6, no. 2, 194–211.

Lawton, M. P., E. Moss, and E. Moles
1984   "The Suprapersonal Neighborhood Context of Older People—Age Heterogeneity and Well-being." *Environment and Behavior* 16, no. 1, 89–109.

O'Bryant, S. L.
1983   "The Subjective Value of Home to Older Homeowners." *Journal of Housing for the Elderly* 1, no. 1, 29–43.

Poulin, J. M.
1984   "Age Segregation and Interpersonal Involvement and Morale of the Aged." *The Gerontologist* 24, no. 3, 266–69.

Rosov, I.
1967   *Social Integration of the Aged*. New York: The Free Press.

Shuval, J. T., R. Fleishman, and A. Shmueli
1982   *Informal Support for the Elderly: Social Networks in a Jerusalem Neighborhood*. Jerusalem: Brookdale Institute of Gerontology.

Sundeen, R. A., and J. T. Mathieu
1976   "The Fear of Crime and its Consequences among Elderly in Three Urban Communities." *The Gerontologist* 16, no. 3, 211–19.

Yin, R. P.
1980   "Fear of Crime among the Elderly: Some Issues and Suggestions." *Social Problems* 27, no. 4, 492–504.

Name Index

Subject Index

Contributors

JAMES R. ANDERSON is a Professor at the University of Illinois, Champaign-Urbana. He has a joint appointment with the School of Architecture and the Housing Research and Development Program. Involved in research in housing evaluation for over ten years, his academic background is in architecture and urban planning, fields in which he continues to work as a private consultant.

KENNETH K. BAAR is an attorney and urban planner in Berkeley, California. He has served as a consultant to cities in California and to the State of New Jersey on rent control issues, taught housing courses at San Francisco State University, and published numerous articles on rent control.

TRUDI E. BUNTING is an Associate Professor of Geography at the University of Waterloo, Ontario, Canada. Her major research interests lie in the interdisciplinary area of environmental behavior. Current research projects include inner-city residential change and comparative aspects of urban development in U.S. and Canadian cities.

HARVEY CHOLDIN is Professor of Sociology at the University of Illinois, Champaign-Urbana. After studies at the University of Chicago, he did fieldwork on family planning and community development in Bangladesh. He then taught at Michigan State University where he conducted research on the Mexican-American community. He has published articles in *Annual Review of Sociology* and *American Sociological Review*, and is the author of *Cities and Suburbs: An Introduction to Urban Sociology* (1985).

SYLVIA F. FAVA is Senior Research Scholar in the Ph.D. Program in Sociology at the Graduate Center, City University of New York. She has written on urban sociology, new towns, suburban society, and housing. Currently she is conducting studies of the "suburban generation" and of the role of gender in community life.

GUIDO FRANCESCATO is a Professor and Chair of the Department of Housing and Design at the University of Maryland, College Park. Since 1972 he has published numerous articles, book chapters, and monographs on housing quality and residential satisfaction.

KAREN A. FRANCK is Associate Professor at the School of Architecture, New Jersey Institute of Technology, Newark. She is currently completing a National Science Foundation project on recent social and spatial innovations in American housing. Additional research interests include the history of public housing design, women and environments, and architecture and social change. Previously she collaborated with Oscar Newman on research about the relationships between housing design, crime, fear of crime, and community instability. She has published articles in *The Journal of Social Issues, Population and Environment, Sociological Focus, Sociological Inquiry, Environment and Behavior*, and *Ekistics*.

YONA GINSBERG is a Senior Lecturer in the Department of Sociology, Bar Ilan University, Ramat Gan, Israel. In recent years she has been studying various housing types, rehabilitation areas, and the central neighborhoods of Tel Aviv. Currently she is conducting a study of the housing problems of single-parent families.

ELIZABETH HUTTMAN is Professor of Sociology at California State University, Hayward. She has written *Housing and Social Services for the Elderly*, coedited *Housing Needs and Policy Approaches*, authored "Transnational Housing Policy" in *Home Environments* (Altman and Werner), and is coeditor of the forthcoming *Handbook on Housing and the Built Environment*. She is co-organizer of the International Committee on Housing and the Built Environment.

E. C. M. MACHIELSE studied social geography with special reference to physical planning at the University of Utrecht, the Netherlands. She is currently with the Department of Urban Studies in the Faculty of Social Sciences of the same university. Her present research is focused on the housing of middle- and upper-income households, particularly in the large cities of the Netherlands.

WILLIAM MICHELSON is Professor of Sociology at the University of Toronto, where he is also associated with the Center for Urban and Community Studies. His research interests concern how people's contexts bear on their lives; this has led to work on such topics as housing, urban children, and maternal employment. His most recent books are *From Sun To Sun: Daily Obligations and Community Structure in the Lives of Employed Women and Their Families* (1985) and (coedited by Robert Bechtel and Robert Marans) *Methods for Environmental and Behavioral Research* (1986).

TANER OC is Senior Lecturer in Urban Planning at the University of Nottingham, England, and currently Vice-Dean of the Faculty of Law and Social Sciences. Dr. Oc has taught at the Queen's University of Belfast and George Washington University. His publications include "Public Participation in Planning: The British Experience," which appeared in *Planning Comment* in 1978; "Migration Problems in Turkey: Arid Zone Society in Transition" in *Design for Arid Regions*, edited by Gideon Golany; and "Ethnic Minorities and Rehabilitation—Comparative Study of USA and UK" in *Renewal, Rehabilitation and Maintenance* (1983).

DAVID POPENOE is Professor of Sociology at Rutgers, the State University of New Jersey. He has been a visiting faculty member or research scholar at New York University, the University of Pennsylvania, the University of Stockholm, the National Swedish Institute for Building Research, and the Center for Environmental Studies, London. A specialist in the comparative sociology of communities, housing, and the family, his most recent book is *Private Pleasure, Public Plight: American Metropolitan Community Life in Comparative Perspective* (1985).

JOAN C. SIMON was an Associate Professor at the University of Guelph, Ontario, Canada, responsible for housing courses in the Department of Consumer Studies and a partner of Simon Architects and Planners, Toronto, until her death in a traffic accident in 1986. Her practice, research, and teaching interests focused on the social and cultural aspects of residential design. She also served as Chairman of the National Advisory Council on Aging, a task force of Canada Mortgage and Housing Corporation on housing for the elderly.

REBECCA L. SMITH studied urban geography at the University of Minnesota, where her dissertation on the concept of neighborhoods won the Nystrom Award. Joining the University of Massachusetts faculty in 1982, she has focused her work on institutional constraints influencing housing choice.

RAYMOND G. STUDER is Dean of the College of Environmental Design, University of Colorado, at Boulder. He formerly held faculty positions at Arizona State University, Rhode Island School of Design, and Columbia University. He headed the Planning Analysis Project at Brown University and the programs in Man-Environment Relations and Community Systems Planning and Development at Pennsylvania State University. His teaching and research interests include methodological issues in sociophysical planning, programming, design, and management; application of behavioral technology and behavioral ecology in sociophysical intervention; and the utilization of sociophysical research in architecture, urban planning, and public policy. His current focus is upon the implications of the rationality debate, critical theory, and related developments for sociophysical decision-making methodology.

C. LEE THOMSON is currently finishing her master's thesis in geography at the University of Massachusetts. She is Research Coordinator for the Atlas of Massachusetts scheduled for publication in 1989.

EVA VAN KEMPEN is a Lecturer in the Department of Human Geography at the University of Amsterdam. Her research interests include the social implications of environmental planning and design, urban development, and social segregation in cities.

WILLEM VAN VLIET— is on leave from Pennsylvania State University, visiting in the Department of Sociology and College of Environmental Design at the University of Colorado, Boulder. He is editor of *Housing Markets and Policies under Fiscal Austerity* (1987) and the forthcoming *International Handbook of Housing Policies and Practices* and coeditor of *Habitats for Children* (1985), *Housing Needs and Policy Approaches* (1985), and the forthcoming *Handbook on Housing and the Built Environment*.

JAN VAN WEESEP is an Associate Professor at Utrecht University, the Netherlands, where he teaches urban geography. He has been Visiting Associate Professor at the University of Western Ontario and European Research Fellow at the Center for Metropolitan Planning and Research at Johns Hopkins University. His current research focuses on the causes and consequences of tenure conversion in different national contexts. He has coauthored textbooks on field methods and urban geography and contributed to various geographical and planning journals.

SUE WEIDEMANN is Professor at the University of Illinois, Champaign-Urbana. She has a joint appointment with the Housing Research and Development Program in the Graduate College and the Department of Landscape Architecture. She has been conducting research on the evaluation of residential environments since 1972.

GERDA R. WEKERLE is an Associate Professor in the Faculty of Environmental Studies, York University, Toronto. Her research over the past decade has dealt with various aspects of women and environments: housing, transportation, public space and safety, responsive neighborhood environments. She is coeditor of *New Space for Women* (1980) and cofounder of the journal *Women and Environments*.

ALISON E. WOODWARD is Professor in the Program for International Politics and Policy at the University of Antwerp and at the National Higher Institute for Architecture and City Planning in Antwerp, Belgium. Until 1986 she worked

as an academic researcher in Sweden on issues of new town planning, gender roles, and experimental housing policies. She has contributed to several books and published articles and reviews in *Sociology*, *Acta Sociologica*, and the *International Journal of Urban and Regional Development*.

KAREN WUERTZ and TON VAN DER PENNEN are employed by the Research Center on Housing and Regional Development at the University of Leiden, the Netherlands. They have studied participation in housing by squatters, ethnic minorities, mobil home owners, and housing associations.